THESE MANY

A bicycle journey across Eurasia

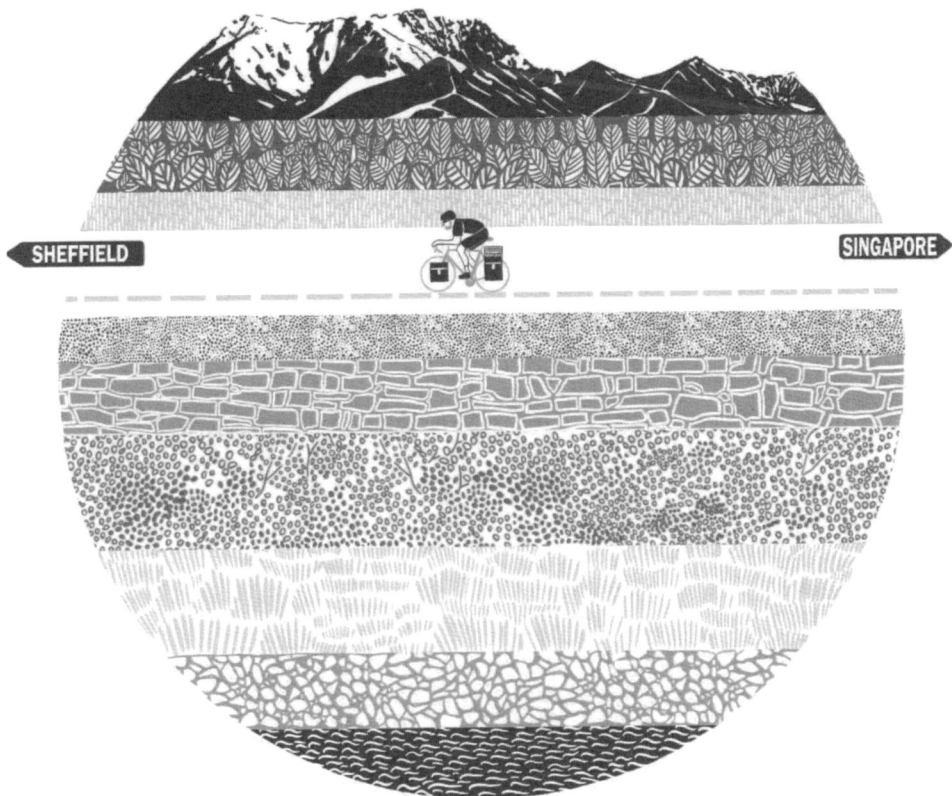

SHEFFIELD

SINGAPORE

Jake Johnson

Published in the UK
ISBN: 978-1-7394037-0-6

First edition 2025

Dedication of These Many Worlds

This book is first and foremost dedicated to the memory of my little sister, Lottie Johnson, that still permeates through these many worlds.

It is then dedicated to my family, who supported me when scraping the barrel, and were my tailwind through myriad joys. A special word to the Johnsons down-under. Thank you for your openness and warmth. To Pierre, thank you for dreaming up this trip and planning it with me. To my friends following from afar. Sam and the Peterkens, Seb, Sally, Martha, Liz, Alan, Tim, Sandra. Thank you. To Célie, thank you. To those who supported Pierre and I through gofundme, thank you. To the Alpkit foundation and Get Exploring trust, thank you.

Very importantly - to the strangers in this world who kept me pedalling, thank you.

Three favourite quotes from Eurasia

человеческая жизнь очень коротка, надо жить красиво.
Human life is very short, you have to live beautifully.
- DJ-cum-sim card salesman, Samarkand.

If you love a person like to say it don't let it regret.
-Back of a t-shirt of a Thai motorcycle passenger, somewhere in Thailand

如果喜欢花，你会摘掉它。如果爱花，你会保护它。
If you like the flower, you will pick it. If you love the flower, you will leave it be.
-Lany, hostel attendant, Xining

Contents

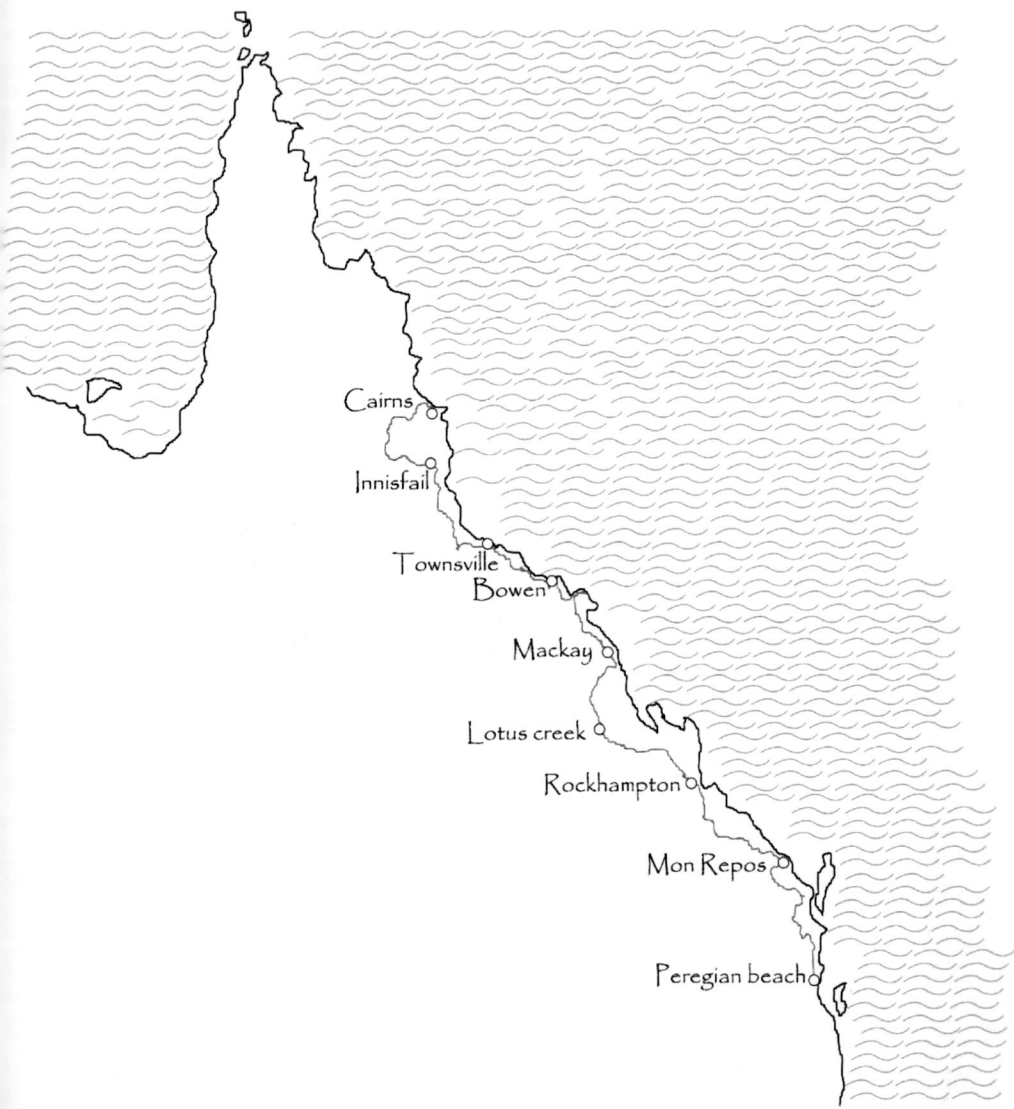

Cairns

Innisfail

Townsville
Bowen

Mackay

Lotus creek

Rockhampton

Mon Repos

Peregian beach

Prologue

I had just told my friend, Pierre, with whom for one year I had planned a rather long bicycle ride from Singapore to France, that I could no longer do it with him. I was emotional, fraught with self-contempt and self-loathing at my own stupidity and willingness to break off such a painstakingly planned trip in a single conversation. After the few terse days that were the tailing end of our companionship, we finally went our separate ways. It was one of those moments of no-return. Pierre headed north to work on a farm in Gympie, just a hundred or so kilometres to the north-west of the Australian sunshine coast. I, in the meantime, saw no reason to hang around. Perhaps it was the emotional feather-ruffling that compelled me to begin and leave my comfortable surroundings for the right direction, also North and West, but towards England on the other side of the world.

For the last month or so, we had been based at Peregian beach, a laid-back village utopia on the Pacific. It is a quaint suburbia where tanned retirees periodically saunter along the sand, meditatively wandering back and forth. The sort whose generous midriffs are partly obscured by translucent white cotton shirts and whose heads of silver hair are crowned with straw hats that shade their plump rosy faces from the south-eastern sun. I would sometimes watch as they parked their podgy bums down on the sand to flick insouciantly through the latest crime novels pulled from tote bags. I would think about how easy it seemed for them to simply bathe and bask in this world of calm, undisruptable comfort, having quite clearly made it, whatever 'it' was. It just so happened that this was also the world of my Uncle and Auntie who had fashioned a life for themselves by our world's greatest ocean, having sailed it for much of their lives. When Pierre and I were planning the trip, my uncle had offered us this place to rendezvous, to gather ourselves, and to use it as the starting line for the crazy journey that we had conceived in our heads. The soft existence here had lulled us both by its all-permeating serenity. But now that the ties had been broken, and the plan shattered, it felt that this serene backdrop was imposterish to the interior turmoil that was churning within my gut. I could not stay here, I had decided. It was time to leave. I would head north. My destination was Cairns, some 2000 kilometres away. I would try to get there in three weeks before heading to Singapore and taking on Eurasia by bike.

And so it was that I stopped working with the labourers who I had joined to keep my wallet in shape. I stopped looking at podgy bums in the sand. I stopped the morning sunrise beach walks and the visits to the cute coffee shops in this paradisiac Butlins. I packed all my belongings for the next three weeks into my two rear panniers supplemented with enough food supplies for the next couple of days. The tent that had served Pierre and me on a previous six-day trip to the outback was wrapped in a trusty orange bin bag and strapped resoundingly onto the rack. With my home in place, I could turn to my Uncle and Auntie and say final farewells. They had done so much to make me feel at home to the extent that I was almost tempted to stay. When I began stipulating that another week couldn't hurt, they were very sure to usher me strongly and enthusiastically off. This, I am sure had everything to do with their support for my adventure and nothing to do with the frequency at which they had found the fridge being emptied the previous month. It was with their gleeful au-revoir that I wheeled off up the road, northward bound. Pacific Ocean to my right, rows of posh hinterland houses on my left. The comforts were behind, and the unknown ahead. I was positively charged with nervous anticipation at what was to become of me. The wheels hummed on the tarmac. The next stop would be Cairns.

On the three-week trip up north, I had plenty of time to think everything through, none of which I used to do so. I got caught

2

up in a number of other preoccupations, not least panicking my way through many electric storms, or picking my way through the Bushfires that were raging in Queensland in the early Austral Summer of 2018. In between escaping the blazes, I made acquaintances all the way up the coast and somehow in the stifling heat and through my dog-tiredness, I managed to get a first impression, a fleeting glimpse, of what it meant to be a long-distance cycling rambler.

I had set off in a spirit of naïve happiness, with the friendly open road embracing me onwards. I imagined that this state could rarely be disturbed. What could possibly be more consistent and predictable than turning one pedal after the other down straight long roads? I quickly learnt that roads could always throw up surprises. Even on the first day out of Peregian beach, I got to sample one of the most basic of all uncertainties to which a cycle-tourist is subject. The day had begun with the sun pouring down from a sky of brilliant blue on which a few stray cumulus floated along. Eucalyptus trees perfumed the air. Crickets chirped. I whistled my way through the smattered and sparse civilisations of Queenslander tin-roof houses trailing from the Sunshine coast. I was still very much high on that beautiful anticipation that marks the beginnings of adventures, and was sure that no ill-fate could ever befall me. I felt a warmness in my stomach that brought me to be convinced that anything was possible. I could not help but succumb wholly to this feeling and made the move to depart from the straight highway, and onto the Cooloola way, a far more adventurous trail that wound towards the great sandy national park along a single sandy track.

Kilometres passed by, and any remnant of the civilised world was far away, behind leagues of densely packed trees. The anticipation that had warmed my stomach had gained a nervous tang as I cycled along, as the road deteriorated further and further. Great drifts of shifting sand stopped the laden bike in its tracks, and for much of the way I was brought down to a walk. Time was marching on, and the sky that had previously hosted but a few fluffy floating clouds mere hours ago now hosted a menacing front coming from the sea. I was acutely aware that these dark ribbons were rolling inland, shading the forest canopy a frightful hue. Their arrival coincided with dusk. I stopped and listened to the shrill earie wind-cry that rustled the sand and made it hiss, and shuddered in the beginnings of fear. The warmness of anticipation had now already evolved into an immense loneliness out in this wilderness. I decided I had to push on through to where the next town might be, but my sand-stunted progress served only to frustrate. I sometimes attempted to mount my bike, only for it to sink into the sand to a halt a few metres later. My breathing hastened, and I could feel electricity building. To the east an odd flash of light made its way through the trees. I was in awe and shock at how such a simple and easy day had given way to this scene, and I took stock of my vulnerability. I was out here, very much alone.

After ten more kilometres, around one hour, nothing had come of the threatening storm and I had made it to the civilisation of Cooloola cove. Relief displaced the nervousness that sloshed around in my stomach, and at the end of this first day, I realised that I could probably never trust one to go as I would expect it. That night, I pitched up on the beachfront, in a place where camping was technically forbidden, as all the best camping places are. Darkness had settled, as had the air, and I began once again to feel content. A couple of fellows in utes came along to the beach to pull up their harvest of some type of worm that buried in the sand. They stopped to chat, and asked if I needed a place to stay for the night once they heard of my plans. In spite of their generous offer, I wished for nothing else than to stay in the tent, allow the emotions to settle, and to steady myself for whatever the road would throw up next.

It turned out that the road did indeed throw up many an exciting adventure, none of which I could have ever predicted or imagined. As mentioned previously, the constant backdrop of

4

this Australian coastal journey were the horrendous forest fires that blazed beneath a searing heat that would often top out above 40 degrees in the shade. I was easily drinking around ten litres of water before midday that presently evaporated straight out of my sun cream-lathered skin. It wasn't smart or funny to cycle much later than this time in such conditions. I often found myself pedalling hard from 5:30 or 6:00 until 12:00, resting for a few hours, then making the most of the cool evening hours before sundown to pedal a little further still. Sometimes, as the hour grew late, storms would roll off the coast as if to mock or rival the fiery day time heat. I would erect my tent with jarring dances of light defibrillating the Eastern horizon, never knowing whether they would come my way or not. While such moments were always the source of a certain nervousness as they were lived, and that I can still sometimes feel when remembering these evenings, the thoughts now of their sublime power have matured into something that I realise to be very special and very humbling.

Above these spectacles of nature, the most important adventures of this first foray into long-distance cycling came almost always as a direct consequence of the people that the road threw my way. These meetings were seldom more predictable than the weather.

The first remarkable people that I had the privilege to encounter were Michael and his family. They had agreed to host me in the tiny village of Mon Repos, comprised of only seven houses, just near the Southernmost point of the Great Barrier Reef, and just a few tens of kilometres from where forest fires were ravaging the coastal communities to the north.

Michael welcomed me with open arms, and I must say that few things have felt sweeter than the cold shower I took there to wash away the sweaty crass of a few days in 40 degrees. After some much-needed mon repos relaxation, the night began to set in. Michael began telling me about his involvement with a team of marine biologists who had a long-running experiment, just a few hundred metres away from his house. My curiosity and excitement multiplied as he began explaining that the experiment was to observe the behaviour and ecology of majestic loggerhead turtles. I naturally fell quite easily into persuasion when he offered to take me along for the night. Within a couple of hours, we found ourselves padding along the sands in buttery moonlight searching for loggerheads who were coming ashore to lay their eggs. At a certain moment, we found tracks in the sand, that looked as if a huge sack of potatoes had been dragged from the ocean. Michael quickly put this hypothesis to rest, and we alerted the biologists and followed the tracks. Here, at the end, we came upon a mother who was digging her nest into the sand, completely entranced in the act of birth. We watched in awe as she meticulously covered the eggs by clumsy but instinctively purposeful movements, shovelling the sand flipperstroke by flipperstroke. Then, she just left, job done, back to the ocean. Her eggs were soon dug up by the scientists to be counted, before they would hatch in mere weeks. If one returned then, one would witness legions of cute loggerheads bursting through the sand to fend for themselves. Once they do so, those that survive embark on a sixteen-year swimming tour of the South Pacific, which puts my little journey to shame, to say the least.

At the end of the night, I returned to Michael's, replete with awe and wonder. Never has such a restful feeling been felt when I awoke the following morning. I still could not quite believe my luck at chancing over such people as those that let me so briefly but so warmly into their world. I left with my bike, airy-hearted, feeling free as a loggerhead hatchling.

It was a few more days of sweating my way over the tropic of Capricorn, in those conditions described earlier, before I would meet the next truly remarkable folk. The road cut across the Great Dividing Range, away from the main highway, which is where I figured out that most of the magic happened. I had taken with me enough water to last just until midday, which is when

I hoped to reach the ranch of Sue and Simon Gedda. I had contacted them on an app called 'warmshowers', that puts cycle tourists in contact with each other. My clothes and skin were crystallised with salt, and I dared not dip in the crocodile-infested creeks for a wash. A shower and a bed for a couple of days could certainly do no harm. This is what was on my mind as I turned my wheel towards the Geddas, who had accepted to take me in.

A hundred and twenty kilometres down, and midday had gone by. The sun hung leaden in the sky that seemed to creak and sweat beneath the weight of the unrelenting heat. I was sat under the scant shade of roadside shrubbery, whose sparse branches barely had the girth to shade my skin. I sat in the dust, with a few drops of water to my name. Lotus Creek, where Simon and Sue should live, didn't seem to exist. I had reached where it ought to be on the map, to find nothing but the same parched and cracked earth with desperate tufts of grass that had covered much of the landscape of the previous sixty kilometres. I despaired and worried at my stupidity for underpacking water. Magical H_2O. I had refused to pay the few dollars for an extra bottle at the last roadhouse, a hundred kilometres earlier, and now my tongue felt just like the expansive drought-earth that rolled infinitely on, either side of the glimmering mirage-tarmac. Minutes that felt like hours passed, when finally, a truck danced its way onto the distant horizon. It stayed there for more minutes, unmoving but for its convalescent thermal dance. I willed it onwards, and on it came. Slowly, but it came. I heaved myself from my sliver of shade and waved it down to a halt. Two burly men peered down from the window to enquire as to what on earth had driven me here. They laughed when I told them of my cycling trip, and replenished my bottles from their cold esky. Water never had so sweet a taste.

With full bottles, I mustered onwards, and found that Sue and Simon lived only twenty kilometres up the road from the previous Lotus creek, that had been levelled by a cyclone eighteen months earlier. Once again, that fine cocktail of deliverance from suffering, and human warmth that brought me from it, bucked my spirits and rested my body. I napped away the whole afternoon, before gently being shown life on the ranch by the Geddas.

Sue, Mrs Gedda that is, had herself ended up there as a British traveller a couple of decades ago. Unsuspectingly, as she was passing through the range, a cyclone struck land that was so violent that a whole community was wiped off that map. She stuck around when the rescue efforts began, which is where she met Simon. He arrived in a helicopter to deliver supplies and he left with a wife. This couple were now in the business of hosting travellers like myself, as well as a herd of cattle, whose task it was to find and eat the rare blades of grass that defied all odds to grown on these parched mountains. We spent our couple of evenings talking together about how life can spread people to such improbable fates. In between our discussions, Simon would periodically leave to check the radar. Rain was forecast for the first time in months, which would be the difference between life and an early trip to the knackers for many of his cows. Like for the traveller, life at the ranch was left to the cruel stochastic whim of the elements. On the morning I was leaving, I rose to a beaming Simon looking excitedly out of the window. Drops of steady rain danced down the pane, and I could feel the dusty grasslands glugging down the water from the skies, as I had glugged that of the truckers.

With the rain, came wind. The first cyclone of the year – cyclone Owen - had formed over the Solomon islands at around the same time the first rain had come to the rescue of the Queensland cows. Within a couple of days it tracked towards the Australian coast, bringing epic deluges and palm-bending gusts. I relished the wind that blew my jacksy merrily up the coastal road that I rejoined after leaving the Gedda ranch. Finally, the fires and unbearable heat was being quenched. In these conditions I crossed the first cycle-tourist of the trip. I was rather ecstatic at seeing another soul as mad as myself appear on the horizon. I readied myself for spending the rest of the day sitting, chatting, recounting our travels with tips for water and campgrounds. As such, when a burly Hollander with an unflinching gurn barely stopped to shout hello through the headwind, I was a little disappointed. It seemed that my tail-wind smile immediately put us on different footings, despite the likeness of our situations. I cannot understate that the wind changes everything for the cycle-tourist. Here I saw that the one facing the wind saw was so irately disturbed by it, that it was almost impossible to assimilate his case to my own. He bitterly recounted his terrible day as I held my tongue to gloat about my easy mileage. He moved on within only a few minutes, grimacing, facing the pelting rain once more. On the other hand, for me, the miles flew on by. The road-signs to Cairns were showing smaller and smaller numbers, and besides the complaints of my backside, it looked like I was going to make it there more or less unharmed. The temperature had cooled off, and as the tropics approached, roadside banana, mango and pawpaw provided me with almost unlimited fuel to march further North and West.

Much to my ignorance, while I was lapping up the kilometres, cyclone Owen that had skirted Westwards with little consequence, had redoubled its strength over the Gulf of Carpentaria. It had since boomeranged back towards the Cape York peninsula and was predicted to make landfall between Cairns and Innisfail. So was I. A couple of women in a roadhouse where I was filling water warned me that my tent might not be the strongest match for a category three cyclone. It seemed I needed to find shelter for a couple of days. I reached out to Aarn, a warmshowers host who lived in Innisfail, 170km away. I had a day to make the distance. With a considerable effort that left my backside in tatters, I just about did it. Owen was weakening overland and when it reached the next day, it was little more than a tropical depression. My trusty tent would have been just fine, but I was still glad to be tucked away inside drinking Aarn's fortified home-brew. For the couple of days spent with Aarn, we engaged in intelligent discussion all through to the evening. He regaled me with tales of his travels in Cambodia, studying tiny river fish. This was his absolute passion. In his own cycle touring times in South East Asia, he had one goal: to see something truly amazing every single day. When he spoke, a fire and a twinkle lit up his eyes that filled me with inspiration and almost adoration. Then, at around seven in the evening, the homebrew would take its toll, and his inspiring words weakened and degraded into slurring gibberish at the telly. I retired to bed with a pang of sadness and wondered if he had gone cold turkey on his fix of amazement.

On the last detour in Australia, onto the Atherton tablelands, I began thinking about my own goals. *What did I want to get out of what I had set out to do?* I had a bunch of expectations to deliver. I had set out to raise money for a charity called Newlife. This charity had once helped my younger sister, Lottie, who could not walk, talk, eat, etc (but who could smile incessantly). The trip was conceived in the spirit that Pierre and I would make full use of our mobility, to raise money and awareness for those that don't have that privilege. I had no idea how to fundraise, especially now that I was alone. My strategy of how to involve Newlife in my trip was completely hazy. My promise to them was that I was to provide a story of such extreme challenge and hardship, that people would simply be compelled to empty their wallets. But now that life seemed rather simple, could I still spin such a story? Then, there was my family, my friends and their impressions. I had esteem to uphold: an image I had created for myself as an adventurer. I didn't know if I was courageous enough to change this. I had presented my journey as a serious feat of physical endurance. Did I really want this? Maybe at one point I did: that time when my heroes were the pioneer racers of the Tour de France. How they flew across mountains! How they gritted their teeth in driving rain, not stopping to sleep for hundreds of kilometres. That was the image I had of my trip. I wanted this for myself. Grit. I would get lost in the desert and not drink water for a week until finally I would rescue myself by slaying a camel and drinking its hump dry of sour milk. My experiences in Australia told me this would be unlikely. When I ran out of water in the searing heat of the remote expanse of the Great Diving Range, all I needed do was flap my arms by the roadside. Before ten minutes expired, my water was once again full. Perhaps my trip would not be so adventurous after all.

In any case, the coast was now clear for Cairns, and after the three-day detour to the verdant tableland delights, where aristocrat cows thrived on green fields nourished by constant humid rainfall, contrary to those in much of the rest of Queensland, I descended the Kuranda range, ecstatic and full of pride. Cairns. This city marked the end of a somewhat arduous jaunt. After 2000 kilometres and 21 days I welled with emotion as I rolled into the city. The bike was in good condition and my only concern was how sore my back and arse had become. I had born witness to the sublime and had proved to myself that I could navigate what the road threw up: from bushfires, to cyclones, to backpackers. I felt marginally more confident in my own abilities, even if most of my time was spent in fear only dulled by the mundanity of endless pedalstrokes.

In the city, I reflected on the fact that for much of these three weeks, I had been mostly bored, aching and hot. I could not help but reflect that if the merits of cycle touring were to be judged and told in a timewise proportion, nobody other than a masochist would recommend it. I had experienced the mundane in abundance. I had also found that it was precisely the mundane that was the perfect playground for the exciting and the out-of-the-ordinary. It's easy to think of cycle touring as an *escape* from routine: the perfect freedom. And yet for most of the time, this escape from routine simply translated into routine once more, arguably even less stimulating. Wake up. Pack panniers (knowing before long exactly where everything lives). Pack tent. Cycle. Eat. Cycle. Eat. Cycle. Eat. Put up tent. Sleep.

Most of the time is spent in routine boredom. The great benefit of cycling, however, is the potential for routine to be broken at any moment. On the bike you are out there, and out there, the world has a funny way of conspiring against too rigorous a routine. I still had my goal. That was to get back to England. But how I wanted to do it changed in light of this first trip. I felt that it was the people who had made it so special. Those whose small gestures and fleeting connections were the breaking of intense monotony. I wanted to my trip to become a story whose main characters were the people of this world that I would meet along the road.

Taunggyi

Lao Cai

Loikaw

Luang Namtha

Op Luang

Thabarwa

Mae Sot

Bangkok

Kao Sam
Roi Yot

Surat Thani

Alor Setar

Petaling Jaya

Singapore

13

Alone in Singapore

I spent the first night in Asia in the tent of a homeless man on the East coast park of Singapore.

The delayed flight into Changi delivered me into the humid night. Hunger panged the stomach and thirst parched my lips as I had refused to be extorted for bottled water on the aeroplane. It was already dark outside when I began putting my bicycle together in front of the sliding doors of the arrivals hall. The enormous box that it was packaged in was stood to my right and when I had finally tightened the last bolt, fixing the pedal to the pedal arm, I turned my sights to the box. *What to do with this?* A Chinese man was smoking the last drags of his cigarette and ogling me with curiosity. I felt like a freak from a far-away land, and I was. He smiled fleetingly and stubbed his butt in a small black bin in front of the taxi rank. I looked around shiftily and when nobody was looking, leant the box gently against the bin, feeling it was almost the same as putting it inside. I had heard that Singapore was the cleanest city in the world, and I didn't want to bring down the tone. With that final detail nicely taken-care of, to the snigger of onlookers who I had not remarked, I mounted the bike and headed to the centre of Singapore to find first water, then food, then a hostel.

I had studied the map for the best part of two minutes and set off onto what turned out to be a motorway. The drivers barely batted their eyelids and I felt immediately happy. Nobody hollered or ran me over as I suspected someone might have done if it were the UK. As swiftly as I joined the motorway, I left it and joined the slightly more pedestrian East Coast parkway that spans a large section of the South of the island. I glided through the still, humid air, passing runners, roller skaters and cyclists out for their evening recreation. A bunch of food stands that I later learnt was called a *hawker centre* blared in gaudy neon light against the backdrop of the manicured tropical trees silhouetted against the glow of LED streetlamps. Hungry and curious, I floated over like a moth. There was a cacophony of voices speaking Chinese, English, Malay and some sort of Indian language. Vendors busied themselves in their tiny stalls preparing fish ball soups and noodles, while the servers swiftly flitted amongst the tables. I found a seat and reclined into Asia. I was finally here. It wasn't as I had expected. For one, Pierre wasn't here with me and for two, I felt far too comfortable. In the hot night-time air, the conversation, laughter, flash fry sizzle and optimistic slurps from dry glass-bottoms were betraying my *expedition* for a holiday. I mused on how all this might soon change, or whether hawker stalls might exist all the way to Europe. I ate my fishballs and continued on, tired and anxious to find a place to stay.

Further along the East Coast Park I noticed a camp of a few tents. Feeling bold, I proceeded to ask the three scruffy men milling outside what they were doing camping here. *Was it possible? Could I camp here too?* The three men immediately welcomed me to sit down.

"Hello my friend, where you from? Welcome to Singapore! Rambutan, cola?" Not waiting for my tangle of confusion to unravel into a response, the man grinned a toothy grin and rummaged in a cooler-box producing a bottle of cola and a handful of spiky red fruit.

"Rambutan!" He grinned. "Try, try."

He peeled back the spiky red skin to reveal a translucent flesh – the size of a small plum, and just as juicy and sweet. I was immediately made to feel like a guest, despite meeting in a park. I mustered the courage to ask about camping here for the night. Bursting with enthusiasm and an infectious smile, he told me in somewhat broken English that I could certainly stay. What was more, I didn't even need to unpack my own tent – he had a spare.

I spent the night confused and on edge, in a flimsy tent next to those of two of the three men I had just met. What a bizarre situation to end up sleeping here in the middle of one of Singapore's most popular parks on my first night on the continent! I sniffed a laugh when I retired into the canvas, amused, bemused and incredulous. I had no idea what made these guys so graciously accommodate me. I barely spared a thought as to why they were here and especially why they had an extra tent. I was only reassured by the fact that nobody paid any particular attention or surprise to the camp – and the fact that a Chinese father and son were camping alongside us. The men who had invited me weren't particularly shady, but doubt gnawed at my thoughts. *Was I going to get mugged: My bike lock picked in the dead of night while I was snared in the canvas trap?* I could see the silhouettes of the two men standing and smoking and drinking and I could hear them chortling and cackling. *Had I been done?* I fell into a light sleep, lullabied by Singapore's murmurs.

When I woke in the morning all my worldly possessions were still alongside me and my bike still attached securely to the same palm as last night. I felt guilty for my unfounded doubts and judgements: especially after reading about the kindness of strangers in so many travellers' stories. Ludovic Hubler, Jamie McDonald, Leon McCarron, Sarah Outen, Alastair Humphreys, Harold Tillman and countless others all spoke of being on the receiving end of sickening kindness, but I never expected it to happen to me.

The men awoke shortly after me at daybreak and I spent the morning relaxing and finding out more about their lives. They were homeless but had been given let to camp in this designated area on the East Coast Park. The spare tent was for if they had family or guests to come and visit (yes, seriously) but when nobody was there it was used for storage. They made a living by catching worms on the seafront and selling them to fishermen, or if they were feeling lucky themselves, would use them to catch fish that they would then hawk off to the seafood restaurants. All this they were doing until they could afford a house and better work. I took my leave from these fine gentlemen in the humid mid-morning, curious to discover more of Singapore and its strangers.

I had first dreamt of coming to Singapore roughly one year prior. I was here because it was the starting point of mine and Pierre's 16,000 kilometres cycling route across the Eurasian landmass. Pierre was already about 2000 kilometres up the road. He had gotten a flight to Kuala Lumpur a few weeks ago. Even the prologue hadn't gone to plan, not that we ever had a tenable one. I guess we only ever acted on ideas. I can remember the first one. The chilly February rain flicked steadily at my steamy Withington window back in Manchester. I was about to announce to the world (but in reality, probably just my mum and dad) the culmination of mine and Pierre's discussions that began as a half-hearted joke and ended with this. *A Frenchman and an Englishman walk into a bar after having cycled from Singapore to France*, ha! Who even does that?

What a buzz when my friends began asking of my plans for after university. Was I bound for the civil service, or for a PhD in Quantum theory, or would I look dreamily onto London's lights from the upper floor of a Canary Wharf tower? Could I drive profits? Would I design game-changing software platforms to please plump shareholders? Was I made to consult, or to code? Client-facing, office pacing or profit chasing? Was I a front end or back end kinda guy? I didn't have an answer to any of these questions that to me were just as relevant as wondering whether it was the Martian or the Lunar surface that was the best place for a vegetable garden. I was just sure that the world was an open place and when I sheepishly replied that I was going to cycle across a couple of continents with my friend to raise money for a charity called Newlife, my belly flared with a nervous passion. My friends hardly believed it, and neither did I, even when I was brushing the pedals by Marina bay.

I had planned the whole trip with Pierre. Pierre was a guy from whom life flowed in abundance. He had taken me on my first ever hitch-hike, up my first ever Alpine mountain and cycled with me from Lyon to Montpellier, the city where we had first met on an endless blazing summer evening some years ago. He was Dean Moriarty and I was Sal Paradise and although I had always dreamt of hitting the road on my bicycle, after my first long ride to Amsterdam back in the promising summer of the year before, I'm not sure I would have had the gusto to set off on a transcontinental without him. Yet here I was. Gusto or no gusto I was alone in Singapore with a bike to pedal and a tent to kip in and a bunch of panniers where every morning I would stuff my worldly possessions, to take them a step closer to home.

I had split from Pierre just as everything was finally in place for the trip. We had built up an image, a concept, and what almost became an obligation to each other. It was called 'Half the World away'. We had received help from a small number of organisations. A cooking set from the Alpkit foundation, a few hundred pounds from the Get Exploring Trust, two sets of repaired panniers from Carradice and even bikes on loan from my Uncle's dental company. We had a *gofundme* account to support our journey and all the equipment that we needed to cycle together. I had arrived in Peregian beach under a heavy grey sky at the start of Australian Summer. Pierre was already there. I remember how the bus from the airport pulled into the lazy suburban street. I gazed on in wonder at the tropical thicket beyond the houses that abruptly dissolved into the sands of a buttercream white beach that stretched on for miles. Leaving the shuttle, I could hear the sedate sloshing of the Pacific and taste its saline tang. I felt an intense sense of anticipation. Here I was. I remember how I breathed deeply before knocking at the door and allowing mine and Pierre's processions of events to meld into one. I remember the easing of the existential dissonance, as ecstatic, free and wild, we ran barefoot through the strip of bush, to the sands, stumbling in a clumsy sprint across the deserted beach beneath the heavy grey clouds and leaping across the waves before plunging into the pacific. We were going across Eurasia!

We didn't hang around too long, and on my Uncle's recommendation we set out on our first tour as partners, into the enigmatic depths of the bush, the vastness of Australia, away from the coastal cocoon. We spent a week doing exactly this, testing our equipment, our resolve and each other. We rode on a rocky track over the hinterland of the Great Dividing Range, where the sky hung over the distant layers of forested hills in a melting swathe of indigo and lilac. Clear of the coastal hills, we soon discovered the mundanity of cycle touring on the unfaltering straight roads, where vehicles would stay on the horizon forever. After a number of adventures and misadventures on the bike, we soon found work on a farm that was managed by a friend of my uncle. In between the hard work of dismantling a passion fruit farm, we shared moments of unforgettable simple pleasures: bathing in the shaded creek where trickles of sweat were washed away by trickles of cool water, or in the lake where we could swim to the crack of whip birds and the chuckle of insouciant kookaburras. At the same time, we had shared the tent for two weeks and we were slowly beginning to grate on each other, as almost any two friends would. The dynamic seemed to be changing. We headed back to Peregian beach having each fattened our wallets, but there seemed to be a little more uncertainty in our relationship. And what were we going to do about this whole cycling around the world business?

As more time was spent in Peregian beach with Pierre, making final preparations for our departure to Singapore, it became more and more clear that we were in very different positions. It seemed to me that Pierre wanted to get back to France quickly.

He mused on getting back for summer, on taking trains and on studying again. I was very much open to long detours and wanted to traverse the continent uniquely by bicycle. I had also, with farm and labour work in Australia, managed to save almost £5000 for the rest of the trip, with Pierre having accrued substantially less. I hate that money came into my considerations. It dampened the exciting romance of travel by which Pierre and I were completely besotted, but it weighed on my mind nonetheless. I couldn't bear the thought of this trip I had sacrificed so much for, being one of compromise. I had given up stability: turned down a PhD, left behind friends, family and weekend evenings in pubs. I had broken-up with the girl I loved, because I loved myself more, and this trip, if I am honest, was about me. How could I justify such a selfish trajectory for which I had cut so many ties, if I was going to let myself be strung along by Pierre's changing ideas? I couldn't. My whole life had been about opening doors but all I wanted was to slam them shut and cycle out to an open plain, where doors don't exist. Pierre was beginning to think about doors. At the same time, how could I tell all this to Pierre? I felt like a rancid cheat, like I had led Pierre down a rutted path where I would leave him, clueless and alone, while I revelled in pre-meditated freedom. I was manic with indecision. After a few torturous few days mulling and pacing and writing and ragging out my hair I decided that I needed to broach the possibility of no longer doing the trip with Pierre - of separating.

After having spent the best part of the last year creating a vision together for how we would travel, it seemed so awfully momentous to scrap everything. Not to mention the question of how we were to proceed about telling the people who had so much sponsored and supported us. My heart was in my mouth as I headed to my cousin's house to meet with Pierre and tell him how I felt. On the surface I went under the pretence of chatting about the *possibility* of separation, but deep down I knew I was on my way to *tell* him that I was going it alone. The 'we need to talk' conversation was a haunting moment. I felt wretched and traitorous. I remember clearly the walk back down the beach after the *break-up* chat. I felt heartbroken, but in the same instance a renewed sense of freedom and the possible welled within. I looked up to catch the inert gaze of the full moon, and down along the infinite sandy expanse it goadingly illuminated. I sighed a sigh of freshness into the cool night air. Through my tears, I knew it was the right decision to make. From this moment, it was up to Pierre and I to reinvent our visions of the future based on the new present that just a week prior had been unforeseeable. We would both make the trip back to Europe solo. In our own ways, under our own steam. This is why I found myself alone in Singapore.

Acorns

Singapore is a city of the future, where one would struggle to imagine any circumstance of crime or misfortune. Things advanced in a clocklike manner everywhere, with the exception of little India which is the city's token pocket of chaos. This is where I made my base for two nights, after the stay with my homeless hosts. The marigolds, the hollering, the jingling of trinkets and turbulence of aromas filled the air with an atmosphere that changed slightly but noticeably with each step. Scruffy-looking Indians sat on tiny stools and shovelled rice and dahl into their mouths from banana leaf plates, staring at the constant stream of mopeds or creaky bicycles that ambled past – more often than not on the wrong side of the street. One could wander down the same street dozens of times and each length would be different. It was a fascinating little world that was a massive contrast to the smartness and sharpness of much of the rest of the city. On the third day, after stocking up on everything I thought I might need on the road, my feet became itchy. The deeper delights that were held in this city-state-island were doing little to tempt me. Though the lights, soundscapes and sky-trees of marina bay were nothing short of astonishing, they were not what I was here for. My goal was in the other direction: England. I certainly wasn't working toward it by goofing around this place, however much utopian fascination it held. I was also trying to dodge the thoughts of being at too loose an end. Alone in a city whose endless possibilities turned my compass in endless rings, with no network and no immediate friend to orientate me... A far less frightful proposition was to begin cycling across Eurasia. It was a trade of freedom for purpose.

With the orientation of purpose, I packed my bags once more, as I had done in Peregian beach. The anticipation as I rolled away my clothes, and buckled the panniers was familiar, but amplified. I was about the hit the road, for real. Pierre and I had already planned a route whose trace was etched in my mind. I repeated it to myself in my sleep. It began in Singapore, made its way up the Malaysian West coast, and into Thailand. In Bangkok we would get visas for Tibet and Pakistan, which is where we would go next. So up through Laos and into China and then to the world's greatest plateau before coming down to Kathmandu. From Kathmandu it would be west to Delhi and then Lahore. Pakistan would lead us to Iran, and Iran up to Turkey. Then from Turkey there would only be little old Europe to fly across. We envisaged arriving in France, welcomed by friends, partying for weeks, and never having our hands free of a beer. It still seemed like a reasonable idea to me, relatively of course. I knew that the crux of this plan would be getting all the permits and visas, but I would worry about that down the road.

At the stage of imminently leaving Singapore, this was the route I banked on following. Along with this came my basic, but hopefully effective game plan. Cycle an average of 100 kilometres a day in the right direction. That was head and tail of it. Head and tail can always be made of everything but it's the guts that prove the problem. I believed that the diplomacy and the visas and the few restricted regions would probably be the main issues. Indeed, when Pierre and I had researched the documentation that we might need, we hastily drew the conclusion that we might need to *wing it*. It seemed that the papers were nigh on impossible to obtain on the road. We held nonetheless a steadfast conviction that such diplomatic blockades could easily be overcome with the power of innocence and naivety. I had read in books that travellers had attempted to bypass the Police checkpoints in Tibet for example, and if caught, simply feigned the dumb tourist. *If Ludovic Hubler could talk his way onto a vessel bound for Antarctica, we could talk our way across Tibet,* I would muse. I was inspired by the contragrain audacity of such travellers. It was a game, and like any good superhero film, the brave and virtuous would win and the caped villain of bureaucratic restriction would fall unmasked, one way or another. Even alone, I had the utmost faith that I could find a way to and through these lands. I was willing to wait and beg and plead and generally do whatever it might take, but I didn't need to consider this for now. I had a game plan to get on with. With the guts pushed out of my mind, all that was left was head and tail. If I flipped a coin, both sides would be for go.

And so, in the stewing Singapore humidity of the morning of the 4th of January 2019, escorted over the motorway by a pair of concerned Indians in a delivery truck, I crossed the Woodlands bridge and the border into Malaysia.

Waves

The concerned Indian escorts in their battered red pickup truck forked away to the car lane of the border crossing with a wave. They joined the backlog of traffic waiting to cross the immense bridge while I passed my first international land border crossing with ease. I sailed through in the motorcycle lane and savoured the uniqueness of my situation. No other cyclists to be seen. Sore thumb would be an understatement and I constantly received honks and waves of encouragement from the friendly Malays who whizzed past on their mopeds. Even the border guard was jolly as he stamped my passport and allowed me through with little ado and a hearty "Welcome to Malaysia!"

I hadn't realised this previously, but on the other side of the bridge from Singapore was Malaysia's third largest city: Johor Bahru. I had half expected to quickly join quiet palm-lined lanes where pygmies stood on doorsteps of tin huts. Instead I was met with a 4-lane highway with 2-lane slip roads. Cars and mopeds and busses thronging with people careered in legion towards this sprawling Asian mega city. At every slip road I had to leap from the saddle and shift myself with furious acceleration into the merging traffic. Once up to my lowly maximum speed, I drifted across two lanes of motorcycles and cars to make it back to the safety of the hard-shoulder. My heart was in my mouth for most of this stint, which was rather unhelpful as I was gasping in adrenaline-driven fright. After a good hour, and with my eyes watering from fear and thick pollution, the traffic gradually thinned. The road skirted away from Johor Bahru, and I took the highway exit on the road towards Pontian Kecil (Kecil meaning small in Malay, which was promising). Very abruptly, the palm-lined winding lane finally settled into reality. Now only the odd motorcycle or pickup loaded full with some strange enormous fruit that looked like a cross between a blackberry and a porcupine passed by. My expectations and preconceptions were constantly being dashed. I looked around and now in a calmer state could take stock of my surroundings. I had imagined the Malaysian palms to be tangled in jungles of bush and vine, wild and uncultivated. What I saw was that it receded many hectares beyond the road in ordered ranks. Most of the trees bore that strange fruit that was stacked in the pickups. The words *Sime Darby plantation* were plastered on signs everywhere. After some time, I realised I was not in the wild, but a vast expanse of agricultural land. This landscape ended up being the one I would be most commonly immersed during my passage through Malaysia. It didn't take much more thought to connect the dots and realise that these vast areas of cultivated trees that were pushing back Malaysia's jungle were plantations of palm oil.

This road passed through miles and miles of the homogeneous ranks of the oil palm, on its way to little Pontian, my goal for the evening. It seemed natural to have a town as a goal for the end of the day. I would find food, light and civilization. I arrived in the town, passing though districts of what seemed to be uniquely Chinese electronics shops or garages. Their faded signs dissolved into the flaking paints of pastel creams and pinks with the onset of dusk. All roads, each flanked by such shops, seemed to converge towards the bustling evening marketplace. Here, I descended my bike and wandered amongst the hiss and smoke puffs of flash fryers and woks. Young children ran about trailing their *Air* (pronounced eye-ear) *Kelapa* while parents prospected the *Nasi Lemak* and *Mee Goreng*. It was a festive atmosphere that felt like a huge family party. Pleasantries and jokes were being exchanged everywhere that fed the swelling cacophony. I let a market vendor choose my meal, that he generously packed into a box at the cost of about five ringgit, or £1. The Malays sure were proud of their food and for good reason; each bite of vegetable and slurp of noodle packed a burst of flavour that tingled with hints of spice. It perfectly complemented the atmosphere. Replete with noodles, air kelapa and good vibrations, I still didn't feel as I was on an expedition as much as I was on a holiday.

26

Well fed, I moved my attention to the next of my needs, which was rest (it seems I skipped over cleanliness). Ending the day in a town sure was conducive to a good feed, but less so to a good sleep. It would take me a long time in fact, to realise that having a town as a goal for day's end would always preclude the simplicity of just pitching the tent somewhere in the countryside. Luckily, my maps software indicated that there was a hostel in the main strip of town. I set off optimistically but found the address to correspond to a dilapidated old shack surrounded by hessian sacks overflowing with litter. It looked like it had never been a hostel at all. I trundled back to the market to see what some Pontian residents had to say on the matter but they all pointed me in the direction of the expensive looking hotel, that made my wallet shiver. Turning back to the map, I noticed a small park on the way out of town and away from the incessant din of the mopeds humming down the busy main road.

Upon arriving at the site, with no alternative prospect, I decided that this was to be my first lone-campsite. I hid behind a couple of alien trees, in the most secluded place I could find. The hornblasts and moped-buzzes barely settled, and lights flitted into the shadow from the street nearby. The night-time heat was still quite flustering, despite the sun having set a couple of hours ago. I pitched the inner section of my tent, as discreet as I could manage in the public park. Here, I simply lay for an hour, sweating, staring, not wondering, but dozing awake in that state of brain emptiness that a day of exercise in the sun almost always leads to. From the thronging market, to this solitary ingratiating campsite. I fell difficultly to a light sleep, feeling lonely and small, a speck on the tip of this Asian continent that seemed to dominate me.

As the hazy morning light filtered through the tent lining, I felt somewhat renewed. I had not been swallowed by hungry Malays prowling for dessert after their market-snack or the stray dogs that slunk along alleys and roadsides. In fact I had been quite undisturbed, and felt rather thrilled at my town-camp, even comfortable. Although, I don't believe I had stopped sweating since leaving Singapore.

The second day was all about moving further up the road to Batu Pahat. Here I would mercifully be rescued from the prospect of camping in my own sweat and loneliness by a *Warmshowers* host by the name of Sebiji. He welcomed me late in the afternoon to his humble but beautiful Chinese food canteen and led me to the empty room above. I was rescued from the heat and mundanity of the road in a sudden swing of the door. Inside, the whole place exhumed a spiritual calmness. An eclectic mix of minimalist Ancient China and cycling inspired deco left no space unpleasant to the eye. I could have spent days exploring the confines of his canteen! He showed me to the shower in the backroom upstairs. It was a large bucket with a small tray for pouring the cold water over the body and it was absolutely perfect for the heat and humidity. Refreshed, I set off once more to cater to my most basic of needs, while Sebiji was occupied cooking for his customers.

At another of the hawker centres, that so far proved to be almost as ubiquitous as pubs in Britain, I made the acquaintance of a nutty Chinese bachelor. He couldn't have missed me in my outlandish floral shirt and trusty blue decathlon hiking shorts clumsily trying to converse with a stall owner. He beckoned me to his table to share his cockles and drink a beer with him. I accepted with glee, especially as beer was expensive in Malaysia, and went to hear what he had to say. He exuded an emphatic charisma as he began banterously laughing with or at me. With him were two Vietnamese companions who didn't speak any English, or Vietnamese for that matter. They seemed wholly unmoved by the gesticulations and jibes of the nutty man, whose jokes and words I seldom understood or kept up with. A word that all four of us understood, however, was karaoke. This was the materialising goal of my evermore drunken new friend, that he was coaxing the rest of us to assume. We walked a short distance and reached a car that he unlocked. The young Vietnamese couple got inside and I hesitated at the door, expecting only to be walking.

"Uhm, I'm not sure about getting in the car, I have to go back to my friend's house soon."

"No Jake, no problem! Get in, not far!"

I hesitated, but thought back to the strangers in Singapore. How awful I felt for mistrusting them. I wouldn't make that mistake again. I got in the car. As soon as I did, I regretted my decision. The man's tone suddenly changed. We drove into the traffic of Batu Pahat and he incessantly whispered, "Everything's going to be just fine Jake. Everything is going to be ok. Jake, you will be ok."

We rolled on, cutting the neon-cast shadows of Batu Pahat.

"In life you have to know who are good people and who are bad people Jake, you will learn to tell the difference."

I wanted to scream *STOP and let me out!* but I remained fixed in my seat and stifled a nervous giggle as I fidgeted with my fingers and did everything I could to not look anywhere except out of the window. The tension at red lights was thick. The fifteen-minute drive to the karaoke bar took an eternity and I felt relieved as we pulled up and I stepped out of the door. Why I did not take this chance to run away, I do not know, but instead I followed this strange man and his two strange companions down the pavement.

We quickly arrived at the karaoke bar. It had no signs, no indication of KTV, no gaudy flashing lights or slogans, just a black façade with a black door inconspicuously fitted into it. One of two Chinese-looking men in suits fitted to their bulging chests and arms opened the door and in we went.

Inside was a dark empty bar and a few tables in front of a projector screen. We sat, three in silence, and one enthusiastically shouting for attention. Scantily clad girls came presently holding a bucket of iced beers and microphones that they placed on the table. My mind was still torn between two actions. Sitting with these three unlikely companions to sing cheesy pop songs, which it goes without saying, I no longer had the appetite to do, or taking my chance to sprint away into the night. We had already been served with beer at the table before I could follow what my mind was sure it had to do. We remained the only people in the establishment as the karaoke began. After two heavy Vietnamese power ballads, it was my turn to pick up the mic and muster some enthusiasm to flatter Queen's "Don't stop me now". Meanwhile, in between each sip of beer, one of the suggestively dressed women would come and make strong eye contact while bending over a little too far, taking a bottle of Tiger from the iced bucket in the middle of the table and topping up the tiny glass to the top. I sipped as gently as possible so as not to bring her over, but to give the illusion to the others that I was having a good time. I sat in nervous horror as the 60-year old Chinese bachelor belted his heart out to Frank Sinatra's "My Way" and the woman, who I was now sure was a stripper, stared into my soul, pouring me beer I didn't want, while witch-like giggles escaped the Vietnamese girl's mouth at her assumed boyfriend's fondles. I *needed* to escape.

The Chinese man went to the toilet and I sat immobile. When he returned, I collared him and pleaded him to take me back to my friend right away. He protested and told me that a big night out was on the cards, and more friends were arriving. I surprised myself with my firm response.
"You've brought me here. We've had fun, and now you have to take me back."
"Ok Jake," he sighed in resignation, "ok".
I breathed a sigh of relief. He shouted something in Chinese to the Vietnamese lovers, who nodded at me, before we left under the hawk-like eyes of the bouncers at the door.
The drunken Chinese man drove me back to where we had come from and I got out as he told me that the life of a bachelor was one of freedom to do whatever he so wished. I felt sick at the thought of this slimy sextegenarian having his way with

some poor young woman who he would likely pay for sex, which is exactly what he had been banging on about for the last twenty minutes in the car. I texted an acquaintance I had met in Singapore to ask her opinion on the situation, and her response confirmed my hypothesis. She told me that in South East Asia, quite a few brothels are organised in this way. She also warned me that when left alone in the room, the bouncers come over and force the naïve karaokephile to pay for sex with one of the girls. I was lucky to have got out when I did and clearly also lucky to have the Vietnamese lovers with me so I was never left alone. One thing I did at least take from this creep was that I now had another compelling case study for the continuous lesson of being able to discern the good from the bad in the world.

Arriving back to Sebiji, I recounted my misadventure. He was just cleaning up the kitchen and seemed mostly unphased. He played down the experience, but I was sure I was on the cusp of a dark situation. In any case, I knew I would never be tempted to participate in a karaoke night in the near future.

Sebiji saw me off in the morning as I rejoined the coastal road Northwards. It seemed to me that many adventures and misadventures were already coming my way. Much more intensely so than in Australia. I calmed myself by acknowledging the difference in scale and context. Here, the journey through Malaysia was always going to be about finding my feet in this starkly different environment to anything I had known before. I was willing to take my time to acclimatise and to detour and to not rush and to try not to look too much at the map. I remember distinctly looking lots at the map. It was laughable. My GPS tracking application, Polarsteps, roughly recorded the progress on the bike. After three days of cycling in the stifling humidity I felt pretty well spent. *I must be close now*, I thought, and opened up the tracker to check. I zoomed out first to Malaysia, where progress seemed tedious at best. Then, at the scale of South-East Asia, the trace became a dot. I then prospected the size of China and then all of Eurasia against the minute distance I had already covered. I gulped. I may well have bitten off a bit more than I could chew.

The distances were simply so vast. A vastness so impossible to confront by bicycle. I thought back to the first time I broached the distance between Manchester and Sheffield on my Triban-300 road bike. The freezing squalls and biting rain. How at one point my feet got so cold that I took off my shoes, removed the gloves from my hands and proceeded to clumsily put them onto my poor soaking feet. My gross lack of preparation and lack of suitable clothing. My jittering teeth and shivering body. But, at the end, the pride of taking on a full 72 kilometres and the sense of entitled deliverance that came with a hot bath and cup of instant coffee. At the time, Manchester to Sheffield seemed almost as vast as the continent that now lay before me. I felt like a madman for doing that on a bicycle. *Was I now in a similar position, just scaled up a bit?* I took solace from these humble origins, even if it was evident that by analogy, I was barely beyond my South Manchester cul-de-sac. The biting rain on the lonely moors of the bleak peaks was yet to come. I quickly closed the map and quelled these dangerous thoughts and tried to melt harmoniously into my surroundings where my mind was more at ease.

On the fifth day, the first real problems began. I had done two hours of riding on quiet roads in the midst of the eternal Sime Darby palm plantations, when a wave of weakness washed over me. I had a striking headache and was losing focus quickly. At first I thought I might be dehydrated and so I drank and drank and drank. I was drinking slightly less than in Australia but the temperature was certainly a little cooler here, although this was compensated by the high humidity. Either way, I didn't *need* to drink as much as in Australia and felt like I had not been under-watering myself. I then wondered if I needed sugar so I gorged on fruit. It didn't seem to help much. I pedalled on in the mounting heat and humidity regardless, not even considering stopping or resting.

By midday I was bordering on delirium and found a small sheltered platform next to a heap of waste where I lay for an hour in the foul hot stench. I was unable to get up from this position and my head pounded and my stomach was squeezing itself into a prune. It didn't take long for impulse to take over and I hurdled the trash heap and onto the sand of the nearby beach to throw up. I was on my hands and knees, spluttering and retching when a curious Malay passing by decided it was the perfect moment to squat next to me and inquire as to my religious affiliation. Needless to say I was feeling rather godless at that moment and I certainly made it known to him. I am still unsure how I managed the extra 40 kilometres to Port Dickson on this day. It took me a long time. In the evening I made the decision to move from my roll mat where I had collapsed, eyes closed and rolling gently back into my skull, and into a nearby hotel.

I sauntered zombie-like to the nearest one and checked in with little regard to my wallet. The hotel owner who greeted me was snarky and I could feel his sour menace over the counter. At any other time I would have gone elsewhere, but drained of all energy, anywhere I could attempt to exert some degree of control over my bowel movements and vomiting was just fine. For two out of the three nights here, I didn't need the bed, just the toilet. As I woke on day two, I prised apart my sticky eyes to take in the scenery of my lodgings. The wafer-thin drape curtains that smelt like cigarettes let in curdled light onto the decaying sofa where I was laid, mouth drooping open like a dog having a stroke. It was obviously dawn at Sunrise beach hotel, but for me, there had been no night before this. I resentfully switched off the smooth jazz that had been eking out of the telly all night in a feeble attempt to soothe away my shits (It didn't work). I looked around at the depressed kettle on top of the sad fridge and forced myself to trek over the peeling lino to boil some water to drink. I titillated over, all the time feeling like death could be imminent, filled up on boiled water and flopped onto the springs hidden below a thin coating of mattress until midday. No hope. At 13:00 I called for the hotel boss to declare that I must see a doctor. He knew he had me. "Ah, so you stay one more night then, my friend?" Hook line and sinker.

I willed myself as strongly as I could to get over this sickness and within 72 hours was back on the bike, having meticulously researched all possible toilet breaks on the route to Klang. During my time laid on that bed inside sunrise hotel, I began thinking about getting a flight home. The episode scared me. I wasn't prepared to be so ill so soon. If this were my state after five days, how would I be in a month, or even a year? I shuddered at these thoughts but learned to take solace in my gradually improving condition. My tune changed to the sound of *if I can surmount this: I can surmount any illness this trip will throw at me!* Still, It didn't make the eight other times I shat myself any easier.

I was glad to have researched all of the toilet points, as I think I made the most of almost all of them. Nonetheless, my form was coming back. Klang was the last port of call before heading to the spaghetti-like road plan of Kuala Lumpur. Wei Ann, a friend from university, had agreed to let me stay with her parents for a few days in this sprawling city. They lived in the outskirts – the still expansive metropolis of Petaling Jaya. From there I could commute into the centre to explore and importantly get stuck into the guts of my trip. I wanted to get myself a Thai visa for 60 days, that should give me time to organise the more complicated ones once I make it to Thailand.

Once more, I managed to avoid Malaysian traffic death by the skin of my teeth and turned up to Wei Ann's family home intact. I was welcomed with open arms and mirth by the Hengs. For it probably looked like I could benefit from a bit of hospitality.

Alongside minor explorations into the engulfing humidity and hi-rises of Kuala Lumpur, I had managed to gather all documentation for the Thai visa. I joined the queue outside the grand gated embassy building just around the corner from the famous Petronas towers. A young Moroccan man was in front of me and we shuffled slowly on towards the splendid entrance of the gates manned by two guards. We had made it to the front and just as he was about the cross the threshold, a beefy arm stuck out and barred his way.

"No more entry today. Come back tomorrow."

We looked at each other in annoyance and disbelief. We began protesting to the guard but he was having none of it. I departed empty handed with my new friend and to ease the bitterness, we took a no-visa coffee over which we debated the source of morals for Muslims versus atheists. His compelling arguments made it the closest I have ever been to converting to religion.

I left him behind with an embrace, once again dumped into my visa-less, godless and gutless reality. It wasn't *such* a big deal, although it was a disappointment. I had spent most of my time in *KL* preparing the documents to obtain the 60-day permit instead of the 30-day waiver issued at the border, and the uncertainty that comes with it. I had planned to organise my Chinese visa in Bangkok and if I were to look at options for Tibet, Pakistan and Iran here too, I would probably need more than these measly 30 days. I swept these thoughts under the carpet once more. A keenness to press on and leave behind this disappointment welled within. It felt like I had taken enough advantage of the warm and friendly Heng family hospitality, where I could have happily spent weeks.

The now familiar routine of meetings, departings, sleepings, sweatings, pedalings, eatings and drinkings led me towards the 1000 kilometres milestone. The line I had ridden by this point covered much of Malaysia, having cycled up to and down from the cool haven of the Cameron highlands. In Ipoh, when I checked the map, there was only 400 kilometres to the Thai border. My excitement to progress was getting the better of me and I pushed on to cover that distance in three days, in spite of worsening issues downstairs.

Three days, 400 kilometres. I looked at the map over a stodgy morning porridge, reclining in the early morning silence of my £3 hostel kitchen. Kuala Kangsar, Taiping, Selamat: these places would be my stepping stones to Thailand. I set off like a puck on ice, frictionlessly sailing up the coast. This sensation endured a great five minutes. Then the slog of headwind began. Then I realised how sore my undercarriage had become from wearing cycling shorts in the humid squeeze of Malaysia. I stopped. I changed shorts. I carried on, but for the rest of the day I felt like a female emperor penguin incubating quintuplets. I was constantly shifting my weight, clenching my bum cheeks and getting up off the saddle. *Kuala Kangsar, ha! I'm sorry but I cannot even think about stopping here*! All I could think about is how my poor gooch was suffering hell down there. My respite came briefly with one of those cheap and flavoursome Indian banana leaf spreads of Malaysia that had become a staple and one for which I was extremely thankful.

The rest of the first day along these 400 kilometres was wholly uneventful. It was turning pedals. Listening for cars and trucks and thinking about turning peddles and cars and trucks and occasionally an idea that would never develop into anything more, ever. There was no deep contemplation, few long trains of thought. Just machinal forwards motion. Little had changed throughout much of Malaysia. Sime Darby palm still encroached the roadside, obscuring the dreams of dense jungle that would stretch out beyond. Pickups and mopeds still ambled along. Muezzins still shouted into crackly microphones from mosque towers. The sacks of litter piled on the roadside did not change in content or frequency. People still smiled and waved hellos. On the other hand, I began to feel more at ease with spending lonely nights in tents and lonely days on the pedals. What started as loneliness was now maturing into solitude and the daunting sense of the ride I had ahead of me dulled the intensity of the early misadventures of Malaysia. I felt above all relaxed and harmonious in the act of pedalling imperceptibly Northwards. Uneventful has its perks.

That night, I set up camp in a clearing in a spot of actual unmutilated natural forest by a clean river in which I took a dip. An unpolluted Malaysian river is a rarity indeed and I relished the wash while praying for no parasites. Just as I was beginning to drift off, once dried and back in my tent, a family of three on a motorcycle came by to check me out. A ten-year old kid was driving, with a middle-aged woman in the middle and a young girl at the back. I roused myself to welcome my guests. They spoke no English so in broken *Bahasa Melayu* I began to explain, "Basikal dara Australia Ke InGlant na sleep here in tent, cam-ping."
They nodded happily along. For the following thirty minutes the young boy reeled off names of famous cricketers. The only one I recognised was Ricky Ponting. The boy managed to communicate that he was from Bangladesh and the Malaysian woman on the scooter was not his mother. I was sure they had a fascinating story. The pseudo mother went to take a look at my tent and squatted for fifteen minutes while the young boy opened up his Bengali to English phrase app. He told me he loved me, and I asked him whether he should get to know me better before making such bold statements. He cocked his eager head in momentary confusion. As I would later find out in Thailand, 'to love is give' but please, not to everyone. After thirty minutes of laughing at the absurdity, I grew weary and I told them I was calling it a night. *Trêve de balivernes!* I crawled into my bed at 11pm as the incredulous trio jumped back onto the moped, surely to go off in search of other campers to bewilder.

With just one day to the Malaysian border left, somebody entered this story who would leave a huge and lasting impression on me. I entered the hostel at Alor Setar and a kind faced Chinese woman approached me. "Ah Hello Charlie!"

"Hello, I'm not Charlie, I'm Jake, I haven't reserved anything!"
I smiled back, amused at her bold presumption of something as improbable as my name. I thought nothing else of it until another white man appeared at the door of the hostel just a few minutes later. The Chinese woman elegantly rushed over taking fairy steps to greet him. As she opened the door, the white cyclist roared at a troop of motorcyclists outside blasting their horns with impunity. "Oh shut up you daft bloody morons!"

He turned and walked past the woman, who was trying not to let her surprise show through her courteous smile. "God it's just been one of those days, some people just don't know how bloody irritating their horns are!"

The woman trailed his confident strides with her fairy steps once more. "Ah Hello Charlie!"

It all made sense now. He calmed down and after his initial outburst, manifested himself as quite a charming, if a little opinionated fellow.

Charlie was old enough to be my Dad. Indeed, that became a running joke between us as we set off to cycle together after our chance meeting at the hostel. Charlie, as it transpired was quite the character. He had been cycling for none less than the last 22 years of his life and had covered an astounding 340,000 kilometres with his bicycle. It made the Tour de France seem like a ride to the shops. To put this astronomical distance into context, it is about 90 percent the distance from the Earth to the moon. He, like me, was currently cycling towards China and eventually onwards too, to England! For him this was but a jaunt on the tour that had become his life. Beyond the impressive mileage that he had accumulated and the fantastical stories that such mileage necessarily generates, the most extraordinary thing about Charlie was just how ordinary he was. He will always win the best stories pissing contest, with no doubt. But what made him such a fascinating person was his insatiable curiosity to get to know the stories of the people and the lands that he passed through. I was humbled and a little star-struck that we were cycling together, but I tried not to let that show too much as we crossed into Thailand, the land of smiles, him for the fifth time, I, for the first.

Smiles

The calls to prayer of Muslim Malaysia slowly dissipated behind us as we crossed the border into Thailand, the first predominantly Buddhist country of the trip, although there is still a significant Muslim population in the South. I expected all cultural change to take place in infinitesimal increments, but on either side of this border were two very different worlds. The Thai people don't come close to resembling Malay people and impossibly they seemed even *more* smiley than the Malays, whose choruses of *Hello! Hello!* throughout the day were a source of continuous warmth and motivation. I felt nervous crossing the small border. I acted as if I had something to hide and felt under pressure when filling in the entry form. "Shit, what shall I put for accommodation? We can't put tent! What if they suspect us, or call up the hotel where we say we're staying?"

Charlie cast me an amused glance as he handed the form to the immigration officer, with the address of a random hotel in Bangkok. I followed suit and the immigration officer didn't even read what was written and with a beaming smile ushered us onwards. "Welcome to Thailand!"

I felt like it was too easy.

In Southern Thailand there were two massive global products that flanked most of the roads that we took. One was the palm that spilled over from Malaysia, and now there were the rubber plantations as a supplement. It was in the latter that secluded and relatively comfortable camp spots could reliably be found. On the first night, I fell under Charlie's guidance. I was curious to observe his technique for finding camping spots. *Would his barriers for acceptable comfort and seclusion be different from mine?* After dusk we cycled out of the village where we had eaten dinner and bought beers (necessary to celebrate completing a country) and once civilisation had thinned to only the odd house, we slinked into the ranks of rubber trees. Tents put up on the flattest spot we could find, we cracked open the beers. We sat on our roll mats amidst the ambient stillness of the trees and I listened in fascination to Charlie's wealth of stories and views on the cycle touring lifestyle. *This is a man who has lived,* I thought. I envied his life.

 After we clambered into the tents, the silence of the night contoured a tension in the atmosphere, despite Charlie's companionship and snoring. The trees had become ominous and the shadows cast in a frightening texture. I could almost imagine the fleeting figures spying on us in the night, waiting to strike. I slept lightly, until, at about 03:00am, when I awoke to a flitting light that couldn't have been more than a hundred metres from the tent. I watched as it came closer. *Thief? Murderer? Police?* The light wasn't moving in a straight line but seemed to stop, then dart quickly off, then stop, then dart. Hiding, appearing. Hiding, appearing. When it was very near I unzipped the tent as slowly as possible and poked out my head. There, I could just make out the silhouette of a man wielding a torch in one hand, and in the other, a knife. I remained immobile as he came nearer. *Shit,* I whispered to myself. He glided over, while I held my breath. He darted up to the tent, then with a courteous nod and a smile and a *sawa-dee kap,* skipped straight past it. Stunned, I continued observing him on his flitting between the trees, scoring the bark of the trunks. It suddenly made sense what he was doing! He was collecting rubber and our presence barely even caused him to blink. Reassured that he was not here to slit our throats, I fell quickly back to sleep. The next time rubber workers came in the middle of the night, we shared a ridiculous midnight laugh before they scuttled onwards from tree to tree.

Thailand was an easy country to traverse by bicycle. The humidity of the Southern Malaysian peninsula had dropped off. The temperature was lower, the people were reliably kind, the food was amazing and cheap, the roads were perfect and it felt like there was never any wind. The language was fun to learn and speak and people were receptive to this minute effort that allowed me to connect, if just a little, to people who couldn't speak English. In addition to all this, there was the Thai Royal police. Charlie told me of his past experience with this public order branch. He recounted anecdotes of being offered places to stay, coffee, WiFi, water... I just had to see this for myself. He wasn't wrong. Frequently I would knock on the door of these small roadside buildings and ask for water. It wasn't uncommon to leave with a couple of coffees in the belly and an armful of bananas and a broad smile. They truly wanted to help. Whether or not this service is provided uniquely to foreigners on bicycles remains a matter of debate, but it is impossible to deny that the bicycle is a great tool for ice breaking. It is an instant indicator of identity and of humility. People just seemed to connect with that. It almost felt not as if the bicycle was an extension of myself, but as if I was an extension of the bicycle.

In Surat Thani, Charlie and I split ways after some 600 kilometres together. We weren't particularly heading in different directions; indeed, from Southern to Central Thailand there is only the thinnest sliver of land that channels all traffic between North and South. His wit and mixture of good-humoured conversation, trivia knowledge and ability to appreciate silence meant that we got on famously. On the other hand, he already knew the country so well and had such a wealth of experience, that I felt like I was discovering Thailand under his wing. I wanted the freedom to make my own mistakes, to work out my own routes and to set my own pace. I also wanted people to stop admiring Charlie for being able to keep up with his son, and me for accepting my dad's presence on my holiday.

That day I took my time. I hugged the coast as much as I could to escape the bulk of the traffic in favour of the soothing waves lolling in from the gulf sea and lapping the pandanus-lined shores.

The trucks transporting oil-palm fruits were replaced by small pickups trundling along with huge piles of green coconuts, secured in place by skinny topless men who always seemed to have half a cigarette drooping from their mouths. They waved and hooted greetings invariably. The day passed by in a succession of charming fishing villages. Brightly painted wooden boats whose protruding bows were decorated with marigold wreaths were moored by the jetties and rocked lazily in the gentle swell. Other than the odd sprint to escape a ravenous dog, I steadily made my way along the coast, as if to make a point that I had too much time on my hands. As night was not long from falling, I suddenly heard a bellow that broke my quiet meditative mood.

"Oi! You!"

I turned around and Charlie was there again, grinning toothily. "What are *you* doing here?" I laughed. "Shouldn't you be a bit further up the coast by now?!"

He had clearly savoured the day even more so than myself. We resolved to camp together again that night. In our search for a camping spot we came across one of the myriad Buddhist monasteries that are to Thailand what the masjids are to Malaysia. There must be thousands up and down this country where religion plays such a central role in society. In fact, the white of the Thai flag represents the religion that links the guiding Royal blue at the centre to the red of the blood of the Thai people at top and bottom.

It was on the grounds of one of these many monasteries that we camped for the evening – right on the headland. The whole monastery was deserted but for a pack of about fifteen dogs who came yapping and barking as we approached the main building. There was an open toilet block, sleeping quarters and oddly enough, a huge full-size replica of some sort of war ship, complete with a foot-thick steel door and canons. I climbed the mast to have a vantage point over our outdoor hotel for the night, and to choose the perfect space to plonk the tents. I was almost considering sleeping inside the ship itself until Charlie suggested it would be a bad idea if the monks were to turn up, only to find a foreign vagrant or two stowed away in what must have been a historical, or otherwise very kitsch monument. We settled for a couple of small shelters further from the main building, in case our presence was disturbing to the monks (although given the number of dogs that were howling and barking and scratching around, the monks must have become desensitised to disturbance of any kind). When I woke in the morning Charlie was packing up to leave, while I lingered a little while longer in the tent. This time, the goodbye was to be for a little longer than a day.

The coastal cycle continued to be nothing but pleasant, with perfect roads, little traffic, plenty of cheap eating establishments and delightful weather conditions. It was never difficult to find camping spots on the beach, other than when I attempted to do so in a militarised zone, from where I was swiftly ousted. The next stop from the militarised zone was a small city with the fabulous name of Prachuap Kiri-Khan, where I was set to meet a very special person from back home who just happened to be working in Thailand.

Sam Peterken was *the* person in my entourage who was up for anything. In fact, it was with him that I did most of the 'stupid' adventures of my university days. We walked ninety kilometres to Sheffield from Manchester in twenty hours, climbed all the 3000 feet peaks in Wales in fifteen hours (after sleeping on the damp floor of a mountain hut the previous night and ending up in an old slate miners' tool shed the night afterwards) and later, hitchhiked around the Alps sleeping in hammock. Most of these trips were Sam's ideas, although he would perhaps argue the contrary. It was Sam who had invited me to the South of France that fateful summer, to spend time with his friend, Iseline, who took us to the party where I met Pierre. We hardly knew each other at the time, but that quickly changed after a week in la Lèque. We ran through lavender fields on dulcet mornings as tractors chugged by and garlic punched into the air and the sun bore down and time sometimes froze and we asked each other whether we would work in offices. Now, here he was working in Thailand and I was cycling across the globe. By pushing some nobs, he had managed to get the time off to spend a few days with me on the bike.

When I arrived in Prachuap, I booked myself into a cheap and cheerful guesthouse called Maggie's, where a bunch of old French folk fussed and chirped over the preparation of their evening meal. They had been coming back to this same guesthouse for many years, using Prachuap Kiri Khan as a base to explore much of the rest of Thailand. It seemed that their adventurous spirit hadn't waned with age and they were great company for the night, although none of them could suggest a dingy, smoky bar where I had hoped to await Sam the next day.

I ended up meeting him in a light and airy coffee shop, where he stomped over to me with his infectious grin slapped across his cheeks. "Good to see you mate!"
We collided in a big hug and spent the rest of the day catching up on lost time, as well as planning a jaunt to Kao Sam Roi Yot national park, where inevitably, we ended up causing a stir. One of the French biddies at Maggie's agreed to lend Sam a bike for four days. With the settling of this final detail, we set off on the fifty kilometres or so to the park.

England beautiful Thailand beautiful

The park of Khao Sam Roi Yot sprang out of nowhere. The flat road that we had taken was suddenly flanked by great silvery monoliths, fissured with verdant strands of climbing vegetation that breathed up the salty sea air. We pitched our camp on the idyllic Sam Phraya beach, where breeze ruffled the sand and Sam swang in his hammock. We ate unaccompanied pineapple jam and mulled over a programme for the next few days. The main attractions of the park were the caverns set into the limestone hills. It appeared that the smallest, Sai cave, was included with the national park entry fee, but the larger one, Phraya Nakhon, came at an extra cost. Being tight wads, we opted for a relaxed visit to Sai the following day, although relaxed certainly isn't a word I would have chosen in retrospect…

After trying and failing to get the Thai ticket for the national park instead of the tourist ticket (by claiming that we were in fact Thai nationals), we cycled the ten kilometres through Sai village right to the foot of the path leading to Sai cave. The ranger checked our tickets, took a sneaky photo, and let us pass. We hobbled up the steep winding steps until we reached a gaping opening in the rock. The cave was ethereal. Never had I heard such silence. The rock formations were enchanting and the seclusion engulfing. The syncopated drips of water from stalactite tips seemed to slow down time and echo forever in the unknown depths. The enormity encapsulated us in our own little bubbles where we sat meditatively. This hole in the hill left us both a sense of appeasement and wonder at once, that ran through us as we broke back into daylight. This was supposed to be enough. On our way back down the path, in spite of our airy appeased meditative state, we noticed a well-concealed path cutting through the thickly jungled headland. The map told us that if we followed it, it would bring us to the larger and more expensive cave before joining the tourist path back down to civilisation in the form of a fishing village. We looked at each other.

"Shall we?", Sam asked with a cheeky grin.

"Hm I don't know." I replied dubiously.

"Oh come on. Its only a couple of miles!"

The jungle was thick. It sure looked as if this would only be trouble.

"Oh go on then," I said, "If we must!"

I knew full well there was little choice in the matter. We began bushwhacking; the path wasn't maintained and a quick battle against the thicket of branches and undergrowth led us to postulate that it might be an impasse. We agreed to try another hundred metres to see if conditions would improve. To our great surprise the undergrowth thinned and the path became more apparent. With only three kilometres until the larger cave we decided it would be a shame to turn back. It wasn't an hour later that we found ourselves cursing and scrambling over jagged toothy rocks and skirting the odd abyssal hole that would be a one-way ticket into the caves and chambers that veined through the rock beneath us. In one hour one would normally hope to walk a steady five kilometres. With such technical terrain and the odd pause to admire a Spectacled Langur, we had walked a stunning 900m. It felt like we had been trekking for days. The path did have the odd marker here and there though, to assure us that we hadn't just wandered aimlessly into the forest. Red plastic ribbons knotted around a tree, aluminium cuts nailed into the bark and even an indulgent arrow from time to time. This did not prevent the occasional erring... After three hours, and a couple of precarious balancing acts on the toothy rocks, we finally came to a ridge where through the trees we could make out our first tourists.

We skipped down to the concreted pedestrian highway like two very excitable primates, content to find other similar, albeit probably more civilized ones. Phraya Nakhon cave was just in front of us, and we entered, smug that our adventure had saved us a couple of quid. The cave was much larger than Sai, but left us with only superficial admiration. Perhaps we had saturated our capacity for appreciation? We jogged away from the cave, down the pedestrian highway. We saw civilization ahead and were already thinking of a beery reward, but the rangers had other plans. "Hey! Pharang, pharang come, come!", they shouted towards us. "Come you, hey!"

We sheepishly walked over to the gesturing group of men.

"What do you think you are a doing?" They asked, sternly. It seemed that their buddy who had let us up to Sai cave and took a sneaky photo of us got worried when after three hours we were apparently still in there. This appropriately zealous man who was doing an excellent job went to look for us and when he couldn't find us, obviously spread the message to the other rangers. Look out for these suspects: one twat in a bucket hat and one ginger in a FELA t-shirt. We had been busted. They told us that the path wasn't meant to be walked by tourists and that we were very naughty and should *not* do it again. We coyly apologised for our misdemeanours. With enough adventure for one day, all that remained was to hitch hike back to the bikes and ride home to tent and hammock.

It only took two separate pickup trucks to get back to Sai village. Both of the drivers let us clamber into the back without fuss. With the wind in my thick locks and on Sam's slowly balding scalp and thinning hair we savoured the ride, passing the flat marshlands and shrimp farms, surrounded by verdant lime towers slowly receding into the bleached light of the evening. It was blissful. Our second driver left us 500 metres away from the bikes. We just had to walk in a straight line, collect our bikes and go back to camp. We decided to take a little diversion, coaxed possibly by the sound of a Thai power ballad being played live. The path took us onto the main street of the fishing village that ran along the beachfront. What we found was absurdity.

Here is the scene: there was a monk, clad in white and holding a ceremonial bouquet of flowers. Next to him, his friends and close family, donning soft smiles of calmness, pride and appeasement. Panning to the left, we saw a large truck with speakers for walls on which four musicians were stood, blasting Thai rock. Panning again to the left, was the rest of the village who were raucously gyrating or flitting around holding overflowing beer bottles or boogying away in front of the speaker truck or jumping up and down as if they were at a football game. Almost all their t-shirts were stained with beer that was being consumed with impunity. Then there was Sam and me: mouths limp with incomprehension at the nature of this spectacle.

Before long we were ushered to the dance floor and in the next 45 minutes we made the brief acquaintance of a few of the village people. 1) The forthcoming woman. She immediately latched on to Sam, shifted her body about in strange ways then proceeded to ask for £8 for two beers. We said no and moved away. She later asked for £8 for the one beer we had just acquired for free. We refused and she wasn't seen again. 2) The village hustler. He drank his beer from a silver chalice and had one too many buttons of his shirt undone. He donned a moustache and did not indulge in frivolity but was pleased that others did. 3) The supplier. He was sat on the back of his pickup with a polystyrene box stocked with various beverages. Everyone knew he was the man. Before he gave Sam and me one free beer (to the disgust of forthcoming woman), he also supplied a young boy with water. You name it. He had it. 4) Two outrageously drunken men who were the football dancing type. They tried to converse but only managed a rasp, a slur then a stumble which could have been interpreted as a hug. 5) Nouveau-riche villager. His Adidas trainers, flowery shirt and designer sunglasses said it all. *Look at me.* He stayed with us for 30 minutes repeating to us incessantly that he loves England and that he loves Thailand and that both countries are beautiful. This polypatriot had not been to England. His conversation with

us should have lasted three minutes but his insistence to be seen as the one to entertain the Pharang (*foreigner* in Thai, originating from Arabic *Ferenghi* to refer to European traders) prolonged this beyond what was comfortable. He gave us two beers. We paid him the more-than-fair price of 60 baht each. 6) The monk for whom the party was called. He noticed us but did not talk to us. He was joining the order at the local temple, so this whole party was for him. The truck was advanced by the villagers pushing at a very, very slow pace. For the first forty minutes the monk and his companions professionally inched their way behind it. They then apparently gave it all up and went to the buffet that was still being prepared. Sam and I decided to join them. We offered to pay but the cooks just smiled and repeated *buffet buffet buffet!* We were ushered to the village hustler's table who moved his chalice to accommodate us. He welcomed us and ensured we filled our plates full with rice and curry and prawns. Just as we were tucking in, a panicked chatter rippled through those who were seated. A girl who spoke English was summoned and she came to speak to us. "You must leave now because someone is coming to fight you."
"Eh?" We looked at hustler with confusion. He took a sip from his chalice and said gravely, "Eat go, eat go, eat go."
We did.

We didn't want to stick around and as we rushed to the bikes, we ran back through our minds who we could have riled to such an extent as to want to fight. *Was it 1?* She lost out on her beer money. *Or 3?* Maybe he resented that he had to give one of his beverages to a pair of twits from Britain. *Or 2?* Who was just about to throw over the table and pull a gun? We didn't hang around the find out. The villagers seemed to be on our side and coerced us through back streets and away into exile.

That evening once we had reached the safety of our tent we mused on the most likely culprit. We both agreed that 5 was the main culprit, on account of being snubbed in favour of the enticing buffet. For the rest of our stay here we remained off the heat, opting to lay low and collect shells and go to the seven-eleven convenience store. After this one day of misadventure it seemed like everyone in the park knew who we were. Rangers smiled at us and said, "I know you!"

We were slightly disconcerted and left this place as an unlikely infamous duo with a glance over our shoulder to make sure we could not see *1,2,3,4,5* or *6*.

Sam had to take the bike back to François, the French gentleman, and I had to move forwards to Bangkok. I cycled almost back to Prachuap Kiri-Khan with him before our ways parted, having gone through an ordeal that we would not quickly forget.

Eddies

The smoggy route to Bangkok was speedy and flat: especially the 100 kilometres along heavily trafficked roads that would lead me to this chaotic city. I arrived late on a Wednesday afternoon and blended into to the throng of motorcyclists that congregated in front of every red light. When the light turned green it was free for all. I have no idea how, but amidst the hectic motion of everyone moving away at once, order formed and miraculously I didn't see a single crash. This was how it worked here. There was a hidden order in the criss-crossed lines and hidden messages in the horn blasts. I was still far from understanding them, but somehow everyone made it forward, in the least efficient but most joyful manner.

It was exhilarating to weave between the cars stuck in convoy and to leapfrog the song-teows that swang in and out of the road to pick up and drop off without any apparent signal from passengers. From the two benches on the back, kids jumped and waved alongside their snoozing parents. Monks sat squeezed in between market hawkers and their produce. The drivers remained unmoved by the isotropic hustle, and as always, a half-burned cigarette drooped out of their mouths. I passed and was passed by the same group of excitable school-boys shouting "Sawasdee kap" and girls giggling "Sawasdee Ka", all the way until Bangkok Noi, where I found my lodgings. Here, on the other side of the Chao Praya river from the main attractions of the city, I could consolidate and finally look into the guts of my journey.

Bangkok was thinking time. It was here where I would apply for my Chinese visa. I also wanted to inform myself about cycling through Tibet, although hearing the stories of other travellers, it seemed the base of this endeavour was built on shifting sand. I had heard tales that a dozen or so travellers had to gather all their means to pay a guide through the region. Or that Tibet was closed off to foreigners entirely until April. Or that a bunch of climbers who wanted to scale Hkakabo Razi had been arrested at the border. On the other hand, the handful of travellers I met that had made it to South East Asia overland from Europe talked favourably of the Stans of Central Asia. Taking this route back to Europe would mean a rather massive detour into the wild North West China, effectively skirting the entire Himalaya. I was warming slowly to this idea as I mused on its implications. Thousands more kilometres. Unknown countries. Unknown people. Unknown landscapes. This was certainly appealing. Given that time was of no limit to me, any route permissible was possible. In any case, it sure would avoid days of diplomatic faff or potentially prison if I decided to run checkpoints. I thought back to the wise nuggets of wisdom from old Uncle Perry. *The best thing about having a plan is that it can change.* I needed time to massage my indecision into clarity, or the road to throw something up for me; to block one way or another and guide me down a singular path.

At breakfast time in the hostel, sipping on a cha, I looked through the curling steam wisps at the map on the wall as thoughts of where to go streamed turbulently through my head. I appraised it closely with a focus on South East Asia. I looked back at where I had come from, on the spit between the Andaman sea and the Gulf of Thailand and Charlie's voice came in to my head. *Why don't you go up through Burma?* In an epiphany I realised that this was the road I had to take. I do not believe in destiny. Rather, when searching for a sign, any sign will do. This was my sign. Anyway, if I headed into China straight away, I would arrive in the highlands with snow still lingering on the passes, and the temperature would be in negative double figures. Clearly, this is not the most delightful of conditions for the cycle tourist, and so on a whim I bought myself a Burmese e-Visa to see what this country held in store. All I had heard about it were the atrocities committed by the military and that it was, for want of a better term, diplomatically fucked. I was about to discover if this was a reflection of the true Burma.

Awaiting my trip into this new country, I traipsed backwards and forwards to the Chinese visa application centre with applications, revised applications and revised revised applications. The sixty days I wanted, to keep all possibilities open, was initially rejected. According to the officials at the visa centre, it was far too long a time for my proposed itinerary visiting China's main Eastern cities. I went back with a slightly less optimistic and more conservative visa proposal, and once again was made to wait for head scratching and pencil pushing.

The apprehension was mostly forgotten as I spent my days plodding the streets of Bangkok, mostly on the West side of the Chao Phraya. Just one kilometre south of the hostel was the magnificent Wat Arun – the temple of dawn. In an ironic twist, I took my evening walks around its stupas, admiring the shadow chasing the last light up the steps. On one particular evening I stumbled across a small building in the grounds. It was away from the main prang, and above its door was an innocuous peeling wooden sign reading *Meditation Lessons*. It seemed odd that this would be for everyone who visited the temple, as thousands of tourists flock here every day. Unperturbed, I knocked on the door and a small woman peeped her head around the half-ajar door and looked at me expectantly.
"Hi, are there meditation lessons here?" I inquired, speculatively.
"Ah yes," she replied nervously, "but not today." She paused. "Tomorrow! Lessons tomorrow."
She seemed to speak good English and as I asked more about the lessons, it transpired that this building was more than just a meditation hall. As it so happened, she was currently in the process of teaching a few young students English and, having nothing else to do, I offered my services.

The young children aged between 5 and 13 had such an incredible energy and thirst for learning. They did not mess or fidget and they winced with effort to properly pronounce *Hello tea-cher Jake, how are you?* I agreed to prepare a lesson for the following day and Aom – the small woman - promised a meditation lesson with the *Achan* of the centre, a monk who went by the name of Hartanto.

I prepared my lesson that evening, to teach them about my green and splendid home county of Yorkshire and to encourage them to think about and talk about their own region. I took it to the class the following day. The students affirmed it wa' reyt good, but I think anything would have been, coming from the mouth of a real-life Englishman!

It was later when I met the Achan Hartanto (along with Sam – who had come to Bangkok for the weekend). He walked into the dusk-shaded courtyard where we were sat, cross-legged, waiting. There was something immediately profound about this man. His stride, his air, the way he set his eyes upon us with conviction and compassion and presence. Every gesture was compounded with almost mystical calmness. He was well-built for a monk, and dressed entirely in white. He sat in front of myself, Sam, and two others who were present, and began talking in a deep, grave and clear voice. *We spend our time feeding the body- with food, cleaning the body- with water, and exercising the body- with movement. But what do we do for the mind?* He went on telling us about the principles of meditation – how the mind needs all that the body does, and the way that we should respond to the mind's needs is through meditation. Just how he reached these conclusions on how one should treat one's own mind is quite a remarkable story in itself. After our session of meditation under his guidance, he recounted his own personal history that had led him to this temple of Wat Arun.

In his home country of Indonesia, Hartanto was not a monk, but a successful businessman by all accounts. He was CEO of many companies and managed them well, but the intense nature of the work was taking its toll on the man. He would often return to his home tired and irritable. His mother tried to help him and care for him, which tired him even more and in turn, disappointed his mother. One day, the mother of Hartanto's family called all the sons together. The family were Mahayana Buddhists and it was tradition for at least one of the sons to become a monk. So when asked if any of them wished to take the path to ordainment. Hartanto, seeing how he hurt his mother and feeling the strain of the top level of corporate life, volunteered, giving up his life of 'success' for the spiritual journey to monkhood.

He was sent to an order in Thailand, who took rather drastic measures to train his mind that had until then been corrupted by his past life. And so, Hartanto was sent to an uninhabited island, with scant life, no civilization and no possessions save for a book on the Dhamma – the teachings of Buddhism. On that island, alone and with no stimulus, as far away from his previous life as one could possibly imagine, he cried every night. He read the Dhamma to occupy himself and began his practice of meditation, in between avoiding the snakes and finding and cooking a single meal a day. Hartanto was here for *two whole years* and at the end of this, was finally brought back to Thailand. He was a transformed man, and after two further years intensely studying and meditating, decided it was time to give back. He had understood his own life and now his duty was to help others find their way. This is how the community learning centre in the grounds of wat Arun came to be. The very one and the same where Sam and I were now sat, in owl-eyed amazement. It transpired that the main purpose of the centre was not solely to astonish tourists but to take in young women who are at risk of domestic violence or human trafficking. They are provided with lodgings, food, lessons in meditation, English, cooking and caring and the training necessary to become nurses. Each year twenty-five places are offered and when I was there in February 2019, it was the 20th cohort. At the end of this story, my heart was pumped with admiration and I was acutely aware that I was sat in front of the most inspirational human I was ever likely to come across. If we could each only possess but a half of this man's virtue, then the world would be set to be a finer place indeed.

Meanwhile, outside the temple, my Chinese visa application had succeeded, with thirty days inside the middle kingdom granted. I would apparently also have the opportunity to prolong by thirty days once inside the country, which would be necessary for whichever route I took. The route through Tibet promised untold complication and risk. I knew that I didn't have the patience for organising a guide or waiting around for the season, so my only option would be to travel as a fugitive. With little desire to sneak around Chinese police checkpoints in the dead of night lugging a clumsy thirty-kilo touring bike, I was opting more and more for the 5500 kilometres into Xinjiang through to central Asia. I would need every one of my visa days to accomplish such a feat, without even considering the myriad unknowns that the road was likely to throw up. It seemed that Bangkok had decided my route for me, and it was time to go on with it. It was time for a last good-bye to Sam, who I would likely next see in England. I gave one final lesson to the endearing kids of Wat Arun, before collecting my completed visa and setting off in a great haste before I would be tempted to languish in another stuffy Bangkok evening.

I left the city with the rush hour traffic, feeling somewhat enriched with a lust for the rest of my life. It felt like the future was in a superposition of endless possibilities, and I needed only accept those that would come to be content. As it so happened, my romantic vision was somewhat shattered as I ended up camped behind a petrol station to the utter bemusement of myself and the pump attendants. In the heavily populated outskirts of Bangkok, I had come across nowhere suitable to camp. My decision making had been impaired ever since deciding to leave Bangkok in rush hour with a slow puncture (or arguably since I decided to cycle from Singapore to England). My high-on-life attitude led me nonetheless to continue until a busy crossroads where I was dazzled by the light of a Thai petroleum station, resplendent with 7-11, amazon coffee, toilet block and lo – a flat patch of grass on the far side of the forecourt. I asked a security guard in my best Thai if I could camp on that patch of grass. As you might imagine, his face contorted in unspeakable confusion. I asked again, and implored him with puppy-dog eyes to let me stay. He radioed to somebody else and for a tense moment held the silent walkie-talkie to his ear. A crackle and a voice came back. He nodded a couple of times and then said *Ok*. I smugly marched past the pump attendants, then, as if it were completely normal, pitched my tent amidst laughs and expressions of shock and possibly disdain. I spent the entire night enlightened by flashing neon and the headlamps of truckers, far from Bangkok, far from spiritual islands, but glad to be back on the road.

The next five days on the road to Burma were a blur. On the first day out of Bangkok I was molested whilst having my breakfast. A lone slightly-built man pulled up in a car at a Song Teow stop, where I was having my breakfast. He began with charming conversation and quickly began touching my arms and stomach, with words of *oh you so strong*. The fun stopped when he put his hands into my shorts and I froze. I could do nothing else. Nothing else had ever prepared me for this situation. I got up, almost apathetic, mind numbed, and left. Within five minutes, the man passed me in his car with a beep, and within ten, the reality hit. I screamed in rage. Why had I let him get away with it? This was the very worst part! My ineptitude to act. But I could do nothing. No reaction came, just passive, limpid, droopiness. A flop of inaction. Of letting this happen. I then began to feel disgusted with my own body, which seeped and coursed through my skin and lasted about three days. Strangely, this feeling was subdued only when I bought a pair of skimpy yellow fake Adidas shorts, revealing much of my plump cyclist sausage legs to the world. The day I was touched I put my head down and pedalled away the anger to reach a record distance in Asia of 170 kilometres. They passed as if they were nothing, as did the ensuing days, speeding onwards towards the border. I often felt like I was hallucinating and even saw an elephant in the rear of a pickup truck. I had to double take, and was surprised to discover that my eyes were telling the truth the first time! Along this stretch, if there is any consolation for my sorry state, it is in learning that I was able to sleep in monasteries and temples – even when the monks were very much present. This matter really simplified my evening search for campsites as the problem was reduced to finding the nearest temple. I would ask to pitch my tent in their yard and be accepted without fail.

 On one occasion I shared sticky rice and curry with a group of young men who were sleeping out in the yard of the monastery I had arrived at. They were all stick thin and slept on mats with no shelter. They called me over as I was pitching my tent and not much else was said. I sat with them, mostly in silence, while a member of their troop fired up a gas stove and squatted with his bum very nearly on the ground – that comfortable looking position that all Asians can attain (whereas most Western Europeans can barely get their bums past their knees). He stirred the curry slowly that once ready, was passed around to spoon onto the sticky rice we had put into our bowls from the woven cask in which it is steamed. Most of the men had only one spoonful on their measly portion of rice and I followed suit, although my stomach was gurgling for more. I noticed that the men looked almost pitifully skeletal. Most of their upper arms were concave and held in place by pathetically thin and bony shoulders. Their ribs, visible, rhythmically pulsed fore and aft with every breath. Wrinkles, grooves and ridges formed a complex topography on their faces, telling of a life spent just scraping by. I didn't ask how they got here, or whether this was their permanent fix, but I assumed it was. I was humbled that they had shared their rice and curry with me that evening, when they by no means had to. I felt particularly bad for the men who were sleeping at this monastery, as they had to live alongside the ubiquitous monastery dogs that were always present. As night fell, a canine orgy of scrapping, jumping, howling and barking began. No matter how many stones the men threw, or how loud their shouts of deterrence were, the mutts would start over and continue into the night. The poor men could have barely got a wink of sleep. I certainly didn't. Monasteries were safe and easy, but they sure weren't comfortable. On reflecting upon the situation of these men, I vowed never to complain again as long as I had a roof over my head.

The hardest day on the run from Bangkok to Burma was certainly the penultimate one. The heat had ramped up once more that radiated through the steady haze that hung in the sky ever since leaving Bangkok. The sun was definitely there, as I hadn't stopped sweating on the road, but I hadn't seen it in over a week. On this particular day, the heat was particularly menacing. Under its iron press I traversed the mountains that separated most of Thailand from the notorious Burmese borderlands. After the small city of Tak, the road took me directly westwards, where the daunting wooded mountains lay in wait, blasting off a crippling headwind to boot. The road crept up the hillside spangled with bare, fuzzy trees and fallen orange leaves that looked like berets. It didn't seem to gently meander around the contours, but instead ramped up and up, further skyward. I thought that there would be plenty of rest stops, petrol stations and oases of filtered mineral water along the *Asian highway 1* to the main border with Myanmar. Not for the first time, I thought wrong. The killer heat and unwavering humidity meant that as well as finding a flat patch of grass to camp for the night, I would also need to find extra food and water. Just as the sun was departing, I neared the top of a long climb and struck gold. A market!

I met an English teacher whose students I was a little concerned for, but to whom I was very grateful when he passed me a large bag of pork scratchings that I immediately scoffed down. With great enthusiasm, he helpfully relayed to me that my best bet for camping was to go back down the hill I had been climbing for the last fifteen minutes then go down another hill for just a couple of kilometres. He stood smiling and completely ignorant to the pain that those words cause the fatigued touring cyclist. I thanked him for his sound advice then immediately dismissed it and carried on in the right direction, unsure whether the forested hillside would thin or flatten to a suitable campground. After two kilometres of anxiously looking about, I saw a very reassuring sign. The words 'giant Buddha' accompanied with an arrow pointed up a dirt track towards the summit of a hill. Bingo. Along with the giant buddha, was a giant temple, where I was welcomed for the night with a huge plate of rice that was almost as big as the squat woman who gave it to me.

Before any tent was put up, I was taken to see the *Achan*, a *forest monk* who had chosen a path of residing far from civilisation. I was made to sit before him cross-legged on a rug. He was sat meditatively on a raised platform and I looked up to see his bulldog face grinning back down. He puckered his thin wrinkled eyes as he spat some chewing tobacco onto the floor next to me. I thought back to primary school looking up attentively at Mrs Horan perched on her chair, reading slow assured fables while surveying us over the rims of her glasses. We were being prepared for life. Now life had come about and I once again found myself sat cross-legged, discretely picking my nose and looking up at a great wise elder. The caveat was that now I had to justify to a forest monk why I, a western tourist, had come to pester him at his retreat from civilisation. He seemed satisfied with my gestures of riding a bike and sleeping and loving Thailand and wanting to learn about meditation. He laughed and through the translation of the tiny woman proceeded to inform me about *pud taow*, which means breathing in and out. *I will work on it.*

The monks put me up inside the temple that was under construction and gave me a light and a mattress for a comfortable night on top of the hill. As if the fairy tale was missing something, the next morning I was introduced to *the mountain people*, an ethnic minority group who lived on the subsistence of the hills. The men were clad in black cloaks covering bright frilled shirts and the women in long flowery frocks. They all donned some sort of hat (except one woman who had wrapped a coat around her head, into a hat) A forest monk devotee explained to me that the forest monks had shown the mountain people how to cultivate coffee, grow strawberries, manage land and ride motorcycles. In return, the mountain people brought culinary offerings to the forest monks who, like Hartanto, ate only one meal a day. Normally it was a KFC bargain bucket but today the mountain people wanted to impress and so brought vast quantities of curried vegetables, dried fish, pastes, fruits, leaves, sticky rice and meat. The table was laid and the four forest monks arrived. They began eating slowly and peacefully, pushing on tedium but getting the balance just right, which made it look like they were in an advert for Greek yoghurt. Once they had finished, they took their retreat, and everyone else got to eat their fill from the copious leftovers. It was truly a feast. I thanked the mountain people and the forest monks for their kindness and generosity before heading down the sugarplum trail (highway 12) into marzipanland (Mae Sot) on my unicorn (bicycle).

On the 18th February, 48 days into the trip I finally descended from the gruelling mountains over which I had ridden since Tak. Descending from the mountains, I felt like I was plunging into another world entirely. The mountains gave a sense of closure. They were to space as the past is to time. I rode forward towards the embraces of the last town of Thailand. Mae Sot. My suspicions of otherworldliness were founded, and as I rode into town, I noted how it was different from any other I had thus far experienced. The vast majority of the Mae Sot population were no longer smiling Thais, but immigrants from Burma having fled persecution, a crippled economy, or for illicit trade across the border. There were also many NGOs established in the city

to deal with the uncounted immigrants, including many children who would otherwise have no formal education. Everywhere seemed to have a story in this place, but he most fascinating and bustling part of the city, as is the case with the vast majority of Asian agglomerations, was the market. It was one of the first ports of call during my brief stopover in the town. I sat on the steps to the gallery and took in the wild stimuli. *Thanaka*-painted, *Longyi*-clad men and women were selling a whole host of smelly and exotic produce: live eels swimming in wash bowls, putrid smelling pastes made from crushed fish, sticky rice wrapped in vine leaves, fermented tea leaves, betel nut... The dirt-ridden streets hosted a constant stream of creaky tricycles, sometimes carrying huge sacks of waste, boxes of clothes or a sprawled pile of children. It was people-watching paradise. I remained sat on the stairs of the indoor market emporium, slurping mangisteen, trying to be as discreet as possible. Unfortunately, discreet in such a place, and amongst such friendly and curious people, is simply impossible for the cycling tourist. "Hello my friend, what is your name? Where you come from? Where you going?"
I should have brought along a t-shirt with the responses to these questions.

For the next couple of days I frequented the market, revelling in the diversity of the bustle around me. It felt like no two days here could ever be the same and I thought about the lives of the people I was watching for seconds, but in my head inventing the entirety of their histories. Idling all day on the back of a rusty tricycle, vending fruits, cooking wares or knock-off Fila clothes. *Did they know that this was the life in wait for them when they were young? Are they content?* I felt somehow attached to every person I saw by the knowledge that they were experiencing life in the same instant I was. Solipsism seemed to dissolve into this melting pot of humanity, this cross road of cultures that the following day I left behind, onto the other side, into Burma.

Burmese days

The plan for Burma was blurry at best. I wanted to do a horseshoe trajectory from the Mae Sot-Myawaddy border to the Tachileik border with the far north of Thailand. The first stage was to cycle some 450 kilometres from Myawaddy to the old capital of Yangon. The British had once used this port city, then known as Rangoon, as a base to take over the whole of lower Burma. I had slightly more discreet and benevolent ambitions. In the nearby satellite town of Thanlyin was the Thabarwa meditation centre. I had heard of this microcosmic community from a traveller in Mae Sot. She told me it was a place where some of Myanmar's most needy and marginalised are looked after by monks and a team of Western volunteers. This was the purpose of her visit to Myanmar. Now, I too was drawn there for three reasons: the lack of anything else better to do, the inspiring virtue of Ludovic Hubler's experiences volunteering in a similar place in India, and the inspiring vice of fancying the girl who told me about it.

After Thabarwa, the plan I had in my head would take me up along the Irrawaddy river, the huge coronary artery of Burma, and across into Shan state. This region was once the second greatest producer of opioids in the world after *The golden crescent* of Afghanistan and Pakistan and is now still the greatest producer of Amphetamines. I had prospected the route through it while in Bangkok. It looked to be a stunning highway all along the remote Shan plateau that is mostly cut-off from the rest of the world. The road would wind through the assumed verdant hills with a descent into the Salween gorge, and then onwards to the borderlands with Laos and Thailand. The region absolutely fascinated me and its enigma drew me in. Most of the Eastern part of the state does not fall under government control and even traditionally, the region has been administrated by tribal chiefs known as *Sawbwa*, which allowed many separate tribal cultural identities to flourish. I have never before even thought about the fact that areas of a country have been self-administrated for such long periods of time. Countries – especially in my lifetime – seem so fixed and stable and all-encompassing, but here the nature of the plateau seemed to take it beyond the reach of central government. It hardly seemed fair to say that Shan state was part of Myanmar. Indeed, I imagined it as a world unto itself. Nonetheless, it seems that few places are truly isolated on this ever-more accessible planet. *How would the people cope with such vulnerability to change from the rapidly encroaching outside world? What are living conditions like? How will people react to a white foreigner on a bike?* I was hungry for these questions to be answered and I fancied myself intrepid enough to take on Shan state, especially endowed with the humble yet powerful prowess of the bicycle. There were, however, a few flaws in the plan. Namely, police or Tatmadaw (Burmese military) patrolling the borders of the region falling out of government control (essentially a few kilometres after Taunggyi) and further in, the purported potentially violent drug peddlers.

I had previously contacted other cyclists who had been to Burma and they warned that this road was strictly off limits to foreigners. I had them pinned as cotton-wool-wrapped tourists who probably had heard such tales from someone else who in turn had heard that from someone else, etc. etc. My approach was to turn up to Taunggyi – already seldom visited by foreigners since decolonisation -and see what the locals and the police had to say about it. Well, that was the plan at least.

Meanwhile, Pierre was about to cross into Thailand, having passed through Cambodia and Laos, mostly following the Mekong River. He was planning to traverse Burma and cross into India. The easiest and most direct way for him to do this was to take the road across the Shan plateau. If all stars aligned, our paths were almost certain to cross during our respective traverses of the region and I was excited at the prospect of meeting him once more to compare travel notes, especially in such a significantly wild place.

I rolled across the Thai-Myanmar friendship bridge with these thoughts turning in my mind. It was 50 days after leaving Singapore and now feeling border-confident, I got my 28-day tourist visa stamped with ease. A sense of excitement and anticipation tingled through my being as I began cycling into Myawaddy. Even after the transitional city of Mae Sot, Burma proper was a shock – It could have been five thousand miles from Thailand. Everywhere seemed immediately shoddier and more chaotic. Mopeds veered in-between slow-moving carts and the odd stray dog, each fending for itself, slinked along the roadside, sniffing at the gutter for scraps of food before padding off again in the dust. Horns were once again blasted liberally in contrast to the relatively restrained Thailand, giving a sense of business despite the fact that most people were stood idle in front of open shops. "Welcome to Myanmar!"

The ramshackle buildings of Myawaddy soon petered out, giving rise to more heavily vegetated mountain that I huffed and puffed my way over in the hazy, humid air. Nestled amongst the sepia mountains of early March lay a smattering of small huts. Children hung around outside, playing, running, gazing… I assumed the parents were working the land nearby, but in any case, the kids were completely unsupervised. One of them even held a rifle, that merited a second take. I could sense that this country was going to hold quite a few more shocks in store. Aside from the gun wielding children, I passed a couple of police checkpoints where I was made to sit while beady-eyed officers took my paper e-Visa into an office for processing. Two other cops checked me out as I sat down, looking me up and down and laughing with each other. I smiled and fidgeted, trying not to look unnerved while inside I was seething with anxiety. The officer returned and asked where I was going, as if suspecting something. I told him I was on my way to Hpa-An, the most obvious big city that this road lead to. The real plan though, was not to get to Hpa-An. Instead, the cycling would end at Kawkareik, a small town 30 kilometres further along the road. Here lived SuSu, a *Warmshowers* host in a country where hosting foreigners was a dangerous game. I had planned to meet her for a primer on Myanmar culture. Leaving the checkpoint, I certainly felt the need for friendly guidance in this strange land.

Kawkareik was a small town in which the dust from the surrounding mountains settled to a sandy blanket on street sides. Wooden huts were arranged in small lots set back from the roads, where silty comet trails blazed behind mopeds, or trickled behind bicycles or oxen carts. I arrived at one such hut, surprised to find it kitted out as an office with old computers, desks and electronics. I walked in apprehensively, fully expecting that my skin layered up with sweat, salt and dust would frighten any worker immediately from their desk. But when I entered, none of the few people inside so much as batted an eyelid. It seemed they were used to filthy western touring cyclists showing up at the office, as would soon become clear through SuSu's story. One of the workers calmly got up and welcomed me with a huge toothy grin, introducing herself as SuSu. She had an easy and steady manner of speaking, acting and moving. She never seemed to walk, only glide. Despite this, I remember at first feeling that this was a façade to a deeper character. Beyond the smiles and the talk of good food and her local pride, she often seemed to be lost. Not in her town, but in her mind. Beyond her ease, I sensed a very anxious energy.

In any case, she gave up the rest of her day to show me around Kawkareik and gave me the gentle introduction to the innumerable idiosyncrasies of Burmese life and customs that I would likely encounter as a bicycle traveller. The clay pots that were in front of many people's houses contained water that anyone can use for drinking. Camping is not allowed. Locals are not allowed to host foreigners (that night SuSu would take me to a £2.50 guest house). *Laphet yay* is the café drink of choice (a sweet milk tea that had clearly been influenced by the somewhat questionable British tastes). Village life revolves around the pagoda. The list went on. She explained that not many people in Burma were conscious of the environment and yet she was taking a stand by promoting recycling in the community as an alternative to the wanton burning of all types of waste.

After treating me to some of her delicious home-cooking: bowls of curried vegetables, rice, noodles and bitter tea-leaf salads, she mounted her bike and rode with me around town. Her cadence was slow but never laboured, and as while walking, her bicycle seemed to glide elegantly along, like a swan bisecting water. She took me to her friends on the outskirts of town, who were busy making industrial quantities of rice noodles by hand in an enormous cauldron of water. While they wrapped up their work for the day, we sat in the shade of their bamboo house eating fresh jackfruit and some sort of sticky rice dish that had been cooked in vast quantity for the February full moon festival. It wasn't clear if SuSu was *actually* friends with these people whose house we had made ourselves very comfortable in, but in Burma, it seemed that everyone was friends with everyone else. I was filled with mellow contentment at the privilege of relaxing with these people who were at once complete strangers and close friends.

Sitting in a stranger's house eating their fruit while they were busy working, I reflected on the gradient of generosity that so far seemed to scale totally inversely to what people could actually afford to give, financially at least. It is not that the people here were a jackfruit bite from starvation, but the jackfruit did represent a certain proportion of what they had, especially given that some jackfruits can be the size of a small child. Other than the cauldrons, the bamboo stilt-house, the rice cooker, a few plastic stools and table, a poster of a mystical fairytale castle with a red Mercedes parked in front of it, and a lean of rusty bicycles, the family had little to their name. Still, it didn't bother them to share what they did have with some smelly grinning freak from the other side of the world. I couldn't help but wonder what kind of welcome my hosts would receive if they turned up in a typical town in Britain in the same state. I doubt that they could walk into someone's house without a word and get stuck into the contents of the fridge, pausing only to say a broken hello once Ben and Jerry's was oozing down their chin. Having said this, there are probably hundreds of thousands of Brits who would be thrilled to host foreigners at the drop of a hat, but I doubt that a traveller would feel the same constant decontracted warmth emanating from the whole people as one does in much of South East Asia.

These thoughts continued to whir in my mind as SuSu showed me more of her town and of herself. I began to develop a strong admiration for this woman as her stoic personality and inspiring activities came through in conversation. She supported her siblings, taught English to the local children and single-handedly developed initiatives for the environmental cause, so far ahead of her time, all while fighting her own personal demons. I revered how she thought for herself and acted for the good of others all while remaining so humble that I had to really prod to get just how amazing she was. When I asked her what her passions were, she thought for just a second then with a glint in her eye she replied "travel." And yet, she had never left Myanmar. Her travel passion came from welcoming we privileged lot, we cycle tourists passing through Kawkareik, living our dreams. Her passion was lived completely vicariously, through hosting the hundreds of foreigners whose freedoms had brought them her way. Through meeting all these people, SuSu confided that her dream was to visit the Netherlands. But with only around five or at a push, ten days off per year in her government post, and a number of other financial and bureaucratic barriers, her dream would probably remain just that. I felt guilty that I could so easily undertake my great adventure holiday, with barely any thought or regard to my privilege, while SuSu, who had morally earned the right to her dream and more, would probably never get to live it. In summary, I felt gravely guilty, humbled and delighted all at once with SuSu, who in the end left on me such a massive impression, that on leaving Kawkareik just one day later I felt a similar chagrin to leaving behind an old and dear friend.

It took almost a week to get to the Thabarwa centre along Burma's somewhat bumpy roads. The scenery alternated between rubber plantation and paddy field, with the odd stilt-house village to break the monotony. On the first night I made my way into such a small village, with no hotel or guesthouse, to try my luck at a monastery where I had been so successful in Thailand. I knew that it was more dangerous for the monks to host foreigners here, but in a spirit of nonchalance I turned up armed with a naïve smile to see what would happen. I was briskly turned away and even the awful Burmese I had learnt didn't seem to charm the monks who just wanted to see the back of me. I cycled fifty more kilometres in the dark to make it to the next hotel, being too on-edge to camp off the relatively busy main road. I regretted my skittishness to camping as soon as I walked into the depressing guesthouse. It was far more uncomfortable than any camp would have been, and I spent the night in a room being slowly digested by mosquitoes who were avenging their ancestors whose splat had decorated the walls around me over the last few decades. I skipped through Mawlamyine and Hpa-An, keen to make it to Thabarwa to perform some benevolent service that I felt more and more was my due.

Nonetheless, I cycled at a leisurely pace to get there. Slowly spinning the pedals, I had plenty of occasions to keep my head aloft and note the ways the country changed as I moved through it. Moreover, with plenty of stops at laphet yay establishments, I was never short of curious people to keep me on my toes in telling my name, my country, my provenance, my destination and my mode of travel, should I ever forget! What was most startling was that on numerous occasions, even when only briefly satisfying the tea-house loafers with answers to these

70

questions, I found that my tea and snacks had been paid-for. And even when they weren't, I was charged meagre sums ranging between twenty and fifty pence for a meal! It seemed that the Myanmar Kyat was worth less than the paper on which it was printed. I even found myself once get outraged at having to pay an extortionate sum of a couple of pounds for a feast that would have cost ten times as much back in England.

In any case, the people were undeniably amongst the friendliest folk on the planet, always willing to share a smile and a shake of hands. It lifted my spirits on most occasions, to feel this openness and warmth on a near constant basis. There were only a couple of occasions on the way to Thabarwa that I actually did feel unwelcome, and through no fault of the people. This was in passing through some of the more impoverished villages, where I felt that my travel-joy was an insulting reflection of western vanity whose superficial sweetness was dulled by the harsh reality of true struggle. Here, in the tea houses there were still people loafing, conversing, sharing, but the tone was graver. Clothes were more ragged and mannerisms brusquer. These were in the villages that were to be found in the lush green sea of steaming paddies, amongst which the stilt-houses that were barely a few square metres in size, housed full families of six or seven laying together, sleeping away the hottest hours of the day. It took me quite some time before my brain actually comprehended that these open platforms, covered with feeble bamboo and dried teak-leaf roofs were actually houses. These few square metres of wooden planks were all some people would come home to after hours spent labouring in the suffocating humidity. Along these roads sauntered thin children clad in tatters, stooping to pick up empty coke bottles and drop them in a hessian sack that they trailed behind them. While many Burmese children waved, smiled, ran or cycled after me, these ones didn't. They looked at the miserable layer of skin clinging loosely to their grotty bare feet and walked mournfully along, casting an odd glance upwards, then back down. I began to swallow the bitterness of real poverty. It was a harrowing sight that made me feel utterly useless. Pedalling lost its allure and my stomach felt empty, not for want of food, but for want of empathy. Having a friendly villager with stained and rotting teeth and tattered t-shirt come and pay for my next meal after this crippled me with guilt. I smiled my thanks as a terrible sense of injustice seethed within. I really hoped Thabarwa would at least allow me to pay forward the sickening kindness.

It was late afternoon when I arrived. I was sweaty, hungry and thirsty, but mostly glad to finally have some sort of focus other than pedal spinning. I hastened towards the 'reception' to formally announce my arrival and get started on whatever it was that people did here. Here, a couple of unmoved Westerners took down my name and date of birth before telling me to head to the ominously named 'USA hall' where I would apparently live and learn my duties. Before I had the chance to find out even a sliver of further information, the receptionists scurried into the back room on more pressing business. And so I passed between the trotting packs of dogs, that seemed to constitute the majority of life here, towards these living quarters. After seeing only conglomerations of stilt-houses or the odd pastel colonial villa, it was quite a shock to come across a building of more than three stories like the USA hall.

I parked my bike and made my way up the stairs hauling as many panniers I could up to the third floor where a congress of the most white people I had seen in a long time were busy chatting or laid on their beds browsing their smartphones. A few people turned their heads at my arrival and came to help me settle. I ended up leant against the balcony with a Brit, an American and a French couple. The Brit seemed to be a veteran of the centre and he opened his arms wide, as if to address the subjects in the dusty sunset microcosm below, and began to explain Thabarwa.

"Thabarwa is a dumping ground. It is a bottomless pit of possibility and goodwill with but a scratching of resources," the Brit explained. "It was a venerable monk who had first began his work here, with nothing. He welcomed along anybody in need. People who cannot afford healthcare, who have lost themselves to drugs, or who have lost all family and their way in the world. These people came, drawn to this place where no man or woman is turned away, were encouraged to meditate and use the resources around the centre to build a better life for themselves through introspection and labour." He went on…

In the end, however, it seemed to me that many of the people here were too weak to move, never mind to labour, and they just wanted a place to see out the short time left of their lives.

My new pals pointed out the main areas of the centre, starting with the most obvious. In USA hall, forty or so volunteers were spread over two floors in dormitories set out like a hospital. Mosquito nets, steel bed frames, plywood base and bed bug-ridden mattresses were standard, yet this was the most luxurious building of Thabarwa village. The big block to the north was actually two medium sized hospitals, hospice dormitories, public washing facilities and a host of other health amenities. The buildings in between there and here were lodgings built by volunteers and the Thabarwans. There was a pagoda that as SuSu had averted me to, was the spiritual centre of even this village. And otherwise, a few other basics facilities were dotted here and there. A kitchen and a canteen, where one can find cauldrons much like those in Kawkareik to cook for the masses, a couple of basic restaurants (that seemed to thrive!) and centres for raw materials. This however meant nothing without the eclectic inhabitants. Sinners, saints, druggies, monks, patients of AIDS, tuberculosis or other horrible diseases, amputees, the homeless, the disabled, the mentally ill, carers, doctors, physios, nurses, restaurateurs, dogs, more dogs, the group of westerners and one old Chinese man who drank about ten bottles of coke a day (and stored them all under his bed) formed this melting pot community like none other that could exist.

So what could the volunteers do here? In a suitably ambiguous way: whatever they can.

On the first morning, I stood on the second-floor balcony, transfixed gaze cast across the bumpy road running in front of USA hall on which dogs were growling and gnashing their teeth and tumbling in the dust. Horn blasts of motor scooters sounded as they skimmed past wandering children or sauntering monks. There was a juice stand around which a few volunteers slurped avocado smoothie before beginning their day of 'good deeds'. A gregarious group of Burmese were perched on plastic blue stools gathered around a small plastic table straining under an enormous pan of rice. They cast their own gazes onto the bypassing stream of people, smoking cheroot or spitting out betel nut gunk. It was just gone 06:00am.

By 06:30am I had apparently already found my 'good deed' activity for the morning. I sat squished in the rear of a truck with two other volunteers and a troop of monks on the way to collect alms, which is essentially trick or treating except it happens in the morning and it happens every day. We arrived in a non-descript area just south of Yangon. The monks carried huge empty pots and pans, some of which they would pass onto the bumbling westerners. It wasn't long before the barefoot march began. It seemed like we were expected, as trick-or-treatees lined the streets holding smaller pans replete with rice and curries and other donations that they bestowed upon the revered monks. The monks accepted with little ado, mixing similar curries in the big pots before passing it on to us trailing volunteers to carry. As the monks glided by, the inhabitants shikoed and cried in fervour, or maybe because they had just given the last of their curried eggs to the saffron clad taxmen and their band of merry men. We wandered through slums of Yangon, tiptoeing barefoot over sandbags that were piled up and slit open, acting as walkways. I tried to not look into the houses at the private life of the people living there but it was difficult to stifle my curiosity. Living conditions were tough. There was waste in front of most doorways. The smell was bad. Very bad. A miasma of rot around which skinny dogs trotted and sniffed. People lived here. The same people whose food donations fed not only the monks, but in the end all the inhabitants of the Thabarwa centre, including the rich western volunteers. I wondered if they knew that a significant proportion of their food would not in fact be given to monks, so esteemed they were, but to smartphone-wielding, smoothie-slurping Westerners. I doubted this, and even so, I felt that accepting it was nothing short of criminal. Alms-giving is an integral cornerstone of Burmese culture. It gives anyone the chance to contribute selflessly to some transcendent cause, but as one of the people reaping the tangible material essence of the donation, I could not help but feeling like the shady Sherriff of Nottingham.

That night, as we heated our share of the curries, and complemented how delicious it all was, coming together around the canteen table, I cast a brief thought back to the immobile bodies lying in cramped rooms where dust particles danced in slits of light sifting through flimsy wooden exteriors. This is where our food came from. We were eating it like it was god's gift unto us and no gratitude was needed. The worst part was that I complemented the food as well, and ate and laughed with the others, leaving thoughts behind of Yangon slums and the people there who festered in absolute poverty, in favour of the atmosphere of *our* feast at *their* expense.

Despite some of these questionable practices, Thabarwa did have plenty of virtues, and the volunteers there did want to help. Every evening there were meetings to discuss how best to do this. It turned out that some regular care activities were actually planned and programmed. The volunteers either got involved in planned activities or led alternative initiatives in one way or another, often at the request of the long-term volunteers here. The planned activities included physiotherapy, teaching

English, caring for patients, washing the patients, taking invalid Buddhist patients to pray at the pagoda, or 'making patients move'. I resolved to get stuck in more with these immediately more altruistic activities over the following days.

And so, some situations arose that I never believed I would be involved in. *What am I doing here*, I thought, as I stripped a monk of his robes before washing him head to toe with a dishcloth in a bucket of soapy water. Here I was, immersed in the 'activity' of 'patient washing'. Another patient seemed to find the activity much more fun than the despondent monk. I doused this patient's head with water collected in buckets from the large water store, as running water was off for a few days. I massaged his head with shampoo before giving his armpits a good scrubbing. We were in a courtyard outside and Bob Marley was singing out from a volunteer's speaker. I thought of *Shark Tale* and the whale wash and giggled to myself. With the man's upper body now clean, I gave him a forgiving look in his eyes and then down at his manhood. *Every little ting, is gonna be alright!* He began to chortle as his bumbling English hygiene servant sheepishly began to scrub his undersack. I laughed back and pointed my finger at him. "Next time, you're washing my balls, ok!"

The situation was hilarious. Many patients loved the novelty of seeing westerners knelt down, wafting their flannel into where the sun don't shine. Overall, though, there was a mixture of responses from this activity. They ranged from hilarity to gratitude to bitter apathy or even sullen shame.

In other spheres of Thabarwa, it seemed that the presence of the volunteers was largely appreciated. The English lessons, the ridiculous and hilarious exchanges devoid of language, the company given to those who couldn't move, the love shown to children who had no immediate family, the reassurance given to those who had lost hope, were all part of the emergence of glimmers and glimpses of positivity in this tiny world.

In the end, and to my great regret, it was the huge dog population that forced me to leave Thabarwa after only three and a half days. I was gasping for breath, asthma triggered beyond inhaler's help with so much canine activity. Even after such a short time, I popped back out into wider society, very much stunned. After such rudimentary conditions, I thought I was ready for comforts but realised upon entering the air-conditioned room of the hostel in downtown Yangon that the comforts here did not comfort, but repulsed me. I left the hostel to find food and found myself embarking on a cruise of culinary indulgence in an act of self-flagellation that had been brewing for some time. I just wanted to stuff my face with shit to feel just that. Samosas, cakes, a beer. I wanted *more* and the more I wanted, the more I felt ill at myself for doing so.

I was still in a state of confusion about what I had seen at Thabarwa. I respected it for its effort and principle: that anybody could go there to receive care, yet at the same time I felt that the care given was just prolonging the suffering of the many people on death's doorstep. The conditions simply weren't good enough for a hospital and some of the Buddhist principles upon which the whole centre was run didn't help either. Dogs roamed the wards spreading who knows what disease, the bricolage beds caused hideous sores, which could hardly be cleaned since the water was often shut off, physio care was given by the likes of me. I had no medical training and could just as easily have been worsening patients' conditions as improving them. The major saving grace was the exceptional community feel of the place. Everybody was on level pegging, and I'm sure many people reinvented themselves here, in the coexistence of empowerment and anonymity.

At this point, it is fair to say I felt sickened at Western society. As a consequence, the quest to raise money for Newlife only compounded my revolt. It is undeniable that disabled children in the UK were relatively very well-off compared to those in Burma. The tales of what became of disabled people here were incomparably gut-wrenching. Some of these people I saw in Thabarwa, others on the streets of Yangon, others I heard about. They were abandoned, left to rot as a bag of bones and organs, untreated, uncared for. And yet, some of the disabled Thabarwa inhabitants for example, needed such little material care to vastly improve the quality of their lives. Bamboo walking sticks on which people laboriously leant could be replaced by simple wheelchairs, they could have carers, someone reliable – Burmese - to chat to for much-needed support. The most basic of safety nets could be cast that would prevent them from having to beg, limbless on dusty streets or eek out the rest of their existences in Thabarwa. Meanwhile, Newlife were providing battery-powered wheelchairs to replace sleek cruiser chairs, or play sets to replace the boring interactions with loving parents, or high-tech electronic cots so that no-one would suffer in 'normal beds'. I sighed with these thoughts. It seemed I had chosen the wrong cause and I cast Newlife to the further recesses of my mind, while I processed the stifling inequality of this world.

Shan

While I was in Thabarwa, Pierre had crossed the Burmese border but had been prevented by police in Tachileik from continuing any further. The only option available to him was to get a flight to Taunggyi, thus bypassing the restricted road. This put a big question mark over my own plan. Taunggyi was about 650 kilometres to the north and Pierre only needed to get a flight there. It would take me almost a week to get there by which time I would have missed Pierre. My only chance to meet up with him would be to get the train north, cutting out a massive chunk of the Irrawaddy basin flat lands. I was hesitant. So far, I had refused to take any form of public transport. This stubbornness had to be weighed up against my chance to meet with Pierre again. Perhaps motivated by the guilt of our initial separation, I chose to compromise by riding back up to Bago and getting the train to Thazi, leaving only 160 kilometres to cycle to Taunggyi.

I milled around the pastel-shaded stuffy Bago train station for a while, trying to make head and tail of the confusing timetable. It seemed to say that a train would leave northbound (to Thazi) at 01:00pm, but a curious and concerned bystander informed me that I couldn't take a bicycle on the 1pm train and had to wait until 04:00pm. Then another man gave his two pence and told me that the train took an awful long time and that I would do much better to get the bus. Despite having a strong preference for the train, I allowed myself get swayed by this insistent fellow. He led me to the bus station on his moped and expected a tip. I begrudgingly crumpled a 1000K note into his hand. At 10:00pm, the cramped bus finally left the station at Bago towards Meiktila. My bike and panniers were piled at the back with a whole host of freight belonging to the other passengers, barrels of oil, wooden furniture and the odd chicken.

It was a little earlier than 04:00am when the words 'Meiktila Meiktila' sounded over the bus tannoy. I jostled myself into action and with the help of another passenger, descended my bike and panniers. I had barely checked that everything was there when the bus motored hastily away. The air was far cooler and I even felt a chill on my legs. I surveyed my surroundings. The streets were silent save for a couple of stray dogs padding down a nearby alley.

I pedalled away from the centre of town, towards the pagoda that stood overlooking a sedate and hazy lake. Here was a sheltered bench. I took out my sleeping bag, set it up as a pillow and laid myself down to snooze away until daylight. Already at 05:00am, before the sun, the devout Buddhists came to sit in front of the *stupa*. They paid me little regard but still, I felt awkward as people soon came in greater numbers. Dawn wasn't far off, and for fear of disrespect I scurried away, bleary eyed but optimistic at having been transported to a different part of Burma altogether. On the road with the town behind, vague outlines of distant hills slowly came into view with the rising of the sun. They were the Shan hills, exactly where I was headed. I suspected it would take me two days to get to Taunggyi a thousand metres higher in those distant hazy silhouettes.

The road to the Shan plateau weaved its way along the hillside, seeming to follow every meander of the river in the valley below. The temperature in the daytime had ramped back up to the thirties and the hard exertion that the mountain pass demanded made it a tough day. Just as the turning of the pedals was becoming arduous labour I clocked a welcome sight: a monastery perched regally above the village of a few bamboo houses looking down back into the valley and the series of hairpins I had just ascended.

Owing to my previous monastery rejection here in Myanmar, I walked up the stairs with a sense of trepidation, hoping to be welcomed, but expecting to be turned away. The *Ashin,* as it would turn out, was a truly sweet man, a purveyor of the English language and possessor of legendary *chinlone* (foot volley, also known as *sepat takraw* in other South East Asian nations) skills. His attitude was somewhat different from that of the monks I had previously come across. He set a quilt and pillow onto one of the benches of his monastery and stayed up with me, putting the world to rights. My understanding of what it meant to be a monk was continually changing. This particular Ashin added me on Facebook and when I asked if he was getting up at 04:00am to meditate, as seemed to be common practice, he laughed, "Mornings are for sleeping."

True to his word, I left at 06:00am to the sound of a snoring monk in a deep slumber. I suppose that as well as anybody's professions and practices can never fully define them, so the monks were no exception. Cycling away from the monastery, I enjoyed the thought that the special individual flairs and passions of this monk in particular were not bundled away in his crimson robes.

The elevation reached 1300m at Kalaw and a few spatterings of rain fell from the sky. The last time I had felt drizzle was the Cameron highlands of Malaysia and I hummed with contentment as I saw the tiny splashes darken my blue waterproof. Kalaw is a typical hill station town. It was often frequented by British Colonial officers in the springtime before the monsoons when the humidity becomes too much to bear in April and May. Relics of these bygone times still remained, with large, handsome buildings built around the outskirts of the main market area.

At the very back of the town, away from the main road, was a large hill that looked as if it would give a magnificent panorama over the town and surrounding cirque, now being licked by tendrils of low clouds. At the top of the hill, the view became almost completely obscured by the pooling influx of mist: shame. On top was a small shed, which reminded me of a bothy that one might find in Scotland. Naturally, I could not resist trying the door, which ceded open at a light push. Just inside, sprawled on the floor, was a solitary man, half asleep in an uncomfortable-looking position. He stirred slightly at the door creak. A string of saliva drooped from his open mouth. Next to him was a pile of four menacing-looking assault rifles. I didn't wake him to say hello. I froze up and slowly retraced my steps, careful not to make any noise. He hadn't moved anymore and I almost believed myself clear as I carefully closed the door behind me. Suddenly, at precisely the wrong time, a stray dog appeared behind me and started barking. "Oh bloody chuff!" I leapt out of my skin and manically turned to the dog. "Sh!"

The dog kept barking, making a fuss.

"Shhh!"

"Woof woof woof!"

That was enough for me. I sprinted back down the hillside, tail between my legs, not turning to see if the sleeping man had woken to pursue me with his rifles. The builders at the bottom of the hill ogled me curiously as I ran past them, wide-eyed, face white as a sheet. I nodded a stiff hello as I hastened to my locked-up bike. There was probably very little chance of any real danger, but nonetheless - guns unnerve me, the very core of their design being to pull the curtain on life. In any case it wouldn't be the last time I saw them on this trip.

It was almost judgement time. The road descended a great deal from Kalaw onto a plateau, which was disconcerting as Taunggyi was supposed to be 100 metres higher than Kalaw. Twenty kilometres passed like this, cruising downhill through dry scrub-land on a road stretching all the way to the horizon. It couldn't be right. I should have been *climbing* to Taunggyi. Inevitably, with less than ten kilometres to go, the road came to a halt against a dominating hillside upon which the city was perched. Endless hairpins wound up the hill, with cars, trucks, busses and mopeds veering dangerously around every corner and the smell of burning clutch stagnated all around.

Upon arriving on the plateau, I quickly found my lodgings. For the extortionate sum of £8.50, I managed to get a room at one of the few motels priced below 25$. The owner was friendly, familiar with English and had even met more cycle tourists here before, which – perhaps naively - surprised me. He said at least two others had the same idea as mine and both were turned away by the police further down the road. Things weren't boding well for my traverse of the Shan hills. He told me more stories of tribal highwaymen extorting any traveller passing along the road, even Burmese. Indeed, most of the drivers crossing the region would probably begin with about 50$ and end with none. This was nominally included in their budget. I guess in the end it's not awfully dissimilar to the French motorway toll system. With a few more harrowing tales from the hotel boss, I was sufficiently put off to abandon my idea.

In the meantime, Pierre hadn't gotten a flight. He warned me it might be an extra ten days before one makes its way to Taunggyi or even Mandalay. I felt as though I didn't have ten days to wait. My entire trip up this far north seemed completely pointless. In fact, I now felt like making my way back towards Thailand to restart my mission of cycling back to the UK. I was thoroughly enjoying my time in Burma, but it was ultimately a massive detour and distraction from the goal I had set myself. *Get back to England on my bicycle.* Free to meander as I pleased, I felt purposeless and anxious. Although free, I needed structure. From Taunggyi, the only option left to me was a lowly trek back to Mae Sot, where my journey into Burma had begun. It was quite the kick in the teeth, having to end up in the same place I was before, one month later, but there was nothing left for it. I had betted on Shan and I had lost.

To quell the bitterness, I decided to spend a couple of days at Inle lake, a tourist resort only fifty kilometres from Taunggyi.

There I awaited further news from Pierre. Every day he faced the same dilemma, no flights were leaving. Days passed. Finally, it seemed a flight for Mandalay was leaving the following day, but once he arrived it would be a two-day cycle in the wrong direction to meet him, then I would be left with an almighty sprint (or another public transport mission) to make it back to the border before my visa ran out. In all truth I just needed to get back into a headspace where I could feel like I was nearing my goal. Pure vagabonding was difficult to come to terms with. There was surely a balance between purpose and freedom and I felt that vagabonding tipped the scales a little too far from purpose for my liking. My mind was set. I was heading back to the Mae Sot – Myawaddy border. A calm week-long ride, I thought, not quite knowing that things were about to get far more adventurous in Burma.

Roads less travelled

I emptied my lungs, shouting into the wilderness, just 24 hours after having left the cosy tourist confines of Inle lake. My bike jittered awkwardly over the stony track, sending my panniers bouncing and slapping against the rack. For the past five hours, the speedometer had hardly surpassed five kilometres an hour, normal walking pace. Roughly 35 kilometres ago, the road surface had completely deteriorated, leading into a network of tracks that defied my mapping software. I knew my situation was unusual, as whenever I passed the odd local, instead of smiling or waving, they stopped, stared and laughed.

What are you doing here you twit, they must have been thinking. I simply laughed back and shrugged my shoulders, pretending to be nonchalant, but really, suffering. It is worth noting the root of my sufferance was not truly physical discomfort, more the frustration of my inability to advance on such roads, at loggerheads with the spirit of motoring through Burma that I had left Inle with. It did seem curious how the root of suffering lay almost always entirely in the mind.

With no map to rely on, I had memorised the name of the village that I was supposed to arrive at, and stopped everyone I came across to signal what was hopefully the main road south and shout the name of the town. "Hseesaw! Seesang! SiSeng!"
"Ah! Hsihseng?"
"Yes, Hsihseng! teytek?"
Each confused Shan villager would invariably nod, laugh or smile, but never confirm the direction, before bouncing away on their moped, hugging the five centimetres on the very edge of the stony trail where the bumps were somehow slightly flatter.

I continued onwards, suspecting that fifteen kilometres or so of trail remained until the village that I was heading for, through which the main road ran south. But for now, there was an astounding sense of wilderness, as even the odd moped an hour that I had crossed had obviously turned off to some smaller village that I had missed. The only other vehicles on the road were oxen-drawn carts, trundling along. Into the wonderment at the wilderness, my tiredness was folded. The previous night had been restless. With no sign of civilisation save for a monastery perched on a mound above the rocky road, I had headed there. On my way up the dirt path to the derelict building, second thoughts crept in. I paused on the track, a pang of doubt in my stomach telling me to go no further. The panorama around me began to glow. The hills were tinted in twilight bronze and the silence broke only with gentle breaths of wind whispering in the teak leaves. I realised the pang in my stomach was the anxiety at spending the night as a freeloader again, justifying myself, describing my taxonomy, rank and order. Now, with the fullness of nature brimming around me, I was content with the solitude and had no further wants of comfort or shelter. I pitched up the tent on a cleared piece of earth half way up to the building, then ate a dinner of noodles, a few packets of which I always had in my panniers, and settled down to gaze at the celestial beauty of the milky way that streamed through the still sky.

At around midnight a curious rhythmic pitter-patter began to sound. The outer lining was left off my tent, so looking skywards, I expected to see rain falling from blotted clouds. Contrarily, the night was still clear and magnificently star-speckled. So if it wasn't rain, what was that noise? I listened. *Tap tap tap tap...tap tap tap tap...tap tap tap tap.* It sounded as if it was coming from underneath me! I put on my head torch, opened the tent flap, peeled the sheet from the ground and almost jumped up at what I saw. An army of termites were digging their way into the tent! Quickly, I shifted everything away from the cleared Earth and onto the track itself, convinced that nothing would disturb me there for the remainder of the night. Within ten minutes they were back at it! Apparently, there was no escaping these tenacious critters. Eventually, I pounded the ground with my fist, to little avail – for the noise promptly started again five minutes after. In the end, I simply fell asleep. *If they wanted to eat my tent, let 'em have it!* Despite strange dreams of becoming termite fodder, I still woke in the morning, and upon inspecting my tent, it seemed that they must have decided to find a tastier snack elsewhere after all.

Content at not being eaten out of my skin, I packed up and returned to the track. As the crow flies, it seemed that Hsihseng was only a couple of dozen kilometres away, yet the valley trails that led the way there were traitorously long. What's more, with no roads mapped, there was no telling just which road to take. With nothing left for it, I advanced again to the rhythmic spanking of panniers on rack, the road turning the bike into a wheeled jack-hammer. My eyes watered in frustration at these cursed Burmese roads! I wished I could stop, sit down, get a bus ticket out of there. There was, however, no opportunity to do so. Nor even for venting to anyone - not a single villager to gesticulate to. The road, at least at this hour of the morning, was silent but for the slapping, the wind and the churning gravel. It was to these sounds that I had to settle and plod slowly onwards. Nonetheless, a thought for solace was that most roads do all lead somewhere. The end would come sooner or later. My finality was not the endless dusty gravel of Burmese hinterland. And so, as I was crying and pleading for deliverance, the crossroads at Hsihseng finally came into sight. And what a glorious sight it was too, that main road at the end of this excruciating stretch. Tears turned into laughter, and suddenly my bum felt less sore, and the rhythmic slapping of the panniers gained an almost melodic quality. Deliverance at last! I rolled into Hsihseng's first Lah pah yeh joint to settle with a milk tea and nurse the instantaneous trauma that had been endured. Under that shaded veranda and with a milk tea in hand I reflected on that stretch and what it had done to my body and mind. Both exhausted with unexpected strains. However, already, even then, that wild fifty kilometres of road far from anywhere I knew and will likely ever know was winding its way into my deep memories. That clear night sky lit up by the uncountable infinity of the band of our milky way. The blushing sunrise. The grand silence. Even the termites. In those moments, the story was different. How I suffered and wished for nothing but deliverance. And now, funnily enough, if these memories resurface, I realise I wish for nothing but to be there once again.

In any case, though less memorable, the main road South was far easier going. The asphalted way was not at all bad, even outside of Burmese standards. My panniers no longer jittered and jangled as if my bike was a bucking bronco, and I could stream along South towards Loikaw as I had imagined. I felt a pang of sadness and regret at leaving the Shan plateau behind, especially having given up on my initial ambitions to explore the region. Alas, the nature of choice means that not all paths can be trodden.

By evening I had descended back into the clutches of the world at large, to the queer business of folk. The passing of time and extent of space once more took on their ordinary meaning – as they do at lower altitudes. I arrived in Loikaw, the capital of Kayah state and checked into the guesthouse for foreigners.
At the moment of checking in, while already thinking about the relaxing morning ride I would have, simply cruising south, I found a sheet of paper affixed to an information board explaining the restricted zones in Kayah. It read that the government had designated all roads leading in that direction to be restricted: the very roads I relied on for reaching Mae Sot again. I couldn't believe it. It couldn't be so! Kayah seemed like a dead end.

I began to panic and scour the map for my options. All roads leading south restricted. Only roads leading south went to Mae

Sot. The host of the guest house could only confirm the restrictions too. It seemed the only way out of this diplomatic trough would be the torturous stony track I had just come down. Thoughts of pannier slap and sore-arsedness came flooding into my head and I shuddered at the prospect. I had concluded that there were three route options leading eventually to Mae Sot. All of which were out of bounds! I immediately left the hotel to execute my emergency procedure: beer and cakes.

The following morning, to my great surprise, the consumption of embarrassingly high-percentage black shield stout and pineapple moon cakes have not opened up any of the restricted areas that I had initially planned to pass through. In my panicked research I had contacted one person and found out about another person who was living in the area, spoke English and was clued up on the cans and can'ts in Myanmar's volatile paranoia. I also contacted SuSu. I asked whether she thought I could sweet talk or bribe my way out of trouble if I was caught in a restricted zone. She responded anecdotally: an American acquaintance of hers got caught in a restricted zone by the Tatmadaw and received a hearty 3-month jail sentence. I'm not sure even a bribe bottle of Myanmar Glan Master whisky would do the trick. Her advice was clear. Don't be a nob. Don't go to restricted areas. Although I am often adept at not heeding advice, this nugget seemed rather compelling.

It is perhaps worth explaining in a little more detail here the *why* behind the restrictions for foreign travellers and the political and historical mess that still plagues this region rich in ethnic diversity and pretty mountains. Simply put: Kayah had many problems – the most serious being the ongoing state of civil war between the *Tatmadaw* and the Karen National Liberation Army. The reason for this war is rather complex. When Burma was under British rule, what is now Kayah state was left mostly to its own devices. It still fell into British colonial territory but was allowed to continue to be administered by the indigenous population, the Karenni people. It's very likely that the British still exploited this region for its vast tungsten mines, but it wasn't fully assimilated into British Burma. In 1947, when Burma gained independence from Britain after a turbulent Japanese invasion during World War II, the ruling body was unionist. That is to say, the socialist military government led by general Aung San wanted all of Burma to be happy together in one nice post-colonial united state. But the ethnic groups, notably the Rakhine Buddhists and the Karenni said *I don't think so Mr Aung San!* And so the Karennis assembled a resistance against their assimilation into a centrally governed Burma, resulting in civil war between a rebel army and the central government. Similar stories apply to the other ethnic groups whose resistance armies are fighting the military. The history between the moment of the attempted unification of Burma and the present day could, and does, fill many books. Right now, it would be hard to claim that there is widespread outright war, but severe tensions still remain and the whole political environment of Burma is extremely volatile.

As for the Kayah state region, there has been a national ceasefire agreement in place since 2012 (which was unfortunately violated as recently as 2018, when the Tatmadaw entered KNU territory unannounced). The restricted areas are all townships where there is KNU activity that the Burmese military don't want blabbermouth foreigners to visit. It did seem however, to be no more dangerous than anywhere else I had been, and I would anyway be too busy cycling to give a care for having in-depth political discussions with a rebel group. Plus, I could barely make myself understood when asking for a salad, so debating internal policy was out of the question... In brief, it seemed the route was objectively safe for me so I was miffed at not being allowed to take it.

At 07:00am, I left the foreigners' guesthouse in the calm morning chill and was on my way to meet *the foreign guy who knows stuff about Kayah state.* Riding along, looking from side to side, breathing in the exuberance of waking Burma, I noticed the police station. Two officers sat outside puffing on cheroot. I decided to pay them a visit. Ten minutes later, a big grin was slapped across my face. My dear interlocutor, constable Kwe Ye Aung had agreed that one of the three routes (of course, the hardest one through the mountains) was safe for me. This was truly a massive surprise, having so far been under the impression that rules in Burma were not to be broken. My route seemed reasonably remote on the map. A few villages looked to be perched on mountaintops or nestled in valleys and there certainly weren't any guesthouses over this lumpy 220 kilometres stretch. I noted the policeman's name in case I still got asked what I was doing. *Kwe Ye Aung said I could do it!* And so it was decided. I stocked up on dried noodles and extra water, not being sure of how long the route would take me. I hit the road soon after 08:00am, brimming with a renewed sense of adventure.

Nestled in these verdant hills were in the end, many villages, and in these villages, lived some of the kindest folk I met. I strained my way up the punishing gradients towards a village I saw perched atop the road above, two hairpins later. I arrived, utterly exhausted and shimmied over to the first hut that looked like they had some food a-cookin'. Red with effort, bleary eyed and jelly legged, I asked, "Hthamin she lah: Rice, have, yes?"
"She deh, she deh!"
I was in business. A staunch woman with stained teeth that only seemed to accentuate her enthusiastic smile gestured at me to sit. She soon re-emerged from her bamboo hut, carrying a big plate of rice, half of which I scoffed immediately. Then more rice, a soup, a curry, and some vegetable dish that was accompanied with tiny shrimp and what looked like some sort of grub was brought to the table... I wolfed down the lot. The woman who was slowly becoming more and more like a goddess of abundance brought a big plate of watermelon and told me to get eating. I thought I had space for a couple of slices. Seconds later, the plate was empty. At the end of the feast, I tried to pay. She shook he head, "Money, no."

I wanted to give her something, anything! I was learning that the hardest part of being a guest is to accept this one-sidedness with modest grace. It was difficult when I had been brought up on the principle that you don't get something for nothing. I was certainly building up a hefty debt that one day I will pay forwards.

That day, nourished by the hand of the generous Karenni villagers, I had managed to surmount three long mountain passes. The last one especially seemed it would never culminate and just kept cutting upwards, skywards even, through thick jungle. It was twilight by the time I arrived at the summit. The sun was just setting behind the lilac hills that layer by layer began relinquishing their crepuscular glow. It just so happened, that at the top of this hill, was a small house. A skinny topless man was milling about outside, enjoying the last rays of the sunshine. Seeing me crest the hill, he beckoned me to join. He introduced himself as David, affirming himself a Karenni Christian by showing off the cross around his neck. With pride, he welcomed me to the top of the pass, as if he were the caretaker of this saddle point between two valleys. He began by motioning to the fading hills with a big wrinkled smile, his arms amplifying the grandiose sunset. Once he was satisfied that we had sufficiently appreciated this spectacle, he led me up onto the mound above the road where a token virgin Mary shrine had been erected amongst the cleared bamboo thickets. I nodded enthusiastically, all the while prospecting the ground for camping potential. As if reading my mind, we dropped back down to the road, where he motioned at a half-constructed structure: the skeleton of another small hut, perfect for the tent. Together, we moved some planks of wood and nails from the exposed wooden platform beneath the roof joists. He then inspected the planks, took two of the better ones and in less than a minute constructed a ramp up to the platform so that I didn't have to strain to get up.

As I went to gather my sleeping gear, David disappeared round the back of his house. He came back with an enormous sheet of tin and signalled to the open roof structure, then the hammer and nails, making a hand gesture for shelter. In a flash, he had jumped up onto the roof structure with the hammer and signalled for me to pass him a tin sheet. Astonished, I quickly had to shout and gesture that I had shelter already.

"No, no!" I cried, "You don't need to build the bloody roof!"

He leapt down from the roof as I showed my tent. He shrugged the whole ordeal off. I, on the other hand, was in awe at such an idea. I had never counted on someone building a house for me to sleep in for a night.

Once the tent was in place, David and I spent the evening gathered round the fire that he made, taking turns to monologue in our respective languages. I thought I could gleam certain details of his stories and he perhaps some from mine, but that might be utter nonsense. Either way, it was a fascinating interaction. We invented the meaning to each other's words and managed to keep up the charade for hours – telling of our lives, fears, troubles and joys, until the fire extinguished.

Before retiring to my tent, I bade him good night with the promise of cooking porridge for us in the morning. When I did, he took one look at the stodgy gruel in my mess tin and laughed. He refused and force-fed me rice and vegetables instead, telling me it's good for the bike riding! Admittedly, he could equally have been saying *Eat this and piss off you greedy sod!* This, in the end, I did, as both a heavier and richer person, leaving David, guardian of Kayah hilltops, to his remote outpost.

Day two in these restricted mountains brought more of the same delightful hardship and serendipity, but with two major differences. The first was that I was tired and the climbs were somehow even longer and steeper, making it the toughest day on the body thus far. The second was that people gave me mostly free drugs instead of free food. Under the midday heat,

I was feeling particularly low on energy. My legs felt like they were stilled in treacle and my back was creaking like a door swinging back and forth on rusty hinges. Just at the point when I needed to be picked up, something by the road caught my attention: a betel nut stand. Now betel is a drug that almost everybody in Burma seemed to enjoy. It was not uncommon to see men and women alike, squatting by the roadside, slipping a leafy betel package into their mouths, or spitting out the blood-red gunk it produced. At first sight, I thought everyone had tuberculosis until I correlated the spitting to the sucking and chewing practices that preceded it. Evidence of this habit was splattered across almost all the surface of the busier roads leading to towns. I wondered how many square kilometres across the country was painted in this red gunk. Many hundreds at the very least. I would often move out of the way of passing mini buses, less afraid of being run over than being covered by betel slosh that was all too periodically ejected from Burmese mouths through open windows.

Aside from increasing the probability of developing almost every disease known to man, I had a vague recollection of reading that betel increased focus and endurance, so I talked myself into it. "Go on then, only one," I said to the stall owner who proceeded to give me seven. Half of these were then distributed to a group of men chopping down roadside bamboo, in exchange for a lunch of rice and raw garlic they had shared with me. Satisfied I had left betel behind, I continued cleanly on. Just twenty minutes later, a man stopped me, insisting on giving me a gift, that turned out to be seven more betel nut packages!

At the end of the day, the road wound its final descent down from the mountains and into the town of Taungoo. The beauty of the mountain with its passes, its sparse jungle, and its shining people melded into the highway into town, to be replaced with a filthy, bumpy, dusty, rocky road. Horn-blasts and shouts expounded aplenty. The calm and quiet mountains were already far behind and I sighed, delivering myself to another world apart.

Hysteresis

Bago region is not known for its beauty. It is almost entirely flat, scorching hot and filled with dusty villages. After the two mythical mountain days it seemed that not much separated me from Thailand. The border was all that I could think of and so I set off to make it back to Mae Sot as quickly as I could. It was about 06:00pm when I reached the 150 kilometres mark, having slogged against a tickling headwind for the best part of the last eight hours. The road was good for Myanmar standards, and the lack of any topographical variation meant I could hit a rhythm and stick to it. "Pud Taow, pud taow, pud taow"
I experimented meditation while cycling, half afraid to zone out and drift into a moped or a truck, half needing some sort of mental relief from the endless paddy fields and flat stretch of tarmac.

Upon prospection of the map, I realised that there were only 70 kilometres to go to Kyaikto, where there was a guesthouse I had stayed at previously. Feeling energetic, and not wishing to pitch up in the stuffy moist paddy, in a village, or behind a pagoda, I set my sights on this town. I was still feeling fantastic for the first thirty kilometres of the seventy, but as night fell, weariness took over and I cursed myself for not taking it easier on myself. I put my head into the handlebars and kept onwards, ticking over the pedals. With the exception of stumbling across what appeared to be a rave in a forest, where I was almost coaxed into dancing with the drugged-up, *longyi*-clad skankers, I made it to Kyaikto almost without stopping, in complete exhaustion.

The next day was more of the same, Thailand would not leave my mind and in any case there was nothing I wished to do with the day but cycle. Three days out of Taungoo and I found myself once again in the gateway town of Kawkareik. The temperature was above 40°C and when I arrived at the house of SuSu's friend I passed out into a long siesta.

Susu was sat with her friend conversing in the shade when I awoke. I hobbled over to her and asked if there was anywhere I could shower. This suggestion seemed to cause quite a stir. Showering in the heat of the day can make a person sick, apparently! And so I sat, bathed in my sweat, but quite content at being back with SuSu to debrief on the journey through Burma.

I related her my tales back at her place, where we spent the afternoon painting the wooden walls of her house a darker shade of brown. I told her everything from when I last left Kawkareik. The ferries over the river to Mawlamyine, the hazy mountains of Hpa An, the paddy and the poverty around Bago, Thabarwa. The rotting Yangon slums and air-conditioned hostel, the cool north and the ethereal Shan state. The guns. The rocky road. The restricted mountain pass. The rush back. And through this, the unyielding warmth of the Burmese people. This is what I wished to relate to SuSu. The journey, in the end, turned out to be the discovery of how the Burmese people were a constant light source in sometimes dark places, buoys in sometimes turbulent waters, a people whose laughter rippled the sometimes solemn silence. The Burmese people are what make Burma what it is. More so than the rivers, the paddy, the hazy mountains, the buddhas and the pagodas. Although the whole lot melds together into the vast web of culture, the people of Burma truly stood out as the jewels of the land.

I left SuSu with another emotional goodbye the following day and set myself up to tackle the last mountain before Myawaddy, the Burmese border town. I was saying my mental farewell to the country. Everything that I had seen and that had happened here had truly moved me. I smiled, knowing that I had made it through Burma and was all the richer for it. My sub-mission was wholly successful. I now felt a strong attachment to a country that just one month ago I had almost no knowledge of.

As I was relieving myself by the roadside on one of the final inclines, a young teenager pulled alongside me on his moped. "I go Myawaddy!" He excitedly proclaimed.
"And I'm going for a piss!" I incredulously shouted back. *These people have no inhibitions!* He looked at me with a confused expression.
"Oh, and I go Myawaddy too!" I added, laughingly.
He burst into a smile as I snapped my cycling shorts back into place and mounted the bike. On the road, he made a point of driving just in front of me, his headlight illuminating the darkness ahead. In a show of bravado, I gave my everything to overtake him. He laughed and revved up slightly, drawing parallel as my tongue hung out of my mouth. Panting, I continued this ridiculous uphill sprint. After ten minutes (now at a much more settled pace), I told him he could go and I thanked him for his company. He left 30 seconds later. As I rounded the corner at the top of the hill, I saw he had waited for me, and he flagged me down to stop.
I looked at him, not understanding where he wanted to go with this. He pulled out his phone. "Ah, you want a selfie, yes?" I inquired.
He shook his head and removed the phone case, revealing a single US dollar bill. He unfolded it and put it in my hand. I put it back in his and began an earnest protest. "No, no no no, I don't need money, no!"
 He tried to open up my hand to put it back in, and when he couldn't, stuffed it in my handlebar bag.
"Bye bye, my friend," he said, and sped off down the hill, leaving a billowing cloud of dust in his wake. I welled with tears that threatened to fall as I blasted downhill towards Myawaddy, where I spent my final night in this country that has marked me to the core, before crossing the border back to Thailand, and back to business.

Haze

Back in Thailand, I felt sickened by the relative order and needless comfort in comparison to Burma to the extent that I developed diarrhoea. I tried not to let this be too much of a setback and set off for a five-day stint to Chiang Mai where I would for the last time meet up with Sam, in Thailand at least. Half-recovered, I followed the Moei river, the natural border between North Thailand and Myanmar before cutting North East into the Thongchai range. These mountain ranges of Northern Thailand were terrifyingly steep. Taking on the climbs in forty-degree heat with masses of pollution in the air, carried over by the prevailing westerlies from burning crops in Burma, was a struggle, to say the very least. As I descended a minor side road up which I had camped in front of the national park office the night before, my brakes began rubbing on my wheel, so I dismounted to inspect the problem.

"Hallo!" I heard a voice from across the road. It was two older cyclists on half-loaded mountain bikes.
"Har, har, har, look at ze English man vif his bike problames," guffawed the German man from across the road, iPad in hand taking a film of me irately bent over my bicycle adjusting the springs on my calliper breaks after having pumped up my slow punctured tyre. I had forgotten the existence of irksome tourists while in Burma. I pushed a sympathetic smile at the wayward sextegenarian clad in very optimistic lycra. His stalwart sun-freckled bratwurst legs provided a solid platform for the power stance he was pulling astride his trek mountain bike. His wife was chirping and chortling beside him, egging him on with a goofy complicit smile. I smiled at her too, in pity. I knew that while they may be giggling now, their laughs would likely not endure the reputedly cruel mountain passes that the day was set to bring. A veteran cyclist I had met in Mawlamyine described

exactly these hills as the toughest he had ever ridden in his touring life.

Having overtaken the mocking Germans with a terse *have a lovely day,* I turned away from the Moei river, whose company was a joy alongside the soft rises and falls left by a diaphragmatic Earth. As soon as I took the turn, it is fair to say that the road went up and only up. Through the heat and sickness, my headspace became tainted with delirium, and I began imagining the conversation between the road engineer and his stuttering apprentice. *"Well s-s-sir, I know you have p-p-proposhed that the r-road should go s-s-straight over the mount-tains but d-d-don't you think it might be a g-good idea to f-f-follow the hill gently up the valley s-s-s-so the r-r-road isn't v-v-vertical?"*
"Nonsense, boy! Get that tarmac plastered in the straightest line you can!"

I despaired, gazing upwards at the asphalt wall bearing down on me. *I have to climb this,* I thought to myself in hysterical disbelief. The temperature was touching the high thirties. I was having bike troubles. Thirsty. I dismounted and began pushing my bike, physically unable to hall my stuff upwards with feet on the pedals. My tongue hung out like a lizard's. Homeostasis certainly wasn't a cool look and I was glad nobody was around to see. The sound of a chugging motor joined the screeching chorus of *chak-a-chan* (cicadas). A pickup truck passed by with a whooping Doppler-shifted howl of delight. A *German* Doppler shifted howl of delight. The crafty beggars had obviously talked their way into the back of a pickup truck and their light-hearted hilarity in the face of my dogged stubbornness made me laugh my way into a delirium-infused existential crisis that was only just kept under wraps. I kept pushing on, resting in every song-teow shelter I could find. *Maybe I should hitch a ride too?* I wearily pushed these thoughts out of my head, for I was a British man! And British men keep calm and they carry on. I couldn't help think that British men are daft.

The day continued in such a fashion of suffering on uphills and reeling with fear on downhills that were almost freefalls, made only more exhilarating with a rear brake all but out of action. On one section the gradient was so negatively steep I actually whipped up my hands into the air and screamed with fright and delight. I thought there might be a camera that captured it. Perhaps at the end of this run, I could buy the picture of my flogging cheeks and socket-leapt eyes for only £15 or a fiver for a keyring. It would make a great souvenir and I would even get it on a fridge magnet for my Nan. On the uphills, pedalling quickly became pushing, every time. *Make this day stop,* I pleaded in my head. Luckily, as all days do, it did.

After ten kilometres of merciful descent into the valley, I called a stop to the cycling. I went to wash in the river where I found floating bamboo platforms. I couldn't resist putting my tent here and camping. By the river, I met the headmaster of a school who offered for me to sleep there with a bed and Wi-Fi and electricity. He didn't quite get where I was coming from with my rejection. *I'm camping on a river!* It was truly blissful, until in the night when I woke up needing to vomit and release my bowels. There was nothing there. Nothing but the river: the pristine, clear watered national park river. "Bleugh!" I emptied my stomach multiple times in that river.

I waded back across to the riverbank from the river campsite where I had locked my bike the night before, feeling light-headed and woozy. It was only about forty kilometres to Mae Sariang but I felt sufficiently ill that when I arrived there I slept for three hours on a bench outside the police station, while leaving my sweat-imbibed clothes to dry in the pounding sun. I felt slightly better after my siesta but even at 03:00pm, it was far too hot to cycle. I took an extra half an hour in the shade of a palm on the roadside before beginning a climb up to almost

1100 metres. I had to pause to vomit a few times on the way up, but otherwise was making steady progress.

What are you doing?! I thought as for the third time in ten minutes I pulled up to retch. I had to make it to Chiang Mai in two days for Sam and my decision-making was far too impaired to even consider that stopping was a good idea, although it almost certainly was. I was reminded of my illness in Malaysia and the day I crazily continued to Port Dickson. I pushed them thoughts to the back of my mind. *Bad thoughts!* Nearing the top of the climb, I investigated a row of shops, taking my empty bottles inside with the hope of replenishing my dwindling water.

I left the establishment to find my front handlebar bag wide open. *Strange*, I thought to myself. I rooted through, checking everything was there. It was not. My wallet was missing. I started to become frantic and before long had ravaged all of my panniers in search of the article in which both of my debit cards and all my money was stored. It was nowhere to be found.

"Keep calm, keep calm" I repeated to myself as I began to shake. Nobody had seen it in the shop and I hadn't bought a thing. I sat by my bike and put my head in my hands.

The police were called by the shop-owner and when a lone officer on a motorbike arrived, all he wanted to do was take selfies. It wasn't the time and I certainly wasn't in the mood. A bystander offered to take me back down the road on the back of his moped while I looked for the card. Nada. The police officer left and the store-owner retreated back inside. I wheeled my bike away, penniless and unsure of what to do. Then, by some cruel stroke of irony, on the street just outside the shops, I found the only money I found on the entire trip. A 100 Baht note (£2.50). One that had been in my wallet, no doubt! A small boon and a small consolation.

I now had £2.50 to my name and with this securely stuffed away in the handlebar bag, I decided to descend the entire 1000m that

I had just painfully climbed. In true Asian style, I did this on the wrong side of the road, while keeping an eye out for my wallet on the floor. I was clutching at straws. On a corner, a car swung round unexpectedly and almost took me completely out. I jumped out of my dazed state, heart racing. I rejoined the right side of the road. *You idiot man, your wallet is NOT worth your life!* The near miss relativised things a little and drove me to begin accepting the processes I would have to go through. Cancel cards, apply for new ones, somehow borrow some money for the next couple of days until I meet Sam or try to wing it on £2.50 and the half bag of porridge I had left.

Back in Mae Sariang, I went straight to the police station and after some convincing, they wrote me a letter to confirm I had reported the crime. I pitched my tent in their car park and called to friends and family to hear friendly voices. I had got the ball rolling that evening. The cards were cancelled and a new one was on its way to Chiang Mai. I still had little money, but was confident I could arrive in Chiang Mai with what I had.

I allowed myself to hitchhike to where I had got to yesterday, with a helping hand from the police checkpoint situated at the bottom of the climb.

I stood with the officer at the checkpoint until we saw a pickup truck approaching. I nodded to the officer who stood in the road and waved the vehicle down, before describing to the driver his instructions: to take me, beaming cheekily from ear to ear up to the top of the climb in the back of the truck. We hauled the bike in and I jumped in next to it, before the exhilarating rollercoaster up the mountain began. I felt chuffed with my cheek and was having such an incredible time, I almost debated asking the driver to take me all the way to Chiang Mai. He dropped me at the top of the climb and I thanked him with a big thumbs up and a *WOO!*

My vomiting had ceased, which was promising, and the altitude had quelled the temperature and the majority of the choking pollution. The day was joyous, riding the softer climbs and descents cutting across the brilliantly forested massif. I was high enough for pines to be growing, and they did so in abundance, making breathing through the nose an absolute delight. That very evening, after a long descent, I walked into Op Luang police checkpoint, intending only to fill up my bottles. I got slightly more than I bargained for.

Within half an hour, there were two empty beer cans on the table and not many biscuits remained from the full pack that we had started with. Pat was regaling me with some fascinating stories about how he caught Burmese drug smugglers and thieves here in this seemingly peaceful jurisdiction. He also told me that he had served as a representative of the Thai royal police in Haiti, to help with the relief efforts in the aftermath of the tragic Earthquake that rocked the country in 2010.

At the mention of thieves in the area, I couldn't help but relate to him my story of the stolen wallet the previous night. I saw Pat's expression change. "I am so, so sorry to hear that this has happened," he sincerely said, with a polite "kap."
"Yeah, it's a bit of a ballache," I replied despondently, "but it will be okay, don't worry."
"No, this is not the real Thailand," Pat rose, 'I want to show you the real Thailand."
With that he called a few people on his phone and spoke with a mixture of gravity and jolliness. He had organised for a colleague to come and relieve him. He told me that the family in his small village not far away were preparing a feast tonight and were going to spend the night in the hot springs in the national park nearby. We were going to be guests of honour.

We spent a most relaxing night, bathing, cleansing ourselves with the spirit of *true Thailand*. We dined fervently and slept soundly in the tent. The following dawn, we awoke to the tranquillity of the springs in the jungle. It was election day in Thailand, and Pat had to resume his duties at the local polling station. We sat in silence in the rear of the pickup truck that coasted through the national park on a quiet winding road. I loved being in the rear of pickups: the feeling was one of warm engulfing windswept exhilaration. At the station Pat hurriedly prepared everything he would need for the day and just as I was about to leave he called me over one last time. He put two packets of biscuits in my hand, as well as another 100 Baht note. "Buy some noodles for food," he said.

"Ok Pat, I will." I took the note, feeling almost paradoxically grateful for having my wallet stolen so that such kindness could follow.

"Listen thanks *so much* for all this!"

We had a photo shoot in the blue light of the dawn in front of the Op Luang checkpoint sign of which he was so proud and with a hug I set off to cycle the 110 kilometres to Chiang Mai.

The remaining distance was easily brushed off on the relatively flat highway into Thailand's third city. I checked into a hostel and within six hours I was reunited with Sam, who luckily owed me 2000 Baht.

I spent over a full week in this city, mostly with Sam, waiting for the bike mechanic to return from his holiday. It had transpired that my rear rim was cracked, almost certainly on the horrifically bumpy stretch of dirt road from Hpa-An to Kawkareik (that Susu had warned me about). This was also the source of the rubbing brake pads that had been disconnected for the final few days to this city. The bike needed a whole new rear rim, two new tyres, a new chain and cassette as well as a few cables replacing. I had taken the bike to the reputable touring bike shop in the city, the very day that the mechanic was leaving on a week-long trip to Taiwan. Everything would have to be put on hold in the meantime.

This, I didn't mind too much, it meant more time with Sam. A small hitchhike trip was in order and while looking into this, we found a charming restaurant to frequent in the city where the owner, a woman by the name of Jeab, looked after us as if we were her sons. We escaped the asphyxiating pollution into the cooler teak interior and sat, indulged in nothing, denuded of all stress, at complete liberty to watch the world go by or slowly plan our jaunt into the hills. It was a blissful time.

After one week passing by in such a fashion, Pnuc the bike mechanic had finally returned. He had had a lovely time in Taiwan and perhaps more importantly, at least for this story, he had repaired the bike. I had also sent my debit card to his shop that had arrived in his absence. Financial independence and intercontinental transport, in an instant, were regained. I rushed over to the shop, sweating profusely as I ran in the stinking heat that by now I could not wait to escape. I took my card to the ATM. It worked! All debts settled, I was free to move on towards Chiang Rai and then Laos.

Just forty kilometres after leaving Chiang Mai I arrived in yet another national park in Thailand's stunning and verdant north (I was almost bored of national parks at this point). There was a small teak building at the border of the park that served all sorts of culinary delights, and the shaded exterior looked a perfect place to take the afternoon break with a *massaman* curry.

As I went to pay, I noticed a marked lack of something in the new wallet that I had bought. My card was not there. I smiled and laughed nervously and looked in the wallet again. It still wasn't there. I slowly emptied my handlebar bag and checked inside my passport wallet. Nothing. I began to despair. *How stupid can you be?!* I was genuinely concerned for my sanity, as it appeared I was going absolutely doo-lally. I called back the hostel. Nothing there. The bike shop. Nothing there. Pnuc agreed to visit the bank on my behalf but they informed him they couldn't open up the machine until in two days' time. There was nothing else I could do but wallow in my bloody stupidity! My best theory is that I had left it in the ATM, just five minutes after regaining financial freedom.

The problem was less severe this time, as my backup card had been sent to a *Couchsurfing* host in Chiang Rai, where I would arrive in only two days. It wasn't the card that was the worry though - it was my head. So now the ball was rolling. No point waiting around, I struggled over the construction site of a road towards the national park campsite that my Chinese cycling friend Mario had recommended. If you were on the road, going in the opposite direction you would have remarked a man with a stony expression, staring straight forward in unwavering apathy, ignoring the bumps of the road, the watered mud splattering over his bike, open mouth swallowing the dust kicked up by the passing trucks, like a pellet by a gold fish. You might not have known that he was working hard on suppressing all the stress invading his mind, but if you could judge his demeanour long enough, you would probably guess that he was not in a great place...

This wallowing trance was broken when a moped driver slowed down behind me. I spied him out the corner of my eye and stifled a sigh. *Christ what could this guy want?!* I could not deal with pleasantries or curiosa. However, the man didn't even utter a word. He held out his arm and opened his hand. In it was a neck scarf that he gestured for me to take. It would protect my lungs from the dust billowing from the wheels of the trucks and the pollution from the forest fires that were slowly licking their way along the hillside above the road. I eked out a smile of feeble thanks and he nodded and drove onwards. *It's not all bad.* This impromptu act of kindness kicked my arse out of the misery pit and allowed me to regain a more dynamic, optimistic mindset. The guy whose name I didn't even have the chance to ask didn't realise quite how much more than a scarf he gave to me that day.

Only two days later, I reached the Thai-Laos friendship bridge, having secured my back-up bankcard in Chiang Rai. It was time to say good-bye to Thailand for good. I was ready for the challenge of Laos and the start of the bigger mountains that would not cease until North-West China. It promised to be more remote and more gruelling than tourist Thailand. With far less spending on infrastructure, the roads were supposed to be in tatters and I had been told to pack food for days. I crossed the bridge over the Mekong, waited for the Lao visa to be imprinted in my passport and before long I was stamped in. "Welcome to Laos!"

Gradient

The time I spent cycling through Laos coincided with the famous water festival: Songkran. In the early hours of the day, kids would line the streets with buckets and small pistols and amongst the excitable shouts of "Sabaidee, Sabaidee!" the more courageous would give me a welcome dousing down, heavily diluting the sweat that was causing salt to crystallise on all of my clothes. This is the bright side of Songkran. The dark side of Songkran is inextricably linked to the excessive consumption of Beerlao. Beerlao is the part state-owned brewing company of Laos and as a consequence, its namesake beverage is found in abundance and for a very low price. Trucks carrying crates and crates of the stuff passed me on a worryingly regular basis. It seemed that the entire country was fuelled on it. It was truly epidemic. This is without even mentioning the dreadful spirit of Laolao, which is also consumed with apparent impunity. By the afternoon it seemed like many Lao people I encountered were blind drunk and could barely hold themselves up straight. Even kids who looked as young as 13 stumbled out of houses arm in arm, in tears and disorientated.

In Laos, schools served well as a reliable campsite. There were normally raised sheltered platforms on smooth stone verandas in front of the classrooms, or cut-back grass: perfect for pitching up. Water was not too far away for a quick wash (but probably not a drink) and more often than not a small army of kids would come to run around me or play football.

The first couple of days to Luang Namtha passed in relative ease. My legs were becoming accustomed to the brutal inclines but I don't think I could ever get used to the oppressing heat that made the air feel as though it was laden with mercury at all times of the day. I began to see clouds above the haze that each day was becoming thinner and thinner. Clouds! It had been such a long time since I had properly caught a glimpse of the atmosphere above a few hundred metres, owing to the optical trap of the haze. I could make out the nuances of blue of the sky, finally! It felt like I was moving forward. Part of my motivation now for speeding up to the north was to escape the heat. As the crow flies, the tropic of Cancer was only 400 kilometres to the north, where promises of cooler weather willed me onwards.

I rested for a day in Luang Namtha, in the company of Clothilde, a French woman who was exciting and different. She travelled without a mobile phone, a true rarity in these times. She preferred to get lost than to always know where she was going, favouring interactions with locals, no matter how daft, to interaction with the Google oracle. I gave it a go with her and left my phone in the guesthouse for the day. It took us about an hour to find the market, 800m away from our hostel. The key was that such trivialities as time matter not to the traveller: for travellers have the rare privilege of owning it in abundance. We had an amazing time getting lost and asking and not understanding a word that was said to us. Even the simplest of trips was an expedition, but Clothilde's enthusiasm and conviction that this way of travelling was superior, made it a very pleasant expedition. When we said our goodbyes the following morning, I instinctively got out my phone to check maps.me to see where I was going. She walked the other way.

That day, I followed the flow of easy rivers that scored diagonals across the North of the country. On one of the zigs, following a pleasant downhill zag, I found myself in the vicinity of an enormous scale forest fire raging just a few kilometres away. It sounded like a bowl of Rice Krispies except that instead of a small rice puff, entire trees snapped crackled and popped as they exploded into relentless flame. It was certainly a day associated with fire and fright. Although the fires raging never were a problem, the enormous funnelling plumes swirling up from behind the first visible hill layer darkened the sky. For a long time I was preparing for an electric storm to enhance the already apocalyptic atmosphere that accompanied the exile from the low lying civilisation of Muang Xai, 120 kilometres after Luang Namtha.

The storm never came. The day stilled. I was pedalling, feeling lighter and lighter. It was a day to whistle tunes and gently bumble onwards. It felt as if the world was exhaling, relaxing, reclining. That is until all was broken by the hum of a moped driven by a man who had obviously been on the Laolao. He veered clumsily into a verge by the roadside as he tried to put down his kickstand while still in motion. As I passed him, I noticed a large assault rifle on his back that looked an awful lot like a Kalashnikov. Instinctively, I slightly quickened the pace. The moment we crossed on the road was the moment he chose to brake to a halt. He jumped from the scooter and onto the verge, while swinging the gun into his arms. I winced my eyes for a second and carried on, trying to pay him no regard. About 15 seconds later, when I thought I was out of the woods, I turned my head over my shoulder to see if he was there. I only saw the singed barren verge onto which he jumped. Just as I was about ready to release the breath I had been holding in, a volley of shots cracked the air. I did not stick around to find out at who or what they were aimed. I spat out my held breath and my instinct jerked my legs into action. I pedalled, hard and fast. My breathing was quick and I felt my lungs close to my chest. The ensuing 15 kilometres were a helter-skelter technical descent and I ragged my bike down the hill, cornering like a maniac. At the bottom I saw a van of armed police in Kevlar vests making their way up the hill. I would have liked to think this was unrelated, but it didn't seem that way. I will never know.
I finished the day in the safety of a village school after playing a great game of football with the ludicrously skilled kids. Despite this, the world never quite regained its stillness that day after the gunshots.

I had been pleasantly surprised by the road conditions in Laos after the horror stories I had been told. I hummed along a strip of reasonably smooth tarmac and looked up above the trees at one of the many hillsides that were being excavated. Another red truck with a Chinese number plate passed me. The Chinese had certainly got hold of this region and their infrastructure projects were everywhere in Laos. I had little doubt that it was they who had financed the building of this good road, providing an efficient route from South West China to North West Thailand. It is the Chinese who are funding up-front 70% of the cost of the Boten to Vientiane railway that will eventually connect the South-Western Chinese mega-city of Kunming to Singapore. The other 30% is paid for by Laos, but with money loaned by Chinese investment banks. There are also (relatively) luxurious villages perched above the rivers on which hydroelectric dams are being built, to house the Chinese engineers that are working on the hydroelectric exploitation of Laos's numerous rivers. It seemed that the country was being dragged into China's wanton development vision, whether they wanted it or not.

It was initially my plan to cross the border at Boten and into China's Xishuangbanna autonomous district, but I had calculated that this would add on an extra 300 kilometres or so in the country in comparison to if I crossed the Lao Cai – Hekou town border from Northern Vietnam. To get to Lao Cai from Boten was an extra 700 kilometres but I reasoned that I had to cut my route as short as possible in China so that I had the best chance of crossing it entirely by bicycle in the short time that I was allotted. I was going to get to visit Vietnam as another bonus country and I began to get excited as I reared up the final mountain pass to the border crossing at 1200 m on the col in the middle of nowhere.

Passing from a country of barely seven million inhabitants to one of almost 100 million was quite a shock. The last large town in Laos was Muang Mai, which boasted a couple of pharmacies, a school, a few restaurants sat on the edge of the gorge with views over the river below, a row of shops, housing and not all that much else. In between here and Dien Bien Phu was a mountain pass with nothing except the border posts, where I had to pay a small "administration fee" to the Lao officers and whereas the smiling Vietnamese guards hailed me with a "Welcome to Vietnam!" When I arrived at Dien Bien Phu, a bustling city with almost 150 thousand habitants, it felt like I had been transported to another world. Young drivers whirred everywhere on small electric scooters that seemed to make up the vast majority of the traffic in between relatively modern Japanese and Chinese branded cars.

I was in full gas mode, with Lao-Cai just a few days ride away. Ever since Chiang Mai, I had China and only China in my crosshairs. The near two weeks of cycling I had done in Laos and Vietnam were only a means to the end of the road at the Chinese border. I wasted no time in Dien Bien Phu and only after leaving it did I discover its historic status as the climatic battle at the end of the first Indochina war. I wished I had spent more time in these places, getting to know the history, chatting to the people, taking detours, but I could not ignore the call of the road.

Racing on from Dien Bien Phu, I arrived in Muong Lay in the late evening. My suspicions about this place had been aroused earlier in the day when I conversed with a Pho noodle shop owner, who used Google translate to poetically tell me to avoid this town, to attend no meeting, to keep my head down. She cited the lawless bandits marauding the streets and when I asked what was there, through the *Chinese whisper* of Google translate she replied, "No. It is just full of dust and disease."

I took what she said with a large pinch of salt, but for once, the warning of danger was not prejudiced hyperbole. The town was in fact, remarkably shady. Upon entering, a young man skulking by the roadside saw me. "Hotel?" He led me to a room at the bus station. There were no windows and a very DIY mosquito net that had more holes than a block of emmental was draped loosely over the bed. There were also no lights, so when I closed the wooden doors with the padlock that the owner provided, I was plunged into darkness. The walk into town revealed more of this dark-natured place. On the long unlit bridge, I crossed sides to avoid coming across a strewn-out man that a motorcyclist warned me not to approach. I saw people lurking in the shadows, illuminated only by the dull orange burn of a toked cigarette. I was approached by a couple of poverty-stricken blind beggars whose children were leading them around on a cruel carousel of suffering. For the whole evening, the whole town was enveloped in a dark fog. I didn't let my guard down for an instant. Thankfully, nothing happened to me before I arrived back to the humid room at the bus station. I padlocked my door, plunged into darkness and drifted off to distant shouting and dogs barking away into the night. I wondered what made this place so worn and hostile? I almost relished the vibe, but I sure was glad to not stick around.

The following day, I was sat in another of the ubiquitous pho noodle cafés, glad to be basking in the mid-day sun after the interment of the previous evening. As I was observing the comings and goings of folk in front of the establishment at Pa Tan, I spied a tall man wearing designer sunglasses and an open Hawaiian shirt, revealing a hairy chest. There was something odd about this gentleman. Was it his white skin or was it his loaded touring bicycle? "Hey!" I shouted to him as he ambled past. He slowed down and turned to me with a big smile, the sweat dribbling from his forehead following the new contour around his lips. "Hey, man, how are ya?" He asked.
"I'm grand thanks mate, where are you going?" I asked.
"Well, I'm heading to Lao-Cai then to Hanoi," he replied. "How about yourself, now?"
"Ah cool I'm going to Lao-Cai too!"
We chatted for a while at the front of the pho café. He was keen to carry on and I said I would catch him up just down the road.

Within an hour I found him vegetating in one of those gorgeous Vietnamese coffee shops. "So shall we set off together?" I inquired, quite wanting a bit of company on the road after having it all to myself for the previous couple of months or so. "Hell yeah man, let's go!"

The three days with Dave were extremely pleasant. His love for cycle touring rubbed off on me and it was great to have a companion whose outlook completely validated the reasons I had for setting off on this trip. He expounded positivity. "Ya know what man, you just gotta go for these trips like this dude. Look at me. I'm over 40 but I don't let that stop me, it ain't all about doin' what other people think is best, you gotta challenge yourself and you gotta live for yourself!"

And what better way to live for yourself than to be afforded with the ultimate freedom to roam our planet on two wheels, attracting sympathy and inspiring curiosity in the folk that you cross. The bicycle isn't only transportation; it's a magnet for good. My reasons for setting off were always about getting out of my comfort zone and living adventurously. This was still happening, but I was beginning to discover that in the midst of the gratifying discomfort that came with pushing my own boundaries, what I really valued was the connection that my journey was allowing me to establish with people from all walks of life. In living for myself, I had developed a heightened appetite for social bonds, however fleeting they may be.

After a thrilling descent from Lai Chau that had both Dave and me shrieking in unabated joy, we arrived at the foot of the climb towards Phan si Pan, Vietnam's highest peak. At the bottom, Dave and I had slightly different pre-occupations, perhaps contrasting Dave's laid-back attitude against my quest for keeping on top of anything I could. I went to replenish my water from what I believed might be the last source before the climb while Dave fumbled with his e-cigarette, inserting his special capsule of California weed.

"No way are you going to smoke that before this climb!" I chuckled.

"Yes way dude, this shit is epic! Gotta get into the zone for this climb!" He took a toke. "Here, have a puff my man."

Needless to say the climb to the top was funnier than it looked on the map.

At Sa Pa, Dave booked us into a reasonably luxurious hotel, the finest accommodation I had stayed in since Australia. It was here where our paths were to separate. He would stay in the tourist-riddled hill town that reminded me of a ski-station in the Alps. I would descend to Lao Cai: the gateway to China.

A single kilometre and a bridge over the red river is all that separated me from the single country that I hoped to traverse all the way to the Kazakh border at Khorgas. It's a country whose ruthless expansionism and nationalism is all I knew about it. China was an immense territory, truffled with mega cities, vast, barren expanses of desert, mountains that can be both verdant, stark and very, very high. It is the home of some of the world's best athletes, some of the hardest workers, some of the most studious scholars and Kung Fu Panda.

The closer the Chinese border came within reach, the more nervous I began to feel. This feeling did not leave me as I settled for a final day before crossing the border that felt like an extraordinary physical milestone on this journey. South East Asia was behind me now. Finished. All these roads traversed. And so many more to go. I began busying myself with practical details in preparation to cross the border in as strong a position as possible. Download VPNs to keep in touch with the outside world. The necessary maps to see me through Yunnan province at least. Learn the Mandarin words for some of the basic necessities: water (shui), toilet (tse tsuo), I am English man (wo shi Ying guo ren). Buy a toothbrush in case they do not use them in China. Such menial and easy tasks became stressful. My nervous brain had tricked itself into an overdriven paroxysm of fret. I closed my eyes to a mildly sedated mind that night before crossing over, while thoughts whirred in the background: projections of possibility and a cocktail of fright, excitement, anxiety and curiosity to see what on Earth goes on in the People's Republic.

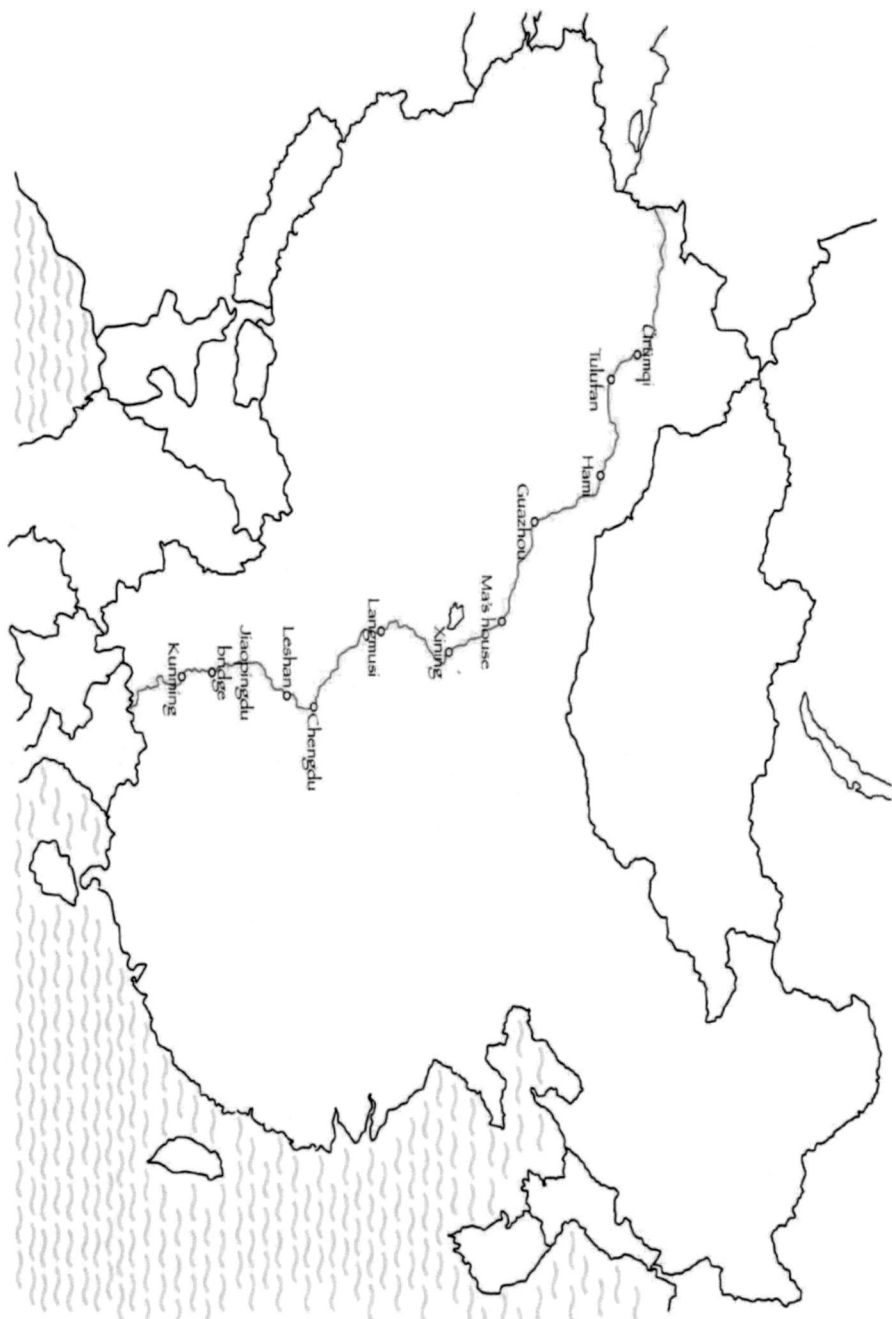

Ürümqi
Tulufan
Hami
Guazhou
Ma's house
Xining
Langmusi
Leshan
Jiaopingdu bridge
Chengdu
Kunming

The Chinese medicine

China is big. One of the most helpful things I did for myself in China was split it into bite-size parts and to not consider it all at once. My splitting of China corresponded to where I would take a rest day (remembering I only had a maximum of 60 days to pass, minus however long it would take for a visa extension to come through) and so there were not many of these places. The first stage was to arrive at Kunming, *the city of perpetual spring*: quite a small city for China with a measly population of just under seven million. Then came Chengdu – over double the population of Kunming. After that was Xining, then Jiayuguan and finally Ürümqi before the final stretch to the border post of Khorgas. This was the plan. 5500 kilometres and 60 days on the clock. Cross the border. Go.

Crossing from Lao Cai to Hekou town were myriad other bicycles, specially designed to be laden with goods and presumably used so that they didn't have to be declared as proper vehicles. Enormous towers of cardboard boxes bursting with merchandise flowed across the bridge over the red river, perpendicular to that of the water below. I walked amongst these cycle merchants breathing in the air somehow scented with rose petals and change. The difference in infrastructure was immediately startling, even in the border centre. Screens explained pictogramatically how best to wait in the queue and how to use the machines that would take digital fingerprints. I had to put all of my belongings through an x-ray machine before being allowed out to the other side.

I was nervous here, having obtained my visa on completely false premises. I had got around the diplomatic red tape at the Chinese visa application centre in Bangkok by writing an itinerary, complete with proof of hotel bookings (that I later cancelled), detailing my intention to get a bus from Vientiane to Kunming, before visiting the pandas and eating Sichuan hotpot at Chengdu, seeing the Tiananmen square at Beijing via the terracotta warriors of Xi'an and experiencing Shanghai, all before getting a train back into Hanoi via Nanning. Little did they know, my intention was to ride my bicycle all the way into the far North Western corner of the country, across the contentious region of Xinjiang. I crossed my fingers and prayed that none of these details came up on the hi-tech looking computer system in front of the border guard.

"Where you going?" The pock-faced man asked in stiff English. "I go to Kunming then to Chengdu," I winced, By bicycle." I looked at him pleadingly with puppy-dog eyes, praying my official itinerary was not displayed on his screen.
"Oh wow!" He laughed. "You are brave and strong!" He tendered my passport back with a stamp. "Welcome to China!"
"Xie xie." I smiled, grabbing my passport and heading out to collect my bicycle, dodging the freight-bikes chaotically darting here and there. That was far less painless than I had anticipated. I was now officially in Hekou town, the clock was ticking and I had a country to traverse.

Hekou was modern in all aspects of the word. Large shopping boutiques filled the tree-lined avenues. Most of the stores were Oppo or Huawei or branches of some other cutting edge technology retailer. In Hekou I learnt that only one bank accepted my back-up debit card (my usual credit card had been sent on to Kunming), this being the bank of China (Zhong guo yin hang) when my card was rejected from about six others. The game of entering a new country was underway. I had to familiarise myself with all of the basics of life once more. It was a rebirth. The first day of a new school year. Where was reliable water? Which were the cheap road-side food joints or markets on which I would depend? Where was it acceptable to go to the toilet? I allowed myself the luxury of staying stood in my first footsteps into China. I surveyed all around. Unusual food was cooking in open kitchens. Sizzling woks drew my gaze down dark, tight alleys. Steam escaped from metal vats or woven towers in shop fronts. I stared around the panoramic street scenes, hopelessly trying to familiarise myself with this new environment. Would the people be friendly and forthcoming? I entered a cash exchange building and via a translate app, was asked to feature in a promotional video for the bank. I chortled an agreement. "You must look happy to receive money," I was told.

The people were friendly and forthcoming.

"Ok, right you are," I agreed. The woman handed me my cash and I turned and showed it to the camera, beaming ear to ear at the 50 Yuan (£6.25) I held in my hand.

It took us six takes to get the smile just outrageous enough to be acceptable and I was added on *WeChat* so that I could contact the film-maker for the dividends that this impromptu moment of stardom would undoubtedly bring me.

It was time, with a nuance of regret at not being able to stay longer, to pedal away from Hekou and make some headway in the 500 kilometres I had promised myself I could cover in four days to make it to Kunming. My legs turned the pedals, their default state. I pootled along the banks of the red river, China's answer to the Missouri. Above me, cars were hurtling along the new national highway that was engineered to be as straight and flat as possible. Indeed throughout China, bridges and tunnels were built to reduce topological constraint to its knees. More often than not, the road would float in the air, suspended on enormous concrete pillars. All of this was great for me, as it meant that the old national roads were quiet, yet the surface still smooth. I beat a bicycle rhythm and allowed my thoughts to wander aimlessly. I was steadily climbing up the valley. To my left I could still make out the hazy ranges and pillars of Northern Vietnam that I had just descended, and on my right was the steep jungled hillside that I would soon have to turn and climb, up onto the Yunnan plateau 2000m higher.

I took the turn right and immediately the road ramped up, following a tributary river at first, then departing onto a road carved into the heavily forested hill. It wound its way up as the sun was setting to the west. I savoured the final golden hour of the day as soft rays interspersed the branches, casting intervals of long shadow and glowing light onto the surface in front of me. These moments of solitude, where I was alone with an instantiation of the vast range of phenomena that nature conjured on the road, were ones that constantly reassured me. That gave me a sort of spiritual pleasure I had never before valued. What I was doing was absolutely worth its short and fleeting while.

The light faded. I could find nowhere to camp, as was often the case on these billowing jungled climbs. The hillside was far too steep either side of the road and there was no sign of a village or any other hope of flat, secluded ground. I rounded a corner and there, I saw a small lone house with a flat roof. I had a flash of inspiration. Visions of waking up in the morning for the sunrise, comfortably pitched on the roof of a rural house after my first night in China leapt into my mind and I set about finding the owner and somehow trying to convey to him my ridiculous proposition. He was in his tiny kitchen. The door was ajar and I could make out his shadowy form, fidgeting in the eaves. He emerged when he saw me approaching. I tentatively waved and smiled dopily. "Ni hao!" I proclaimed.
 "Ni hao!" he replied.
Shit, I thought, as the extent of my Chinese linguist skills had just been exhausted. I began to speak in slow English as if he could understand me. "I come long way with bicycle. Now I am tired. Can I sleep, with tent…" I made the gesture for sleep and a tent motion (hands together at head height, drawn downwards simultaneously, each at 45 degrees to the vertical), "… on your roof?" I pointed to his roof and clapped my hands together. He smiled back, albeit with a slight hint of befuddlement and beckoned me to follow. He took me in to a garage next to the house, to a ladder leading to the upper floor. He climbed up and

opened the door and pointed inside, arm flapping with enthusiasm. There was a cosy little utility room with a wide plank of wood on the floor, the perfect bed! "Ah yes that looks just great!" I said. "Xie xie!"

He helped me bring my bags up, which we deposited on the floor that was dashed with small brown pellets, before descending down to relax for the evening in his modest front room. He intermittently flitted into the kitchen, sizzling some culinary delights, and returning to look at me with a broad and easy smile. I have no idea what he was cooking, but he shared it with me and it remains amongst the most delicious food I have ever tasted. He provided me a bowl of rice with chopsticks. I provided him with half an hour of comedy as I tried to scoop up the grains, hopelessly dropping most of it back into the bowl or on my lap. He shook his head and showed me how it was done, scooping and shovelling with break-neck speed and staggering accuracy and efficiency, as if his life depended on it. Not a grain was left in the bowl.

I retired to the makeshift bedroom after an evening spent with my host, drawing pictograms of our families (our wildly optimistic attempts at Chinglish having fell flat). He wrote a couple of lines of mandarin at the end which I assumed was a charming and flattering impression of myself but could easily have read "You owe me a fiver for the meal, pay me when you get back, you cheeky beggar."

At about midnight I awoke to disconcerting sounds. There were a number of animals scuttling around the attic, making an absolute racket on the tin roof. I got up and turned on the light and suddenly it was clear what the small brown pellets that littered the floor were. Rats. I tried to block out the sounds, but the squeaks and peeps and scuttling and rattling made me feel disgusted. It was soon clear that I couldn't hack sleeping here and so I got out the tent and pitched up right on the roadside at about 01:00am. Trucks kept coming up the road throughout the night and the odd one pulled up right next to my tent, where my host would wake up and come to fill a tank on the vehicle with water, before heading back to sleep. Few sweeter dawns had ever come around than that one. I was implored to stay for breakfast before heading off, and given the flavoursome feast of the night before, I willingly obliged. It was more of the same. I was delighted and I left, filled with the strength that only chilli-fried pork and the kindness of strangers can bring.

For two more days I climbed ever upwards onto the Yunnan plateau along verdant tropical valleys. The landscape changed abruptly: elegantly curved hills suddenly broke into semi-aridity from the lush jungle at the lower altitudes. I passed through small towns, where immense mosques dominated the skyline! *Mosques in China?* I had no idea that Islam even existed as a practice in this part of the world, but I suppose this is what travel was all about, dashing away preconceptions with the evidence rendered to one's eyes.

I had passed through a city that looked like a tiny blemish on the map. It turned out to be absolutely enormous, with vast blocks of high-rise condos stretching skywards. The roads gained three extra lanes and cars zoomed along. A cycle lane had also appeared that was shared with electric motorbikes. The highly developed infrastructure shocked me. It felt futuristic even by European standards. I continued on the road, expecting to reach a centre of sorts, but this never arrived. I didn't seem to pass through any marked change in the cityscape. No big shopping district, no old-town, no town halls or central plazas or high street. It just seemed like the civilization here was supported without vocation, without retail, without entertainment. Without anything other than the unifying goal of expanding *even further*.

On my third day in China, I crashed. The road below me was made of smooth slabs of concrete, each one seamlessly connected to the next. It was covered with two wide wet streaks from the water jets that the ubiquitous red trucks use to cool their brakes. One of exactly these red trucks was ambling slowly ahead. I had not long since woken from my camp sheltered outside an uninhabited concrete residential complex and I felt good. I held the truck in my sights, and not wanting to tarry in its dusty wake, I was confident enough to overtake it just before a corner, brimming with mirth as I did so. As I rounded the corner, completely absorbed in the joy of the speedy descent, I failed to notice the sign warning me of an imminently approaching railway intersecting the road. I looked up and saw that the concrete suddenly deteriorated into a jagged mess of tarmac through which the old lines ran. I braked suddenly and my back wheel locked and skidded out of control on the smooth wet surface. I was shot off and skidded along the floor next to my bike until I hit the deformed tarmac at the railway line. The truck stopped about 10m behind me. It was a good job the driver was paying attention.

I jumped to my feet in pain and panic, shaking my limbs to check that nothing was broken. I was grazed and had a chunk of flesh missing from my hip and I was covered in filth, but otherwise unscathed. My bike had survived but my rear right pannier had succumbed a small tear down the middle. Nothing too serious. I counted myself very lucky and did the best I could to clean up the cuts with tissue roll. I braced myself as I poured iodine solution into the small hole in my hip. "EEEH!"

At the next village I came across a pharmacy. Still not satisfied with the dirt-encrusted cuts doused in iodine, I paid it a visit. The slight, jittery woman there took me outside and showed me to a hose. I doused myself down before she ushered my sodden body into the building. She sat me down and thoroughly disinfected the cuts with precise and business-like motions. She then covered them up with bandage for a meagre £2.50.

Later that same evening, camping on top of a five-storey building under construction in the tiny village of Gaoda (although there was still probably 50,000 habitants, as is the

Chinese way!), I was met by a group of unlikely intruders. I was setting my tent up when a brush of black hair appeared at the top of the precarious ladder that I had used to climb to the flat exposed roof. The first of two heads fully emerged, grinning. "Hello!" The first of the teens said.

"Hi..."

The pair were simply riveted to be practicing their English with me, albeit in a rather odd classroom setting. The sun was just setting over the hills of the Zhuji valley that I had spent the day climbing. I was serenaded to the predictable tune of *Where you from?* and *Where you going?* and *What is your name?* I indulged, and it soon became apparent that this was the full extent of their conversational fluency. British politeness prevented me from asking them to leave when the conversation inevitably dried up after these questions were dutifully answered. "Right, I go to sleep now." I tried to brush off the young gentlemen. Exactly as I was on the cusp of zipping myself in my canvas cocoon, regardless of what these jokers were hanging around for, a new face appeared at the ladder top. "Lovely to meet you, my friend, my name is Wan." He offered his hand before rooting in his bag, taking out a packet of Oreos, a bottle of disinfectant and a vial of odd-smelling powder. "My friends say you are hurt, I have brought you medicine."

"What?" I started. "How on Earth did they know I was hurt and what's in the bottle?"

"This Chinese medicine, it is good for bleeding."

Stupefied, I let the young man pour the powder into the hole in my hip before wrapping it up with a large bandage. "Are you hungry my friend? We can go for our famous barbecue stinky tofu and beer." I didn't need to be asked twice, but I certainly wasn't expecting to receive medical care and an invitation to a barbecue from a group of teenagers on the roof of a construction building. It is just another story of the bizarre, but ultimately heart-warming situations that the whole cycle-touring business seemed to lead to. I slept sound in the knowledge that China was so far much easier than I imagined it to be. I had only 180 kilometres left to Kunming.

Hospitality

Kunming is situated on a 2000m plateau, meaning that in summer, the temperature is not too hot. Being right on the border of the tropic of Cancer also means that the winter temperatures never get too cold. Indeed, the day temperatures apparently seldom leave the 20-30 Celsius range, rendering it an extremely pleasant place to live. With all its parks and tree-lined boulevards bathed in the Freshness of the spring air, it was impossible to remain impervious to the infectious bien-être that seemed to permeate every corner of this great city. Groups of men clad in Mao suits crowded round small tables that glinted in the yolky light, peering intensely at a chess or dominoes game in full swing. Every bench along the boulevards was occupied by early afternoon dozers or old women who sat relating yarns of their days or discussing the price of fruit (I can only assume the content of what I observed to be humdrum, yet absolutely necessary banalities) In the numerous public squares, music pumped from speakers to which rhythmically challenged middle-aged women stepped and clapped. The milk tea establishments bustled with young people wearing t-shirts with cheesy profound English slogans. 'Don't lie but live.' 'It's all easy until it's hard.' 'Big Life Big Game.' 'Love is not real but equal.' 'Stare fast quick' etc. China is perhaps the country where there is the largest rift between young and old in terms of style and attitude. The elderly of China have faces that bear all the signs of heavy ware and toil. Many of them endured the horrific events during the Cultural Revolution. Some would have lived through the famine of the great leap forward. China's recent history is both fascinating and tragic. Many of the youth will not have seen or known the hardship faced by their grandparents, especially due to the abated version of events in the history books. Their urban-centric lifestyles seemed to me to be carefree and full of choice: a far cry from the intense social control to which the elderly were subjugated. It was both sad and pleasant to witness. In spite of all of the Orwellian baggage that comes with a one-party state dictatorship, it is impossible to deny that China's development is generally improving the quality of life for the vast majority of its citizens.

In Kunming I was hosted by Vera – the last *Warmshowers* host I would encounter until France. Vera had cycled from the Netherlands to Japan, passing through Kunming on the way. It was here that she saw a new life for herself and after finishing her tour, returned to its sun-drenched streets to settle. While I was there, she informed me of a small city called Leshan that was famous a few years ago for delivering visa extensions very swiftly. I decided to head for this place before Chengdu to see if I could get the extra time in the bag to steady the ticking of the clock. After two days rest in Vera's warm company, drinking beers on roofs and meeting the international community of the city, I began once more to spin the legs – onwards to Leshan to get that all-important visa extension.

The road from Kunming was stunning. It meandered upwards very gently through untempered pine forests, right up until the border with Sichuan where I descended for 15 kilometres straight down the mountain, on the *inside*, in an impressive network of tunnels. This was odd. There was no straight section on the map. By this point I should be squiggling my front wheel in all directions like a drunken compass. I stopped and checked the map. *Shite.* I had missed my turn-off that would have taken me on the outside of the mountain, on the scary and technical descent to Hongmenchang where there was the only bridge that crossed the river of the Yunnan-Sichuan border. Instead, I was heading down the wrong side of the mountain. In a gap between two tunnels, I looked longingly at the map, waiting for a road to jump out at me that would allow me to rejoin the Yunnan bank of the Jinsha river without having to backtrack. Inevitably, no such road existed and so the cruel climb 15 kilometres back up the hill in the tunnels ensued. I constantly cursed myself on the way up for having been so foolish. At the same time I was tempted to continue the descent through the tunnel to see where it would take me. Indeed, it struck me as very odd that this incredible infrastructure was not built to somehow cross the Jinsha river, but it just felt safer to stick to the roads on the maps that I had.

When I was only a few hundred metres from the top, I had one thing on my mind and one thing only - a bottle of Pepsi or some other incarnation of filthy sugary instant gratification. I was frothing at the mouth by the time I reached the tiny turn-off that I had missed, where 500 m later, was a roadside shop. Exactly what I needed. I flung my bike against the front of the establishment and marched manically through the open door, eyes darting, searching for the fridge in which my sugary relief was kept. In doing so, my eyes met the woman's who was stood behind the counter. Her mouth was wide open as if in shock and before I could compose myself, she let out a long, excited scream, ran from behind her counter and barrelled towards me before embracing me in a massive hug! I was taken aback and loosely patted her back with my awkward hand, confused and still hankering for my Pepsi. After slightly too long, she released me and called out in Chinese. Another woman appeared at the door and she too sprinted to grab me in her arms. *What on Earth is going on?* I thought to myself as I smiled innocently at the most female affection I have ever received in my life. I was swiftly led through to the back room, the second woman dragging me by the hand. There, to my slight disappointment, were sat her male companions: smoking, playing cards and drinking a cornucopia of *baijiu* that I suspected was the source of such wayward merriment.

I was thrust down onto a chair and a glass of *baijiu* was placed in front of me forthwith. I looked up at the grinning Chinese family urging me to down the contents of the glass. Once again, the question *What is going on?* entered my head. At this point I was quite an adept at shooing it away in exchange for kicks. I was raucously cheered when I shotted the burning rice whisky and thus my initiation was complete. For a few minutes I watched the curious game of cards that was being played. I believe I grasped the rules. All players drew three cards from the deck and after a count of three, placed the cards face up on the table. The player with the lowest total would then drink a number of teaspoons of *baijiu* equivalent to the difference between the winning total and the losing total. That was it. It was the lousiest excuse for a day-sesh I had ever seen and after a few minutes (and extra tipples of baijiu), I left with a free bottle of Pepsi and a big hunk of boiled pork that I chewed while being once more hugged to death by the frightfully enthusiastic women. I leapt onto the saddle, waved like the queen, and proceeded to rattle down the scariest and most technical descent I have ever encountered, half drunk on rice whisky.

Now that I was finally on the road I needed to be, it was glorious. The twists down the mountainside saw me pass below impossibly steep rice terraces and settlements somehow clinging onto the mountain edge. I descended further and further and further, seemingly without end, towards an unreachable void below. I knew that this was bad news. On the other side I could only be heading up. I crossed the Jiaopingdu bridge at Hongmengchang above the roaring bluster of the river. I straddled the line between Yunnan and Sichuan. I was lost in the immensity and ferocity of the valley gorge. I shivered. I gazed blankly at the Cliffside above me. It seemed that the road wound its way up there, although I couldn't quite believe it. Surely it is impossible for any road to straddle a cliff, rising from bottom to top. Not for China! The ensuing climb took almost a full day from when I began it mid-afternoon. Fortunately there was a public toilet and viewpoint halfway up the road that was dug into the sheer mountainside where I camped for the night. Perched here, I feasted upon what was undoubtedly one of the most spectacular sights I have seen. The mountains of ferrous brown seemed to glimmer in the sunset as the immeasurable force of the river frothed in the gorge below.

My soul leapt and danced. I was transfixed. A crippled man hobbled towards the viewpoint to join me. He had appeared from nowhere and for half an hour, we silently surveyed the topographical wonder through clouds of dust that were blown from the mountainside and pirouetted lucidly in the dazzle of a droopy sun.

By this point, I was completely accustomed to camping and no longer cared for privacy or stealth. Although, the following day's camp brought with it quite an experience that rounded off a day of almost unbelievable hospitality. I ate my muesli porridge (don't try making porridge with muesli: accept the muesli for what it really is) and with only half a bottle of water left, set out to smash off the rest of the mountain pass. The sun rising behind me provided the fine morning spectacle. It gilded the bronze mountainside and slowly began filling into the valley far below, like a bath being ran with light. I rode in the shadow of the steep cliffs, avoiding the odd spattering of fallen rocks, waiting for the rays to warm my back.

At the first village I asked Guo, a humble restaurateur for some of his water. I had taken to this approach for water in China. I would often be granted it distilled from jugs in restaurants or coolers or boiling flasks from shops along the highway. In the parts of China I travelled, people were superstitious of cold water and believed that hot water brought health benefits. So I often drank water boiled. Guo had a water cooler in the corner of his establishment and along with his permission to help myself, I received an invitation to join his whole family for breakfast. Having already gorged on muesli porridge, I was considering politely declining, but if there is any rule for cycle touring, it is that food is never declined. Especially an expansive buffet of rice, tofu, spicy sauce, pak, two separate pork dishes and watermelon. As if that wasn't enough, he gave me a yoghurt for the road and added me on *Wechat,* the Chinese social media. I left with a belly fit to burst. Not too long after, I met Dora and her eccentric Aunt at their noodle soup shop. I arrived as a family was leaving from a feast. The waitress was just about to throw the rests of the half-eaten hearty dishes to the dogs when I stopped her. The food looked a little *too* good for the dogs, who whined at my arrival. They recognised a glutton when they saw one. Dora provided me with the noodle soup on top of this, on the house. Her aunty attempted to give me a cheerful sun hat. Dora gave me five steamed buns to take away. Her aunty gave me three bottles of water. Later, as my water was dwindling low, I stopped at a truck service point and the woman gave me a bottle. I bought an energy drink and then received a bottle of lime water as goodwill supplement.

I was rather sick of stuff being given to me at this point and after a tiring and long day, wished for nothing more than to crash in the tent in seclusion. Nowhere seemed suitable, and so coming to a village, I asked a security guard who was dozing in his booth. My advice for those who wish for a quiet night: don't ask at an off-grid Chinese village. The guard offered me a place in a corner of the village basketball court and before long a crowd of about twenty curious people gathered around me as I put up the tent. I proudly declared *Wo shì yīnguó rèn (I am English man)* to a murmur of *oaahhhs*. I took a selfie with every single one of them, as they were keen to show their mates this exotic nob from lands afar. I gave a shy young girl, who didn't seem to like me as the others did, the teddy that my Nan made for me before I left. I insisted to the people that I had enough to eat and proceeded to cook noodle soup, hoping that this would bore them away. Then it started coming: a flurry of donations as if I were some sort of deity. I was sure they were going to sacrifice a goat if I didn't ask them to stop after the initial round of gifts: one full watermelon, six small plums, ten pork skewers, two beers, six oranges, and another *bao*. Not wanting to be impolite I ate pretty much the lot, bar some of the fruit. After two hours of being ogled and two offers of staying in the school and tai chi gym respectively, I was finally allowed to sleep. I gained four kilos that day.

In the morning, the security guard wanted to take me for 'mountain noodles' according to the English teacher. One of the chaps I recognised from the night before passed by and gave me a bag full of bananas. I barely had room to fit all of my presents into my bag, and I still had a hard time believing that I wasn't being groomed for some sadistic purpose.

After six days on the road from Kunming I arrived at the point where a smaller country road forked from the main one, went over a mountain pass of unspecified height and then towards Leshan. It looked like the most favourable option for getting to the city, the other being a popular national road like the one I had been on for the last few days. It was never really dangerous, owing to a large hard shoulder that I adopted as my cycle lane, but the traffic was pretty constant. I was looking forward to having some time to explore China by the back roads. If only I knew then what I knew at the end of the three day stretch to Leshan.

Barred

The pass into the valley led down to the Dade River. Along the wide meanders, above which muscular trapezoid mountains stretched to the warm and fuzzy sky, a mining operation of epic proportions was taking place. The road was ran by an even higher than usual quantity of red trucks plodding their way noisily along, dropping deposits of sand, rock and dirt that covered me head to toe in great spatters. *I should have really invested in mudguards*, I thought, chewing on the salty grit of the Earth that was coagulating in my moustache. I was weary. My day became dictated by the incessant deafening *huunn* of lorries. They were like ten-tonne ants and I was in their nest. On some of the climbs, the road became so narrow that the trucks passed within inches as they hooted their foghorns in either merriment or disillusion. I was ground down bit by bit and was on the verge of cracking up. There seemed to be an incomprehensible juxtaposition to the day. I was amongst lush mountains on a minor road. I should have felt awe-struck and at moments, I did. I passed into a gorge where suddenly, the mountains towered to great heights, impossible heights! Trees clung precariously to the canyon walls that rose up so high - higher than any wall should be able to rise. Rivulets trickled down from crannies that split the vertical wilderness. Hollows interspersed the green-silver rock and climbed, climbed, climbed into their other world in the clouds. I had to stop myself on occasions and laugh. This couldn't be part of the same world as my own. As I was stopped, trucks rattled by, quashing the awe, breaking me. I was broken and I was in awe: great broken awe that made me ropey.

The Dade canyon walls eventually opened up, revealing the city of Jinkouhe. Right after the bridge here, I was met by the flashing lights of a police car and was signalled to stop. "Problem constable?"

The officer asked for my passport and then through his translate app told me that foreigners were not allowed in town and I had to leave. "I wasn't thinking of staying in your town anyways. I go to Leshan," I declared.

"Yes Yes, I take you out of jurisdiction in police car," the officer replied with the help of google translate.

"Well, I'm quite happy riding my bicycle on this fine day!" I retorted.

"Get in the car"

"I'm not going to do that. I'm riding my bike." I stood my ground, amazed and unnerved at my audacity.

"It's the rules." He affirmed, as if that would be the clincher.

"I'm riding my bike and if you want to see me out of town you can escort me."

I'm not terribly sure what came over me at this moment, a sudden surge of obstinacy rose within me and I felt empowered and invincible. Invincible broken awe. I told the officer about my journey and the *rules* of the journey. I couldn't get in a car. With my rules battling his, a compromise was reached and I set off under police escort. After ten minutes, he stopped and pleaded that I get in his car again. I politely refused. "I can cycle a little faster but that's all I can do."

"But it's not far now."

"Exactly, you can follow me for not far."

I picked up the pace a bit, and felt a mix of urgency and bitterness at the country for having a restricted area with no prior warning. The urgency of bitter invincible broken awe took over. Part of me wanted to blaze along the road, another to provocatively tarry as much as possible. My mind was rutted with contradiction. All the while horns blared as trucks and vans and cars and mopeds overtook my escort and me. I stared stonily at the front wheel spinning away the kilometres, and began pounding on the pedals, acutely aware of the presence of the van trailing me closely behind. After twenty kilometres I finally looked around and the road was empty. The pesky cops had called it a day. Later research told me that part of the mining operations in this county included uranium ore and that there was an enrichment facility in the town I was stopped and where no foreigners could set foot.

Stressed and a little vexed I continued along the Dade before the road departed from its course and a 700 m altitude-gain climb began. The road thinned. There was no longer a shoulder and the trucks came barrelling past, both ways, horns deafening. Constantly. Often a light truck would overtake a heavy truck, which in turn moved inwards, forcing me right to the edge of the road, squeezed against the crash barrier with only inches of space. Car drivers lacked the ability to wait for five seconds instead of risking their lives (and mine) with overtakes on blind bends. All my previous feelings melted into anger and whenever I saw someone overtaking recklessly I was sure to give them the finger. It was feeble but felt like my only defence. In extreme cases I even shouted at the drivers. "Stupid bastards!" I cried out. Only to be met with honks and spatters of the road. Clouded with rage I start seeing red. Everyone was an enemy and my anger took over. I cursed the country, I cursed the people and the trucks and their animosity on the road. When I passed a pedestrian I gestured a beep followed by a guillotine. When the beep lasted longer than three seconds (which was often) I dished out a mighty finger and thoughts started going through my head of what I would do to such a driver if I caught them. The blinding frenzy of fury from which I wished to escape just kept on multiplying and the angrier I got the easier it was to get angrier. *Pud taow*. But I couldn't think of that then.

On the final night before Leshan, I struggled to find a camp spot. I trudged for over an hour around a scenic lake, but dense trees and steep slopes blocked any hopes of camping. I asked a woman in Chinese if I could camp and she immediately resigned herself to non-understanding, before she had even listened to my plea. "Ting bu dong ting bu dong," she insisted, cutting me mid phrase, shoeing me away.
"You didn't even make an effort you horrible cow!" I shouted back and she definitely didn't *ting bu dong* that! Despair was

beginning to set in. The sun fell away, erased by the mountains at the lake side. I trudged in the dusk, hauling my bike over rutted paths and upturned roots on the lakeside trail. The few people I came across gave me a cold shoulder when I looked at them and averted their gazes. The fury of the road must have still been in my eyes that slowly started to dribble a couple of tears. *Why was I here?* Traipsing and sauntering through China, risking my life. For what? For charity? Validation? Adventure? None of these meant anything to me anymore as, sweaty, angry, hungry and in need of shelter from the fast-encroaching dark, I wandered aimlessly in search of a flat plot of ground.

At the end of the path through the woods, was another street cutting up the hillside. Pushing my bike, I plodded upwards, reaching a house where a young girl was sat outside on her phone. She looked at me sympathetically for an instant, then ran inside. *Typical*, I thought. *Even kids want nothing to do with me.* Just as I was about to turn around, the mother came to the door and called out. I turned, seeing her come towards me, a re-assuring smile on her face. An elderly woman then appeared at the door with a hobble and a smile as well. I was rescued. Explaining in gestures my story and my day, they agreed to let me camp on their courtyard. I was shown the shower and given a bowl full of dumplings. Humans were much sweeter when they were outside of their cars.

Much of my residual anger was soaked up by the dumplings and the fascination of seeing three generations of rural Chinese women all interacting together. The traditionally dressed haggard old woman had come into the courtyard to soak her feet in a small wooden tub of soapy water. She was looking on at her sports-costume clad daughter who was hanging out washing to dry, occasionally shouting out instructions or remarks or platitudes. Finally, the granddaughter was perched once again idly on the wall nearby, dressed in a pretty sequined skirt and a t-shirt with an English slogan. She was engrossed in her phone that was blaring out short video clips, ignorant to all else around her. It was endearing to see all three generations share a sense of togetherness, despite the vast rift between their lifestyles, attitudes, priorities, anguishes and dreams.

When the washing was all hung out, the three women retired into the house and I was allowed to sleep in the cosy cocoon of my tent and close my eyes, letting the simmering frustration from the day slowly cool and float away, at long last.

In the morning, when the birds began to peep, and the dull grey cloudy morning spilled into my tent, I awoke feeling extremely weary. My legs hurt, my clothes smelled of brine, and I had no desire whatsoever to ride my dirt-encrusted bike that was waiting outside. I wanted nothing but to close my eyes once more and be transported away from road that I knew I had to continue along. The trucks. The drivers. The horn-blasts. I wasn't sure I could take it. The mental frustration of the day before had taken its toll, but I had no choice if I wanted to continue cycling. 70 kilometres more torment were on the cards, with the road only promising to get busier and busier as it reached Leshan, a small city of three million people. As I got toppled out of my tent I did so with a moan and a sigh. The road was already in my ears – distant beeps and engine roars from red trucks had replaced the brief dawn chorus of the birds. With no sign of any of the Wa family getting up, I sucked in a breath, and set off for the road to Leshan, where I would make it, one way or another.

The motoring etiquette of China seemed to be something like 'if your vehicle is smaller, give way – especially to bigger vehicles pulling in from side roads with no indication.' As a cyclist, this rule wore thin and almost drove me to mania. Stress simmered and frothed and occasionally overflowed. Many a Chinese driver laughed at a red and fuming European cyclist this day. I was almost in tears by the time I reached the international youth hostel of Leshan. The city where I had placed all hopes of updating my Chinese visa. Having sworn and shouted my way through the final stretch, I arrived feeling small. Like a shrivelled date, pitted of all positivity. As if my soul had melted in a smear along the road, like a silver trail that leaves the snail dry. Spent to exhaustion. Only a shell and a dry polyp left.

No giant Buddha and no Confucian temple. Just hostel then visa office. At the hostel I was immediately told there was no space. I bargained to pitch my tent in a spare room. With that problem solved, I set about getting the hostel receipt that I needed for the visa renewal service. "You can't go there," came the reply. I stifled a nervous laugh. "Oh dear…" I whispered, the final whisker of hope had been plucked.

"This weekend Chinese labour weekend, lots of celebration in town, very good day to be in China! But immigration office closed!" And so after that sordid rush, that emotional battery, the immigration office, the one reason I went down this blasted road, was closed. And it would be closed the following day. And the one after that. By which time it was the weekend, for which the office closes.

All that effort, stress and toil on that damned road to be told I couldn't even apply! Light left my eyes. The hostel receptionists looked at me with an expectant grin. I needed a minute to sit down and let this all sink in. I sat on the table opposite the check-in desk, and stared into the brightly decorated wall. The lift came down with a ding dong and guffawing celebrants came out with balloons and toothy smiles. The receptionist tapped loudly at her computer. A moped and a car honked in unison outside and I finally broke into a good old cry.

It was the ultimate kick in the balls and instead of falling into emotional collapse, I leapt into it. In China, where not losing face or showing emotion is *the* way to act, it seemed to shock the staff there to see me sobbing into my hands. One of the young women approached me with the translate app. She asked, "Can you wait three?"

"Three what?" I wailed, before breaking out into another hiccup of sobs.

"Wait three hours, friend working at the immigration office. might still be able to help..."

After three nail-biting hours, and a secret trip to the officially closed public security bureau, the friend of the hostel receptionist passed on the instructions of where to pick my extension up on Friday morning, in about 38 hours.

Misery turned into elation. The gradient of emotion was certainly the steepest it had ever been in my entire life, and indeed during the whole trip there were oscillations of mood on almost all time scales. Like here, within minutes I could go from a wallowing mess to an energetic chirp. Some days were filled with doubt and moody meditation. These were followed by days of assurance that I was doing something great, coupled with a steadfast conviction that life was meant to be lived as I was doing. Sometimes, even for weeks I could be in high spirits, or simply feel a little melancholy, all the while modulated by mood swings of finer scaling.

This visa situation is also a perfect example of how things work in China: magic. I had my first taste of Chinese magic when that young man of almost perfect English prowess came to the rooftop camp and gave me the Chinese medicine, following a phone call of only a few seconds from one of his mates who had first found me. Another sterling example is when I wanted to buy a SIM card in Kunming. Vera had told me that insistence was key, after I related her my story of having tried and failed to get one in Hekou town.

When I arrived at the SIM card shop I was told that they didn't sell SIM cards. "But you're a SIM card shop," I protested to the translate app.

"No, we don't sell SIM cards here," the app lied back to me.

"But, I know you do."

"We cannot sell SIM cards to foreigners."

"But I know you can because I have foreign friends who have bought SIM cards."

"You do not have a Chinese passport so you cannot buy a SIM card."

"I really think I can, I know I can! My friends have them!"

The shop assistant then looked on his phone and seemed to be swiping, instead of replying back to me. I approached him and peered over his shoulder to see him playing solitaire! I was outraged. "How rude!" I exclaimed.

He stood there, seeming not to lend me any more attention. *Fine*, I thought. *I have time and I will stand here all day.* I remained stood, trying to keep a friendly smile on my face while observing my surroundings. Other than Sir Solitaire were a few other members of staff scuttling around the back of the shop, trying to busy themselves. Within a couple of minutes, a man riding on a moped pulled up in the entrance. He was wearing a leather jacket and he strode into the shop, while pulling out a plastic bag full of what looked like SIM cards from his pocket. I eyed him up as he passed me and made for the desk, where he placed the bag. I was at this moment tapped on the shoulder by Sir Solitaire, who held his phone to my face.

"Which do you want?" it said. I laughed, shook my head and picked the 2-month SIM card, before walking out of the shop. Successful, yes, but utterly bamboozled by the Chinese way.

Five days after reaching Leshan, I had made Chengdu. 1500 kilometres down in only two weeks and with a very healthy 45 days left on my two visas and about 4000 kilometres to go, things were looking pretty sweet and the stress of covering epic distances was slowly dissipating.

Onto the plateau

In Chengdu, I caught up with someone whose trail I had been following hotly for the previous two weeks. Charlie was here! I had left him about three months previously in Southern Thailand, expecting to never see him again. Alas, he entered China only four days before me, and he too had stayed with Vera. He left two days before I arrived. I had finally caught him. When I found him, he was trying to fix a major mechanical problem that could jeopardise his traverse of China. He was stuck in Chengdu for the time being, so I advised him to make the visit to Leshan (by train) while he was there. If he got his mechanical sorted, I would wait for him somewhere, perhaps in Xining, which was about 1000 kilometres away over mountains that grazed the Northeast corner of none other than the Tibetan plateau. I had no idea that the plateau extended so far north but apparently this 2.5-million square kilometre hunk of elevated Earth reached all the way up into Sichuan, Gansu and Qinghai.

The first three days consisted of just one single climb up a valley. In England, the longest climb is Cragg Vale at a whopping 8.35 kilometres. This one was about 350 kilometres. Remember what I said about China and big? The road continued to ramp gently upwards, rarely exceeding a one-degree incline, but an incline nonetheless. Every day I gained about 1000 metres of altitude. On the second day, I encountered a diversion. The main road was closed, which meant an extra 500 metres of climbing, skirting up the steep side of the mountain. On this tiny road that wound tirelessly, up and up, was a traffic jam of epic proportions. Trucks were backed up nose to tail. There were about 15 kilometres of them. After the furore that these rumbling road-giants had so far caused me, I indulged in a great sense of *shadenfreude* as I glided past them. I gave each driver a smug nod. Many smiled at me and brimmed with delight at my trademark thumbs up, returning the gesture in a fore and middle finger V, both ways round. Every so often I would jump out of my saddle in shock as a bored trucker let off a volley of firecrackers to keep the ambiance bearable. While the firecrackers hopped and danced and fizzed a couple of hairpins below, I wove my way carefully between the gridlocked cargo snake and observed the drivers, my sworn enemies, in their intimacy. They were congregated outside cabs, heating kettles on portable gas stoves to brew their cha or instant noodles while loafing and moping. On the other end of business, many were squatted underneath the trailers, wiping their bums, completely unabashed, before leaving the soiled tissue to flutter away in the wind like wedding dress butterflies.

As I reared on the upper reaches of the valley, the climate changed. Gone was the wispy humidity of Chengdu in the valley bottom, the restless cloud fingers beckoning from low skies. I could feel the atmosphere thinning, stepping back, making way for the crisp sear of the sun that belongs to the Tibetan plateau. The final stint of the 350 kilometres climb was punishing, with unrelenting headwinds and a departure from the river, meaning a steeper col to cross the range. As reserves of positivity were dwindling, something on the roadside suddenly flashed in the glare of the sun. Ski goggles! I polished them quickly with my fleece and snapped them onto my face. They were in great condition and made me feel like Arnold Schwarzenegger from the terminator. I instantly loved them. On the road, these attachments are rare and valuable. I took what I could get. Within minutes, as if an act of god, the sun gave way to a sudden flurry of clouds that released the first snows I had felt in a long time. I felt invincible in my goggles and battled on, topped up on positivity and assured that I could now survive in any conditions, no matter how harsh.

Descending down from the climb, I was welcomed onto the Tibetan plateau. The Tibetan plateau! This was what the three-day climb was for. Infinite expansive plains of spring green festooned with tussocks of hay yellow that reached far into the distance. There, impossibly far away, gently contoured snow-dusted peaks rose elegantly in isolated majesty. The plains were specked with odd black forms that I soon recognised to be Yaks. After a few kilometres I came to my first camp of tents, where I drank Yak butter tea and replenished my bottles with some boiled water.

I was torn between asking to camp here, with the first Tibetans I had come across, and continuing onwards. Not wanting to sully my rhythm, I opted to continue along the straight road that seemed to focalise itself and pierce through the distant horizon. After 20 kilometres on the plains, the temperature began to drop off, a punchy chill filled my breath and I hauled my bike off the road and set to walk a few hundred metres to find a camping spot before nightfall. I ate my instant noodles and put on most of my clothes to combat the intensifying cold. Throughout the night, I repeatedly woke and put on whatever I could find to add some insulation. Shoes, on. Goggles, on. I was almost considering putting my feet in my panniers. This night was perhaps the coldest of the trip and I hardly slept. I checked the weather forecast for the nearest town. Minus five degrees. Compare this to the 'extreme' rating of my sleeping bag that sat at a toasty eleven degrees... I shivered for sunrise and have never been so grateful, when little after 8am, the first of the bleached rays snuck between faraway peaks to defrost my tent and indeed myself. *So Tibet is cold*, I confirmed to myself.

Within the first 30 kilometres, just as my shivering had stopped, a Tibetan motorcyclist joined me. He pulled alongside, his face cloaked in a black scarf to protect him from the searing sun at this altitude of some 3300 m. He beckoned me to follow him with hand gestures and muffled shouts. For the next 10 kilometres he motored at my speed (of about 20 kilometres per hour) until we arrived in a small village, where he led me to his house. His mother was sat on a chair outside, her face wrinkled beyond comprehension with piercing hazel eyes that stared vacantly into the distance. She wore traditional robes and slowly but compulsively span a handheld prayer wheel. I wasn't sure whether to approach her and shake her hand or leave her to her prayer wheel. In the end, I decided for the latter. Meanwhile, the son, who was my age, came out of the house and greeted me. With gestures he taught me some Tibetan survival phrases and took me for a hearty lunch of rice and yak-meat stew.

It must be said that Tibetan hospitality from the humans was fantastic, but the hospitality from the animals was a different story altogether. I am, of course, referring to the notorious Tibetan Mastiffs. These creatures are less dog than monster. It seemed that each shepherd had his Ceberus that musters and protects the Yak livestock as a day job. I would soon find out that for leisure, they hunt touring cyclists. Within a few kilometres of leaving the hosts of the morning, I came across a troop of Yak crossing the road in front of me. I whistled and whooped so that they knew I was coming and I would not startle any of them. Shortly after I passed through a gap in the procession, I saw something moving quickly out of the corner of my eye. A shaggy fanged beast was bounding towards me. It approached a fence at the side of the road where I thought it would stop, but shimmied its way under the iron wiring, before letting out a deeply disconcerting bellow.

"Oh shit," I whispered to myself, trying to stay composed. *Just treat it like any of them dogs in Thailand, pedal slowly and turn to it and shout.* "HYA, HYA," I yelled as it got closer. *It should stop any second now.* It sprinted towards me, roaring as it did so, eyes blazing red, fixated on my calf. "HYA, HYA!" I shouted even louder. It wasn't stopping. It was going to have me. "Oh fuck!" I cried as it leapt towards my leg. It missed, redressed itself and sunk its teeth into my rear pannier. My bike jolted backwards for an instant and the dog let go. I shouted for all I was worth and stamped on the pedals. "You bastard!" I yelled as the chase came to an end. My heart was pounding at 200 to the minute and I screamed back at the dog.

"Come on then, you son of a bitch!" I wished my friend of earlier in the day had taught me some curses in Tibetan so the dog could at least have understood.

Throughout the rest of the day, I was extremely skittish. The slightest movement of any small black-object made me quiver in fright. Unfortunately, many of the Yak calves were almost the exact size and colour as the mastiffs that I had come across. In their innocence, they trotted across the plains, unknowingly making me soil myself in pre-emptive fear. At the end of the day, the clouds closed in on the vast plains, blowing over from the distant mountains that were no longer perceptible. I could sense a tension in the air that needed to cede. The pressure dropped. Right at the moment of approaching a camp of tents, the heavens opened and hail pounded down. I hastily approached the first family I saw and asked if I could pitch my tent behind theirs, out of the fierce winds that were now raging and causing me to squint my eyes and hold my hood to my head. They agreed enthusiastically and under the pelting downpour I quickly put up the tent, before a child's head stuck out and the inevitable invitation to enter their home was tendered.

Inside was all one might imagine from a nomadic tent. Thick brightly coloured rugs lined the floor, with sleeping quilts bundled in one corner. The centrepiece of the operation was an enormous yak dung stove that sat in the middle of the room. There was a basket of dried yak dung alongside it that the youngest daughter fed into the heating chamber. Atop was an industrial kettle that I assumed was always on the boil, to provide a continuous source of cha. The most surprising feature inside the tent, however, was a 30-inch flat screen TV that blared out *Xinhua* news. It was powered by a battery attached to the solar panel on the roof of the tent. I never imagined Tibetan nomads to watch telly but I guess the influence of technology has managed to slither into even the most traditional ways of life. Indeed, throughout Asia, I was constantly surprised by how many people, even in remote villages, had

146

mobile phones and how startlingly often their eyes were cast down to their screens.

My sense of surrealism at the crossroads of tradition and change was highest when a man pulled up in a car to help the family to relocate their tent the next morning (probably away from the stray dog that had spent the entire night baying at the moon). With all doors open, traditional Tibetan music filled the air, emanating magical sounds from the car radio. My heart welled with receptive melancholy to the ethereal slow dance of pipe and string. I closed my eyes in a blissful trance, before opening them to the next song in the playlist, wide. It was an electronic remix of Adele's 'Rolling in the deep'. I couldn't quite believe my ears and after finishing packing my own tent, I rolled away for the remaining 40 kilometres or so to Langmusi, wondering whether tradition could survive at all in such a rapid world.

I reached Langmusi five days after setting off from Chengdu. Five days of camping in progressively colder temperatures, culminating in them two horribly uncomfortable nights on the grasslands. I felt putrid, having hardly changed clothes due to the cold weather. I had also not washed for five days. As such, the hot shower at the hostel was not of water but of delight: purified joy and comfort and wellbeing. I basked in relief and felt immediately cleansed, while the steam dancing around me seemed to take on almost magical properties. This is the major merit of all the suffering: the intensity of the joy that comes from its eventual deliverance.

Langmusi straddles the border between Sichuan and Gansu province and is a town whose religious importance is rapidly developing, with new stupas and monasteries being built on both sides of the natural border river. The air was loaded with a fresh alpine crispness: the sort that makes chapped lips smack as it is inhaled and when it fills the lungs, becomes a possession. The thin but full atmosphere was just irresistible for wandering, wrapped beneath layers of hat, scarf and thick coat. Monks and townsfolk unhurriedly meandered through the streets or traipsed up the stairs to the monastery, blowing out billows of sweet and steamy cloud with every breath. Even inside the hostel, this quiet, delicate atmosphere could be felt. It felt like a slow and distant choral melody echoed silently from the walls and it made my soul weep with reverence for where I was. There were always people in the living room, huddled around the stove, sipping away at cha and looking out of the window that let through an interspersion of light and cast it onto the wooden floorboards. I could happily have stayed here for many days, but the road to Xining, where I planned to rest for a day, beckoned me onwards. I left with a full but heavy heart for five more days on the plateau.

One of the first ports of call back on the road was to acquire a large stick of some description, to defend against the Mastiffs. My experience on the day before reaching Langmusi had left me a petrified, nervous wreck, especially since my normal tactic of fending off dogs had fallen completely flat. My new technique would be to dismount the bike, whip out the baton, and give any pooch that deigned cross me an almighty thump on the skull. Within just a few kilometres, I found a downed section of fencing, and managed to free one of the posts that added on a good extra kilo or two to my gear, but was reassuringly bulky to the extent that I thought I would succeed in concussing any dog (or wayward Chinaman) with one blow.

Despite this, I began to feel vulnerable on the plains when no other humans were in sight and I was alone amongst the immensity of the landscape. The powerful scenery became hostile rather than raw and solitude soon became loneliness. The wind had whipped up, and even cycling downhill solicited a great deal of effort. I was struggling and eventually I spat the dummy, rammed my bike against the green-painted crash barrier and sat, back against it, breathing fast and heavy while the road remained mockingly silent to the north and south, bar the strong wind licking the straps of my panniers. I battled the tears that wanted to come and took a few minutes to get a grip of myself. I stood, surveyed the road levying upwards before turning towards the crux of the punishing ascent to the col. I breathed deeply and composed myself. My cleats clicked into my pedals and I shimmied on mournfully, my tenebrous thoughts eating their way into the positivity that I was desperately trying to cling onto. There was only one solution that appeared to me at that moment. 90s classics. I screamed along to *'Don't look back in Anger'*, *'Brimful of Asha'* (except I changed Asha to Asia) and *'Don't marry her'*, trying to impose myself onto the landscape and dominate the silence with my atrocious singing voice.

My spirits were beginning to lift when suddenly a roar shook me to attention. *'WOOF!'* I looked up and saw it sprinting across the field, just as the one that had sunk its teeth into my pannier had done: another bastard mastiff. This time I was ready. I jerked out my earphones, primed myself, stopped the bike and whipped out the post that I had laid on my rear rack, strapped over my tent. I felt like a medieval warrior. *Let's 'av ya pooch!* Right as my beastly adversary reached the fence, a car pulled up and stopped between the dog and me and gestured at me to start cycling. My earphones tangled in my wheel and broke. My heart was still racing, fighting instinct instilled. I began to advance and the dog cowered away at the horn-blasts from the Tibetan driver. The battle was over. I offered him my bitter thanks, almost miffed at being deprived of the opportunity to see if my tactic would have worked. I trundled on, body fraught with an unshakable tension, for two more days, until finally, after a short climb out of Hezuo, the descent began. Confident I was leaving this beast-ridden plateau behind, I even lost the stick.

There were two possible roads that I was considering to reach Xining. One was a rather long 2000m descent to valley level before a slow climb back up to Xining on the edge of the Qinghai plateau (Xining is still 2000m high!). The other was far shorter in apparent distance as the crow flies, but included two epic climbs, each of which carried with it 1000m or so of altitude gain. I had slept next to a grave the night before decision day, hidden away next to a shrewdly positioned prayer wheel that was constantly spun by a small waterfall and played out a repeating meditative chocking sound.

It had rained all night and when I awoke, a thin blanket of drizzle and cloud was still melancholically floating about the hillside. My mood was slightly dampened and as such I was erring toward the easier of the two options: to fully complete the descent I had began yesterday, followed by a gradual climb. I soon reached the junction where I needed to make a decision and against all logic, I compulsively turned my wheel to the left, to the route of the 2 mountain cols. As Fyodor Dostoyevsky explores in his *Notes from Uunderground,* sometimes the interest of greatest import to advance, is one's freedom to take decisions whose consequences will surely be contrary to those of more rational or logically founded endeavours. In short, I was exorcising my freedom of stupidity and took the opportunity to indulge my compulsion. *In any case*, I told myself, *it won't matter which route I took in ten days time, so why not go against the grain. Just to see what happens.* And what did happen was one of the toughest, most lung-busting, sinew-straining, quad-clenching climbs I have ever embarked upon. I had to split the eye-watering gradients into five kilometres sections and upon reaching these, I would rejoice, before recomposing myself to take on the next ones. The wind was howling into my face and stretches of road were no better than a construction site. It took six hours to reach the top, and when I finally made it I punched the air as if I had just taken the stage win on l'Alpe d'Huez. "Come on!" I saw throngs of people held back by crowd barriers, bustling to get a look at me and applaud my majestic performance. Chanting of "Johnson, Johnson, Johnson!" deafeningly rung from the bottom to the top of the mountain, enveloping my victory as my friends and family and managers and journalists rushed towards me, exalting my performance in a bounding frenzy of hugs and tears of joy. I broke from my illusion to the stark reality of the summit. A lone couple of Chinese tourists admiring the view from their car looked on at me and giggled. Nobody was there to applaud me. I looked down at the writhing road I had just conquered, bitterly contemptuous that the only reward was this moment that I had to myself, and myself alone. I could not convey to any of my friends or family what all of this was taking. All revelry was my own, to be selfishly stashed away in my box of memories. It sometimes felt wrong having nobody around with whom I could share these moments.

Nonetheless, I did not dwell on this any further. The descent awaited and after six hours without any food, I was thinking only of my next calorific source, 25 kilometres down a descent that was just as epic as the climb. The total descent, in actual fact, lasted for a full 45 kilometres and finished at the Yangtze: the mythical Yellow river. The scenery all the way was jaw dropping: an instant antidote to the lonely chagrin I experienced at the climb's summit. The snow-capped mountains gave way to a cascade of rugged sandstone, whose irregular ridges looked more like a witch's fingers than rock, clawing at the basin, malevolently encroaching the river that gushed eagerly to meet the Yangtze. As I advanced further, these ridges displayed incredible patterns of erosion, as if someone had baked a batch of brandy snaps into the rock itself. Along the road, armies of Hui muslim school children dressed in smart uniform marched: beaming, waving and shouting as I shot past at what felt like mach-1 but was in fact probably 35 kilometres an hour. This combination of the whooping of an innocent army (not dissimilar to what I had daydreamed on the summit), the monumental geology and lo! tailwind, was exactly the revitalisation I needed. I was descending the Tibetan plateau to join the Yellow river while I had 100 people asking excitedly how I was and I was exactly where I wanted to be and I had to tell this to myself to remind myself it was real. For it was often so easy to allow the monotony of riding to become all encompassing and sometimes I would have loved for somebody to slap me in the face and say "Hey! What you're doing is cool! And where you are is cool! break a smile man, come on, smile! Enjoy! This is life, man, life!" I thought back to Dave, the cyclist in Vietnam. This is what he would have told me.

So, on the final approach to Xining, this is exactly the attitude I adopted. I took a step back in my mind. Reality hit me. I had cycled on the Tibetan plateau. Over 3800 m cols of skybound roads. Across vast planes. Confronting beastly dogs. I felt like I had touched upon an arrestingly enigmatic region of the world and paradoxically it gave me just as much joy to leave as it did to have arrived, knowing that my memories of its hostility, cruelty and imperceptible vastness were already maturing into those of splendid beauty and fondness.

On the fifth day after leaving Langmusi and the tenth since my last rest day in Chengdu, Xining came into view. I indulged in a three-day rest in this city where I met Lany, who worked at the hostel and who made my time here a joy. We wandered around the people's park on her day off, looking at flowers and people watching: two extremely worthy and extremely relaxing pastimes. On the morning of the third day in the city, I lazily sauntered out of the door and very suddenly heard a noise that made me jump out of my skin. "Oi!"
I span round ready to wallop my verbal aggressor. "You!" I retorted, before stepping forward to give Charlie a big hug. "I wasn't expecting to see you here just yet!"
In fact, while I was busy ogling the flowers in Xining's people's park, I had completely forgotten that Charlie was only a couple of days behind me, having fixed his mechanical problem in Chengdu, secured his visa with a train ride to Leshan, and taken to the road only two days after me, hot on my tail. It was great to see him, and we agreed to set off into the wild North West the following day, after an evening of trading tales and sharing ales.

The Long march

As soon as we left Xining, the country became wild. Villages were now few and far-between and the roadside establishments were ramshackle: a far cry from the gaudy milk tea joints in South China. The shop façades were dilapidating. Men, instead of snoozing on benches, or crowing around cards, were squatting shiftily on stone steps, cigarettes drooping precariously from their mouths. In the noodle houses – Mine and Charlie's lunchtime staple, the work-worn ladies who served us would often do so limp-mouthed, before retiring to the shadows of the kitchen hole to stare at us from a safer distance. "I guess they don't get many tourists round here," I remarked to Charlie who was busy appraising the map for the rest of the day. He looked up as a bowl of the £1 noodle soup was placed before him as the server was trying to stifle her titters at the prospect of serving two very wayward gentlemen. He concurred that he had never recalled seeing *100 kilometres up the G227 from Xining* in a Thomas Cook brochure either. "But isn't that just *such* a great feeling," he replied.

It was true that something as mundane as a noodle house in an otherwise mind-numbingly boring village, seemed to take on an exciting quality through the fact that you knew you were a novelty there. The realisation that we might well be amongst the first Western people that the villagers had seen in person – especially the children – filled me with a sense of ambassadorship. I was the image that these people now have of the West: sweaty, dirty, unkempt, living out of panniers, sleeping in a tent and still fumbling with chopsticks. From simply eating in somebody's restaurant, it felt like I was somehow bringing the world closer together. Perhaps those dealing with us in the shops and demanding photos with us would cherish us in their memories and incessantly relate to their peers the yarn of that time two cycling heroes stopped by on their noble quest. More likely they would simply have a giggle over the fact that we stunk and ate like pigs.

If the first day from Xining was about our approach to the Qilian Mountains, then our second day was the traverse, which took us back up to the heights of some 3,800m. The weather was mercifully mild, and the characteristic updraft licked at our behinds as we daintily pedalled our way over the first range. It had been another freezing night and I was thankful for the intense sun that blared mightily in the brilliant blue sky, slowly ebbing warmth back into my body. At the summit, the northern peaks of the Qilian could be seen in the distance, their myriad snow-swathed forms catching the glint of the sun in such a way that drove a sense of delighted wonderment through my entire body. With a 1000m descent in front of me, I brimmed with enthusiasm and wished that I could shout out to everybody that I knew about how much fun this truly was. I waited for Charlie while taking photos and marvelling at everything around. The conditions of the day were perfect. Surely we could even take on the second pass of the day and make it into the flatter steppe of northern Gansu province. "Shall we go for it?" I goaded Charlie who I knew would want to take it easy down this descent. Having experienced a complete break failure once in Northern Spain, he had never quite recovered full confidence in the two thin rubber strips that rub onto the wheel rim to stop the cyclist from barrelling uncontrollably to their death.

In the afternoon, the tailwind that had thus far been joyously pushing us along very suddenly ceded. First with a small puff of headwind, like somebody blowing out the birthday candles, before the direction completely changed. Within a matter of half an hour, clouds gathered ahead, first in a thin wispy haze like tracing paper, then an apocalyptic greying ensued. Over the once crisp mountains, precipitation fell in such a torrent that it looked as if snow was being extracted upwards rather than falling downwards. Everything became cold and squalls of

154

wind howled from the north, forcing Charlie and I to lean into it to avoid being blown into the middle of the road, in the path of the odd red truck.

"We need to stop!" Charlie shouted back to me.

"Let's keep going until we find some better shelter!" I shouted back, voice lost to a gust. I was concerned that if we didn't find any proper shelter the conditions would only worsen and we would end up stuck and exposed. It was better to continue while we could and find a more secure place. Ten minutes later, we encountered a large tent pitched up a dirt track. We took it.

"Ni Hao?" Charlie enquired.

A shabbily-clad man with ruffled hair answered and looked us up and down, trying to comprehend exactly what circumstances had driven us here and what on earth we might want. After a period of ridiculous mimicking of wind and weather and not good, we were allowed into the toasty tent where seven haggard bodies were temporarily living while they were tending to the livestock. They spoke a dialect that sounded very much like an odd mix of Mandarin and Russian. Needless to say, the two hours spent sheltering were not full of conversation, but were full of warmth and tea and bread. The set up was reminiscent of the bunkroom in Steinbeck's 'Of Mice and Men' and Charlie and I were sure that the free time of these men was taken up by three things only: cards, fags and baijiu.

I think both Charlie and I were secretly relishing the company and warmth of the tea, but we thought it rude to prolong our welcome any longer than was necessary. We kept looking outside to appraise the conditions, which for an hour remained much too energy-sapping for cycling. Once the freak storm had somewhat abated, we ventured out, back into the cold headwind, to trundle onwards. It was grim and after only a few minutes, the storm redoubled. *Could we turn back to the tent?* Being far too British, we both felt it would be embarrassing to do so and instead we persevered onwards, putting ourselves in exactly the same predicament as before. Eventually, our toil was rewarded in the shape of a farmhouse on the brim of the hill. Shelter! "Let's try here!" I called out to Charlie. He was already well ahead of me and pulled into the dirt track.

We once more found ourselves in the hands of a stranger with whom we shared no semblance of common language. Ma came out to greet us, almost as if he had been expecting us. *Was he god?* We asked if we could camp in the shelter behind his walls. He flat out refused. Instead, he insisted that we take the biggest room inside his house, with a bed heated by water pipes. *Ma, legend and saviour!* It was Ramadan and so Ma and his Hui Muslim family didn't eat until sundown. In fact they didn't say or do anything with us until sundown. We were simply left completely to our own devices and so we slept lusciously on the heated bed. At the hour we assumed the sun had set (for the grey sky had not lightened), a copium of bread, cakes, noodles and tea was brought to us. Nothing was asked of us. All just given. Not even any questions. Not 'Where are you from?' or 'Where are you going?' It was as if he knew everything about us in advance, including the food that we loved. It was in such contrast to the great selfie-hungry unwashed of the rest of Asia.

Waking up the following morning, we noticed that the wind had settled. The storm was over. There was just one col left before the descent, 2000 m back down to warmer weather in the far northwest of Gansu, before the fabled passage to Xingxingxia at the Xinjiang border, funnelling between the two vast deserts of the Gobi and the Taklamakan. Covering most of this distance was a flat road. The land was poor and arid, albeit irrigated by the industrious Chinese making use of the few rivers that flow northeast out of the Kunlun before dissipating into the ghostly sands.

The descent from the last of the Qilian Mountains was rather special. Toothy spears of rock stood stalwart above the road, like sentinels watching us as we wound our way down alongside the river. Suddenly, the winding stopped and the updraft ceased. There were no more mountains behind the final corner. A magnificent vista of green fields speckled with yellow patches from early-blooming canola fields that draws vast quantities of tourists to this region in the summer months opened up in front of us. The Qilians were behind us, but the descent did not stop there. We broke onto a road lined for dozens of kilometres with poplar trees, breaking up the crosswinds and somehow channelling it behind us. We were cruising at about 35 kilometres per hour with hardly any traffic, surrounded by lush fields. It was one of those days: the perfect ones that are unforgettable and become enshrined in memory as in the moment. That was it. The road was more or less flat all the way to Xinjiang. The mountains that began all the way back in Myanmar were through. We were still at an altitude of about 1500 m and the Tulufan depression where we were headed was 1600 m lower. The border to Xinjiang was only 650 kilometres away, where our freedoms as solo independent travellers in China were set to be somewhat diminished.

On the road to Xinjiang, Charlie and I mused on what we would find there. The situation in Xinjiang is a complex one. It results from a turbulent and fascinating history, and a remote and inhospitable location that has long been the grey zone between empires. The current state of affairs was an ultra-high security surveillance state to quell any resistance to the Chinese identity of the populace. This stems from the rise of Uyghur separatist groups that are politically opposed to the rule of the communist party. It isn't just the loggerheaded interests of the Uyghur separatists that threaten the monopartite principles upon which the nation's political stability is currently based; it is their very existence. Rather than risking the Uyghur separatist groups being allowed to gain momentum on a street level, there is a surveillance crackdown, screaming reminiscence from Orwell's *1984*. In Xinjiang I would discover that the movements of all people are tracked through various means such as checkpoints and hi-tech cameras matched with machine learning algorithms that can identify citizens from as little information as their style of walking. It was a scary prospect knowing that this was the world into which we were currently hurtling. I had heard many stories that I took with a heavy dose of salt, but here in Xinjiang, it seemed inadmissible that something fishy *wasn't* going on. I knew this. I was excited and nervous to see what it was really like. Charlie had already got wind of cyclists and travellers trying to cross the region. Apparently a Dutch couple had to be escorted in a police car for a stretch of almost 1500 kilometres, having been told that cycling was not possible. Another young traveller said that it was only possible to transit by train that stops only in Urumqi and Tulufan and that all other cities were out of bounds. These stories only served to fuel the fire of desire to lift stones in the Xinjiang desert.

In Zhangye, Charlie and I went separate ways once more. I took a detour to cycle over the Danxia Rainbow Mountains, while Charlie was keen to press on, having four days less on his visa than mine. At this point, I had all but won the visa race and the ensuing days drove in the final blows to my temporal adversary. I was in great fitness, other than the fact that half of my gooch was peeling off. With the first flat terrain since Myanmar's Irrawaddy basin, I found that I could cycle seemingly forever. Days of 140 kilometres, 180 kilometres, then 120 kilometres fighting a callous headwind passed by, Xinjiang now fixed in the crosshair. There was one city left before the border, now only 380 kilometres away. I had planned to have a restful morning in the city boasting the westernmost outpost of the Great wall: Jiayuguan, when I received a message from Charlie. He always had half an eye on the weather and he advised me that a strong Easterly was due. He had made incredible progress and was at Guazhou, 280 kilometres ahead. I couldn't miss the opportunity. I hastily packed my panniers and set onto the road. Almost immediately, I found myself in the company of a Chinese cycling squadron who were out for their group ride. They dragged me along with them for fifty kilometres. We were flying. The wind propelling us from behind to speeds of above thirty kilometres per hour while barely having to pedal. 100

kilometres passed, then 150, then 200. I was exerting no energy. It was as if the whole Earth was moving, warping, soaring towards me. 250 kilometres. The sun was just beginning to set and at kilometre 265 I finally ducked from the road into the shelter of a backed-up mound of earth, while the wind blew heartily above, just rattling the top of the tent.

The winds didn't slow the next day either, forcing me to wait for a day in Guazhou to avoid the eighty kilometres per hour air current that now blew as a cross wind. Ahead, lay the last stretch of road before Xinjiang, some 160 kilometres away. The barren, wind-turbine dotted lands of Gansu began to undulate, and lunar hills loomed in the distance, foreboding. The end-of-the-road feel was tangible. I soon reached the small mountains, an infinite expanse of grey mounds, like pimples in the earth, sprawled out. The terrestrial origin of the landscape was only betrayed by a truckers' stop twenty kilometres in. As I cycled towards the last frontier before Xinjiang, the rest of China fell behind the otherworldly mountains, and with the wind now on my back, I was ushered towards the fabled border. It was 18:00 and I had cycled 170 kilometres when the checkpoint came into view from the G30.

Post-Orwell

"Pass-a-port please."

I handed my papers to the SWAT officer behind the booth at the border. He was protected by a glass screen, a Kevlar vest and an automatic machine gun hanging from his neck. He sat, brow furrowed, scrutinising my passport. "Yinguo nada?"

"Yes. English man (*Not American,* as most of the Chinese assumed)."

He invited his superiors with a finger-swish and they too took a good long look at my freaky passport face. There were headshakes and deliberations. Then came the questions. "Where did you enter China?"

"Hekou Town, sir," I answered cordially.

"Where did you stay last night? What's your number? Give me your phone (actually not a question). Where you go now? Where you sleep? We will take you to Hami."

"But I have to ride to Hami, on my bike," I put the words out into the open. The officers began gesticulating and debating. A long stream of negotiation was on its way, but I had the trump card, my jack of spades, a weapon that much of the rest of the world does not possess. I had far too much time on my hands.

"No, you get in the car, to protect your life"

"No, I will ride my bicycle to Hami."

"No, you get in the car." The officer didn't look like he was going to back down. A forceful tone reinforced his words. I decided to change tack and get to the bottom of exactly why I needed to get into the car, without wanting to hit on any sensitive details that I was sure couldn't be shared with the likes of me. "From what does my life need protecting and what is dangerous here?" I inquired, trying to sound innocent and curious.

"Bad road and unpredictable weather."

"I promise you, I've been through worse," I laughed.

"We will drive you with your bicycle to Hami."

"Hmm no, I think I will cycle. I have come from Singapore and never got in a car. I must cycle all the way. That is not going to change now." The officer retreated. The game appeared to be reaching stalemate, until *good cop* Wa appeared. He told me that *if I really wanted to*, I could cycle. I was shocked. He asked where I thought I was going to stay that evening. After 170 kilometres of riding, thirty more kilometres down the road, didn't seem unreasonable. Wa had other plans. He told me that the next police checkpoint was 100 kilometres away and I should try to make it there. "I can't do 100 kilometres now!" I spluttered. The clock was now reading 19:03 and the ticking never stops. Precious time to find a campsite before nightfall was being squandered.

"You must cycle to next checkpoint."

"Ok, ok, Wa, how about this," I tried. "Either I camp here tonight and we leave in the morning, or you come with me and we camp in fifty kilometres."

After a quick call to his bosses, it was confirmed that the checkpoint into Xinjiang was not, in fact, a hotel. Stalemate loomed once more. We kept on chipping away at our ideals until eventually, we reached a deal. I could cycle, yes, but the cops were to stay with me all the way. "Tonight, we sleep where you live," I was told. I warned Wa, who was to join me, that this may be a hole under the expressway. He seemed unphased and he and his wholly disinterested partner in fighting crime and escorting stubborn cyclists, Kazakh Danilili, jumped in their car to get after me. I was already sprinting off down the road. I was into Xinjiang.

The next fifty kilometres were: downhill, tailwind, the setting sun, and the exhilaration of negotiating my way into a region that was putting civil liberties in a vice and tightening it more every week. Behind the wire fences, Martian mounds shimmered in the low light. The odd gust flittered past my ears. Sand slithered on the verges. Ranks and ranks of wind turbines whirred with their backs to the road ahead. It was a vast amphitheatre. This was my soliloquy. I was alone on the road, bucking, galloping, my wheels sang and the clicks of my gears echoed pounding joy. Wa and Dan filmed me as I shot along the open road. I provided entertainment by supermanning and breaking into intermittent sprints. I didn't mind having the company. I wondered whether it was rude or illegal to stop to pee under escort. Would I get arrested for wasting police time (not that I wasn't already)? The police didn't bat an eyelid when eventually I did.

"I suppose we better find a campsite soon" I hollered over to Wa and Dan as I did up my zipper. Light was fading, greying the hue of the alien rocks that surrounded us. I felt a strange sense of responsibility at deciding where two Chinese SWAT officers would be spending the night with me. They very politely asked if it could be a truck-service area. We arrived at one soon after sunset, a long, dilapidating bungalow with a small outhouse. The three of us were relieved to have arrived at this place. It was handshakes and hi-fives all around. Knowing they would be spending the night in their car, I invited them to share the tent but they turned down my offer. *How odd.* It seemed like they appreciated a good joke so I asked whether it was they or I who was buying the baijiu for the evening. "We cannot drink while working!" They gasped. They were straight cops at least.

In the truckers' stop they bought me a meal and gave me some of their instant noodles. We first thanked each other for respecting each other's wishes (them for letting me cycle, and me for understanding that they must fulfil their duty by 'keeping me safe'). By now I was finding it guiltily funny that two SWAT officers were having to sleep in their car at my stubborn expense, but in some ways they probably got a lot of job satisfaction from going above and beyond for the service of their country and their wayward and irritating guest. Affirmations of mutual respect over, the discussion became light-hearted and we joked about their wives and chopsticks and girls and baijiu and beer. Exactly what I expected to talk about

162

with border guards, for some reason. I spent a terribly uncomfortable night next to the loud road and dogs, but it was probably better than Wa and Dan's. They were cooped up in the car. I woke at 6am, packed everything away and banged on the police car window. The sun had not long risen. A dog still whined and scratched around the gravel in front of the truck stop house. The still tarmac beckoned. Danilili sat from his reclined position, rubbed his eyes and grumbled, "Zou go, go." It was still fifty kilometres to the next checkpoint, and I was excited to see what trouble I could cause there.

Throughout Xinjiang, I spent dozens of hours arguing my case to the cops who wanted me to get in a car. They certainly didn't want a foreigner to cycle through the region and especially not their own jurisdiction. The image of the region hung in a very delicate balance in the eyes of the international community. For Xinjiang was, at this moment, a hot topic in global news. The media were reporting on a *cultural genocide* of the Uyghur Muslims – descendants of Turkic people who have occupied Xinjiang for centuries. With mounting tensions, many Uyghurs were made to attend 're-education camps' that the Western media report to be more akin to prison camps. There were further allegations of forced sterilisations and forced disappearances. It sounded abhorrent. As for the extent on which this happens, and whether the allegations were fully true, I am unsure, but they were certainly founded on something. Throughout my time here, I saw the crushing control exerted over the movement of people. It is like nothing I could ever have imagined.

On the second day after the Xinjiang border, arriving into the city of Hami after 200 kilometres of constant police escort, the extent of post-Orwellian dystopia revealed itself. Surveillance cars buzzed around the city like flies around poo. Cameras latched onto pedestrians going about their business, seemingly like everywhere else in China. Police posts lined the road as regularly as lampposts, and khaki-clad *dad's army* men in

Kevlar vests stood guard outside most shops. They sat on wooden chairs, slouched or bowed over, eying up this unscrupulous world in between puffs of cigarette that sagged from their lips. Riot shields and painful-looking spikey poles were rested along their feet or behind the chairs, that I was certain had never been used. I passed the checkpoint into the city and, shaking off one last cop doggedly following me on his moped, appeared to have made it. What rigmarole! I didn't feel any tension or any danger; I just felt outraged for the common person who is submitted to this nonsense day in, day out, slowly ground down into submission. I rendezvoused with Charlie, who had made it here two days earlier, passing through the airport style body scanner into the budget hotel before treating myself with an ice cream. I gobbled it down like nobody was watching, but I was sure that they were...

Charlie and I agreed that from here on, we should stick together. We both wanted to cycle all the way through Xinjiang without bowing to the police pressure to get in an escort vehicle. *The red line, unbroken* was our maxim and as a duo it seemed we might be able to uphold it. We hardly had time to muse on our situation or to stay put too long in Hami to consolidate. Such is the nature of the road. Time is measured relative to our visas, which was in short hand. Distances, on the other hand, on the scale of China relative that of the circumference of our bicycle wheels were rather large.

After an evening roaming the pretty, yet suspect streets, we left our hotel through the metal detector, and took to the road with about 450 kilometres to go until Tulufan. Police presence all but petered out on this stretch. For the next 300 kilometres there were only two checkpoints and the officers let us through unhindered after fulfilling their bureaucratic duties. After three days of this vastness, stony desert with distant rocky forms that never approached, turbines and turbines and just one straight road that we slept under, we had almost made it. We were jubilant, being only ten kilometres from the city and all of that downhill. Thoughts of noodles, water and beer somehow seeped into our tastebuds. We hadn't ate for the last hundred and fifty kilometres or so, and our bottles were dry and empty. Charlie even resorted to drinking for a discarded pepsi bottle that he found on the roadside. Knowing we were so close to being able to fill up, we sped along, willed on by the proximity of these necessities.

As it so happened, there was one last checkpoint to negotiate. And this one was home to the most ostentatious, officious and by-the-book cops of them all. Negotiation was fruitless, and no matter how much begging, bum-licking and bartering we did, the road ahead was, for us, an impasse. We took stock of our situation. Many metres below sea level, famished, thirsty, hot. The shingled rocks around us radiated a stifling heat. My head felt heavy, my stomach empty, my legs stiff and my mood, frankly, foul. We were turned back up the road that we had just descended with a 35 kilometres detour to contest with. "Sister my superior say rules and enforcement cannot be broken," we were told by the snarling cop's translate app. I was furious. *Bastards! Did they have no idea of what we had been through?* However, all pain was totally self-inflicted. Perhaps the rage I was feeling was more a reflection unto ourselves, unto myself, for somehow ending up in this situation where the arguments of moving forward were built on shifting sand. No matter how mad I got, we had to realise that we were the foolish ones in this situation.

These reflections were far off, however, and I shot off ahead, leaving Charlie behind, cursing and strangling the handlebars with shaking hands. I settled at the top of the climb to wait for him, muttering to myself, scared as I was now venting my rage onto Charlie who had done nothing of ill intention. I took a dip in the cool water of the irrigation channel that was gushing back down towards the checkpoint to cool off just in time for Charlie's arrival. He had clearly done some meditating of his own too. The value of having a companion to offload some emotion during this short detour cannot be understated. We soon began laughing and impersonating Chinese cops, while dissipating our anger over the kilometres left behind us, dropping our woes like the breadcrumbs of Hansel and Gretel, until we found ourselves back in the default state of hungry, hot and tired. With only a few kilometres left of our detour, we came across the first eatery of the day. Having consumed only nuts for 170 kilometres, Charlie and I burst into the establishment. "Niu rho mian, la mian!" We sat, bellies cracking, mouths foaming, ogling the hand-pulled noodles that our neighbours were slurping, while filling up on the tea that all Northwest China establishments proffer. That plate of noodles that arrived stands out as the finest I have ever eaten. The kilometres before made it so. The same goes for the first sip of Xinjiang Wusu beer that same evening. Pure bliss. We had made it to Tulufan.

We spent two days utterly reclined in this ancient city. Ürümqi was only a few days and about 1000 kilometres away. The city that is further from the sea of any other on Earth, and importantly, the last big one before the beginning of central Asia: Khorgas. Already in Tulufan, a fascinating crossroad city on the silk road, the transition from the middle kingdom to central Asia was alive. The world of Islam was on its way. The Uyghur people in the scruffy suburbs were brimming with joy. Great Turkic music made the air dance as it filled with smoky clouds from sizzling shish kebabs. We slurped on La mian and great tea, as all around us, people laughed and danced in the flared dusk. We chatted to a teacher who told us that Uyghur people were not allowed out of Xinjiang: what a great shame to contrast the jubilant atmosphere that was perfuse.

Despite the obviousness of the strict measures imposed on Uyghurs, similar to those imposed on Tibetans, they seemed like a hardy folk. I could hardly imagine them as victims of cultural genocide. That being said, the co-ordination of the

166

Chinafication operation was not running evenly across Xinjiang. Perhaps the Uyghurs of Tulufan were being treated differently from the Uyghurs of say, Hotan, where many allegations of human rights abuse were focused: Islamic graveyards levelled into car parks, bans put on Islamic names, and of course, the stories of the re-education camps. These incidences write a different story, one of intense repression of identity and human rights, to the world I witnessed. In any case, that wasn't evident here; the Uyghur quarter of Tulufan was the most vibrant community of China that I had visited. Regardless of the justices and injustices of the unfathomably complex Chinese society, the Uyghurs here were the people who emanated the greatest plenitude of happiness.

It was soon time to leave the cradle of the beautiful Tulufan hostel. It was a paradisiacal place where we ate home-made yoghurt with naans fresh out of the tandoor beneath the shade of the grape vines sprawled over a pagoda in the light-blue painted courtyard. Uzbek style cloth tapestries lazily rippled in the breeze to the sound of smooth jazz and bossa-nova crackling out of a 1970s style radio. On the morning of leaving, light eased through the vine leaves, spangling the table with patches of light and steady conversation occasionally punctuated the instrumental of 'The girl from Ipanema'. This place was the epitome of relaxation and a true sense of bien-être infectiously swelled in the air. So much so, that I smiled nonchalantly at the forecast for sandstorms and weather warnings as we set off. *How could that possibly be true when everything here is so sweet?*

It took three days to reach Ürümqi, setting off from Tulufan, and what a draining three days they were too. Of course, the weather warnings had materialised. Out of Tulufan we had thirty kilometres of fine cycling weather before everything changed. A howling wind funnelled its way in between the dunes, along the shingle rock and fiercely accelerated along the

167

road. We were stunted to walking through the interminable stony desert, barely able to hear each other through the howl of the eternal piston-blow of air. We spent almost 20 hours holed up in a highway police riot-equipment room, where the officers had agreed to shelter us when we turned up, bedraggled and grumpy. The next day we encroached on Ürümqi once the wind had died down a little. Police escorts and checkpoints once again besieged the city. It was no consolation to arrive in Xinjiang's capital. Here, a dullness and suspicion impested the air and hung weighty mass on each end of everybody's lips. It seemed everybody scuttled and nobody strolled. Entire areas of the modern city were deserted too. It strangely reminded me of Muong Lay – the shady town in Northern Vietnam. We arrived in Ürümqi for Eid al fitr. A new crescent moon hung solemnly in the night sky, signalling the end to Ramadan, that none of the Muslim-majority region seemed to have observed. Indeed, walking between the older districts of Ürümqi, under the ever-peeking eyes of surveillance, in between building sites and police boxes we noticed that the gates of all the mosques were chained shut.

After one night in the hostel of stiff interactions, where young African men were laid out on beds, tired from negotiating business and development deals in the region, we set our sights on leaving the city for the last 700 kilometres of China. It felt like it was almost over. 700 kilometres along one straight road all the way to the border was nothing. It was mostly flat but for one enormous climb to surmount just before the Kazakh border. The only thing, we reasoned, that could possibly make this difficult, was the police…

We slowly descended away from Ürümqi towards the northern flank of the Tien Shan that stretch westward all the way to Kyrgyzstan. Just as we were comfortably savouring the free early-evening breeze that rustled in the barley, as gentle waves rustle the shore, a checkpoint came into view. We were signalled to stop and present ourselves inside. The guard, with a focus unyielding to our boyish smiles, scrutinised our papers, We waited for ten minutes, then thirty minutes. An hour passed by. We squatted against the inside wall of the administrative building, reading our books. We were told that our unusual case had attracted one of their superiors who was presently coming to question us. In the meantime, we sat, stooped, incognito against the wall, observing the busloads of Chinese pass through. They were ushered through the metal detector as their travel documents and movements were checked and recorded. We wondered whether they were reassured by the checkpoint or whether, like us, they saw it as a thorn in the arse.

After one hour and a half, a Caucasian-looking man turned up, beaming. *This guy isn't Chinese*, I thought, as he shook our hands and began to speak to us.
"Hello my sirs, my name is Mark and I am here to drive us to the next town, fifty kilometres away," he beamed.
Charlie and I both shook his podgy hand.
"Nice to meet you Mark!" I began. "You do know that Charlie and I have to cycle though, right, and that we cannot accept a ride in your car?"
"Ah very strong very brave!" Mark replied with a slap on my back. "But why will you not come in the car?"
I simply repeated that we could not. Charlie on the other hand began explaining how for the last 23 years he had cycled through African savannahs, through the howling wind of Patagonia, the biting Arctic Frost, and dreadful British summers. He had made it through with no car. He could not begin now.
Somehow, this won Mark over who listened attentively to Charlie shooting off the names of such mythical places. He courteously agreed to escort us. I could sense that he was a good guy. I knew it. *If only the Chinese bachelor of Batu Pahat could see me now!*

We negotiated the fifty kilometres to 25 kilometres and tried his resolve as we asked to camp. Nothing was agreed on. After only five kilometres on the road, and thanks to all the dilly-dallying at the checkpoint, not only was the night drawing in, but a rainstorm was approaching. We signalled to him to stop and asked how far onwards we must go. He seemed confused and phoned up one of his colleagues. I spoke to him on the phone. His English was near perfect, clearly not a minion. He beseeched me to get in the car and was angry when I told him it was against my rules.

"Rules! what rules are you even talking about?" He burst.

I stifled a little giggle as I held the phone away from my mouth. He asked to speak to Mark once more, disappointed. We ran over the possibilities, which were all confused and nonsensical, surely on account of our own nonsensical behaviour. At the last checkpoint the police told us we could not stay there. It also transpired that it was, in fact, sixty kilometres to the next checkpoint, which seemed to be the only option. Mark then suggested that we could turn back. His mate told him to tell us to get in the car. Charlie wanted to turn back. Thunder rumbled in the distance. The situation was just a farce. I took back Mark's phone and attempted to convince the man on the other end that the strict security regime in Xinjiang was making life tricky for us, in situations that would have posed no difficulty in the rest of China, and contrarily, would have been met with support and hospitality. He was not interested and certainly not amused. Plump raindrops began to fall. Charlie and I shivered in impatience and indecision. Mark called three more of his colleagues and after a long conversation with much shouting, told us there was a place some ten kilometres ahead: a hotel. It seemed like the situation had resolved itself.

The rainstorm ride in the dark was euphoric (Charlie found it more grizzly than euphoric). Droplets punched through our conic bike lights and dripped from our noses. Mark stayed at our side in the car and leaned out of the window to tell bad jokes in English or to laugh at us. I savoured the change. Riding in the dark changes everything. The sense of speed through the passing of the landscape is all but lost. The legs turn and the bubble advances, but how much, is just a guess. The world is compressed to the single spotlight projected onto the road a few metres ahead. It is the carrot in front of the nose. The only guide. We pulled into a side street at the beginnings of a town, marked as usual by ranks of seemingly empty towering hi-rise buildings. The luxury four-star hotel was just on the right. We were relieved to be here. It was 11:00pm. We hadn't eaten. Mark offered to pay for our £70 room, to be billed to the Chinese police and the Chinese taxpayer. We thanked him and Charlie asked if he could add on the buffet breakfast for us. *Cheeky sod!* I thought. I thought better when I was stuffing my face with baozi and dumplings the next morning.

We broke fast with Mark, ever smiling and jolly, who never stopped knocking back and forth his jokes. He seemed happy to be doing his job and as he put it, "it's a great opportunity for me to make friends." I suppose that's one motivation for signing up to Chinese SWAT...

Mark was an exceptionally friendly cop out of the large number we encountered on our way to the border town of Khorgas. Not all were like that. I, in particular, ended up blowing my fuse on two occasions, ceding to the pressure that was completely, and ridiculously self-imposed. *The red line, unbroken.* The police also twice lost face with us, which was unusual for the Chinese. I am certain they found it to be the height of stupidity and unwarranted obstinacy that neither Charlie nor I accepted their kind and courteous offer of a lift, given the *'extreme danger'* that our lives were always in.

After emotional farewells to Mark, we found ourselves under the wing of new escorts. They were wholly disinterested and indifferent. They leapfrogged us from time to time. Waiting on the roadside for us to pass, overtaking us, driving into the distance, and repeating the process all the way through their jurisdiction. When I first entered Xinjiang, I felt pressure to cycle quickly when under escort. I was nervous to not keep

171

them waiting, didn't want to agitate them. Now, with Charlie, we almost rode as if they weren't there. We chatted, ambled, played trivia games and took stock of our surroundings: irrigated fields of cabbage, planted poplars, the Tien Shan always in the corner of our left eye. We even stopped for snacks, without a second thought to what our escorts would think.

Alas, our companions passed from friendliness, to indifference, to hostility. The officer of the next township of Kuytun was a very angry man, when he learnt that we were refusing the lifts. I dubbed him *Mr Potato head* or *Captain Morpheus,* for the man held an astonishing semblance to a root vegetable. He confiscated our passports after a long wait and screamed into the translate app, "This is the enforcement of the laws of the people's republic of China!"
I replied with a raised eyebrow, and a goading *ooohh*, like a kid indulged in playground antics. He did not like my reaction and began yelling in Chinese. I got visibly angry. Fortunately Charlie was on hand to quell my seething frustration. The cop got in his car and took us the long way round town. I worked hard on cooling my boiling blood. As we came to the end of the jurisdiction, we shook hands. He squeezed hard, as did I. We and our passports were then passed on to an officious woman who told us we must cycle another 50 kilometres and that we could not camp at her checkpoint. It was 08:00pm and we had 120 kilometres in our legs. She escorted us in her car to a shop in town at our request. It could be a long one, we sensed. We stocked up on essentials. Wusu beer, nuts and biscuits.

Over the next two hours we were passed between three different escorts. They each kept our passports and we followed them, blindly, dogs of our masters. The mood was light and the escorts, once again, disinterested. They were just doing their job. Everything fell into calm. The snow-dusted Tien Shan to the South leant forward from the lilac sky. Behind the mountains, a half moon hung like a knob of butter. The wind was on our backs and shimmied the leaves of the poplars flanking the road. Ahead, all was smooth and empty. The crisp whir of rubber rolling sang of steady progress. As a matted darkness crept in from the East, fast catching up with us, we began to wonder and question: *When would the game finish?* We were urged on by thoughts of a quiet campsite and the psht of the cracked wusu can. We didn't know when this moment would be. *Surely not long now.*

The night drew in and at around 11:00pm a young cop, freshly graduated, still dripping in the amniotic fluid of institutionalism, took over. We saw our chance and pressured him to let us camp. Anywhere! We were exhausted and fed up of being cajoled unfairly forward like packhorses. We beseeched him through Google translate time and again until finally, at about 11:30pm, he cracked. He agreed that we could sleep out, on the condition that he took photos of our exact whereabouts, to be decided by him. The day could soon end. We continued on through the dark until the cop stopped in the middle of nowhere. Crickets chirped but otherwise, silence. The land was cracked, exposed and festooned with prickly shrubs. Nothing was around for miles. His eye for comfortable campsites was substantially less trained than ours. "You camp here," he said, and took out his camera to record our whereabouts. Satisfied with his photos, he left to return to base. Charlie and I looked at each other, half tempted to ride on, but too knackered to be serious. We tramped over the shrubs to a patch of flat earth and lay out the mats under the star-speckled sky. We cooked noodles and finally, released from the grasp of the long arm of the law, cracked open a refreshing tinnie. At long last no cops! We had our passports back. We had food. We had water. We had beer. *Life couldn't be sweeter.* Exhausted, I fell asleep outside in the field. I must have dreamt I was back home, in a bed. Reaching over to my phone on my bedside table I felt only a crack in the chilly Earth. My eyes opened. The crickets hadn't stopped. The sky hadn't lightened. I became aware of a dull ache in my back and rolled onto my side, feeling the bumps of the earth beneath my roll-mat. Reality came into

173

focus. It was 04:30am. I was strewn outside in a dusty wasteland in Xinjiang, North West China. *What was I doing here?*

There can't be too much drama left now, Charlie and I thought, as we rode cop-free for the morning with only about 400 kilometres to go to the Kazakh border. It wasn't long before another checkpoint loomed on the horizon. I felt empty of checkpoint tolerance. *How many more were there?* We entered around midday. It began well, Nescafé and hot water provided as well as rice cakes and sweets. I recognised the psychological priming trick to make you feel that because you have already taken something, you should give back. I took what was on offer, keeping this firmly in my mind. One hour and a half later and we were still in negotiations with the checkpoint boss. A minibus had arrived which would escort us 150 kilometres down the road from where it was promised we could cycle to the border. We politely told the officer that we were not getting in and pulled out the usual phrases. This one was a tough cookie. He didn't care about Burmese roads or Australian cyclones or Charlie's lions in Africa or the rest of Xinjiang. Only, he insisted that the G30 highway was off limits. *Deep breath. Keep face. Remember that we have time.* Two hours was all he had in him, and eventually the minibus left, less two passengers, and we set off on the G30 with the officer's blessing.

On the G30 we were briefly accompanied by an unmarked car that left from the police station to escort us. We passed through the toll-booth to the shouts of the guard that faded slowly behind us. Charlie and I giggled like naughty children. It felt like we had ran rings around all the police of Xinjiang. After forty kilometres, at the next town, a plump middle-aged man smothered in lycra got out of a car to cycle with us. We put him through his paces and elongated our lunch break to the point that it was almost dinner time. "More tea Mr Escort?" I offered him a cup, before Charlie and I took our fifth. He stiffly shook his head and pointed at his watch with urgency. His loss. We reached a hotel in a small town at the end of the day. There was a single dusty square away from the main street, with a few restaurants and technology shops. Most of the shops had stairs descending to the entrance, below ground level. It was a place where people surely only ever passed through. It was almost impossible to imagine people actually living here. *What would they do?* I thought. It was the wild west. The shops bore the same yellow symbols on green or red backgrounds, as did those of the rest of China. Even as far back as Hekou town. That now felt like a different world, but it was the same country. I shuddered at this scale and how things like shop signs could remain constant over thousands of kilometres, while we had passed from the lush tropical jungle, over the Tibetan plateau and into the deserts of Xinjiang.

We walked into the ghost hotel. Here, our unwanted companion left us to check in. Despite moments of apparent friction throughout our ride together, there were handshakes and smiles. We bartered for a cheaper room and got settled. Charlie was in the shower and I flaked onto the bed. I was just about to let out my first sigh of relief when there was a knock at the door. *Room service? Forgotten the tea? Receptionist wants a selfie?* I opened the door to a squad of three police officers demanding to see our passports. My heart dropped in exacerbation. *Give us a break, will ya?* I readied myself for palaver. "You are foreign," noted the man heading the trio in the doorway. He stood with proud, pursed lips, swelling in perspicacity.

I praised his deductive prowess.

"You can't stay here," he continued.

I smiled scornfully and narrowed my eyes. "And why might that be, officer?"

"No foreigner in the hotel."

I was aghast. The escort with whom we had just amicably shook hands didn't seem to have a problem, and so the argument began.

"He was not a policeman," robotically quipped the officer's translate app.

I scoffed. "I'm pretty sure the fact he followed us in a car from the police checkpoint qualifies him as a policeman, don't you think?" I showed the Chinese translation of my voice to the three officers who all squinted to read my screen.

"Not police, travel agent. NO foreigners. Next hotel 70 kilometres." It was my phone against theirs. I was weary of these dealings. I finally broke face. With a trembling voice, I spoke into Google translate. "Look mate, we've been given grief for the last three days by your police pals, made to cycle to midnight, had our freedoms taken from us and now you come here telling us to move after a cop brought us here, can you not just leave us in peace!" Charlie, who had since got out of the shower to join the commotion, reminded me where we were and who I was talking to, and swiftly made me delete what I had just said, but the cop could tell from my voice what I was insinuating. I have never since talked to a phone with such passion.

"Then call the checkpoint and ask them. They will vouch for us, we are not moving on," my phone read in mechanical diction. Our interlocutor angrily shouted to his two apprentices who nodded in agreement. He whipped out another phone. His two apprentices stood, feckless, in the way. They were young and useless, like soft cabbages. The policeman ended the call and told us that the police know us. *No shit.* He then said we can stay and shook our hands, as quickly as that. But, just before leaving he stopped, and typed out one last thing.

"But the man was not police."

Gah!

Thinking about it now, our escort never did have police uniform or an official police car or a police badge. I had to close my eyes and accept what I didn't understand. I was becoming scared that the traverse of this province was making me into someone unrecognisable. Ostentatious, stubborn and short fused sprang to mind. *Was this me now?* It did seem that this was necessary for survival here, or at least to continue cycling: *the red line, unbroken.*

They *were* truly infuriating, these encounters, but paradoxically the shenanigans of Xinjiang were becoming so steeped in routine, that I was almost lamenting leaving this world behind. I had got a decent enough grasp of Chinese to get everything I needed, and the food, culture and customs had become rather familiar. The thought of everything changing in just a few days was almost as daunting as facing up to the bureaucratic faff that we surely faced in the nearer future.

In fact, the rest of the stretch to the border was surprisingly without escort. There were checkpoints, and the checkpoint police scrutinised us and interrogated us, but always let us go onwards. The last adventure of China was thanks to a more familiar enemy: pummelling headwind. The lungs of Aeolus emptied on us, as we tackled the 2000-metre ascent to Sayram lake. We were forced to leave the road and camp in the animal shed of an abandoned farmstead next to a pile of dried shit. It was the only non-exposed place. We didn't quite have enough food and water, but that was soon solved the following day. The last two days to the Kazakh border went quickly and surprisingly unceremoniously. We descended the impossibly green Illi valley. Touristic yurts appeared as the Chinese prelude to central Asia. We breezed past lavender fields and on, on, on to the border! Khorgas! The kilometres of China had almost run out. The limits of the middle kingdom loomed ahead. The red trucks made their way to the border post along side us. They hadn't been absent from start to finish. The x-ray machines of the border post must have eaten them because when we passed from China to Kazakhstan, they were no longer to be seen. Everything changed. Our phones were scanned for incriminating videos at the smart and modern building, the last of China. We moved on and passed through the ramshackle Kazakhstan border post with ease. "Welcome to Kazakhstan!"

Kazakhstan! Yes! We emerged on the other side. The road in front of us was empty. Gone were the nondescript lego towers of deserted Chinese towns. Sand dunes bordered each side of the strip of concrete that was like the horizon's outstretched tongue. You could have heard even a whisper, were there a creature around to stifle one. China was behind. All 5500 kilometres of it traced beneath the wheels of a bicycle. Charlie and I sailed onwards towards Zharkhent and I welled with pride at having taken down the largest country of the trip for which I was so terribly, terribly nervous.

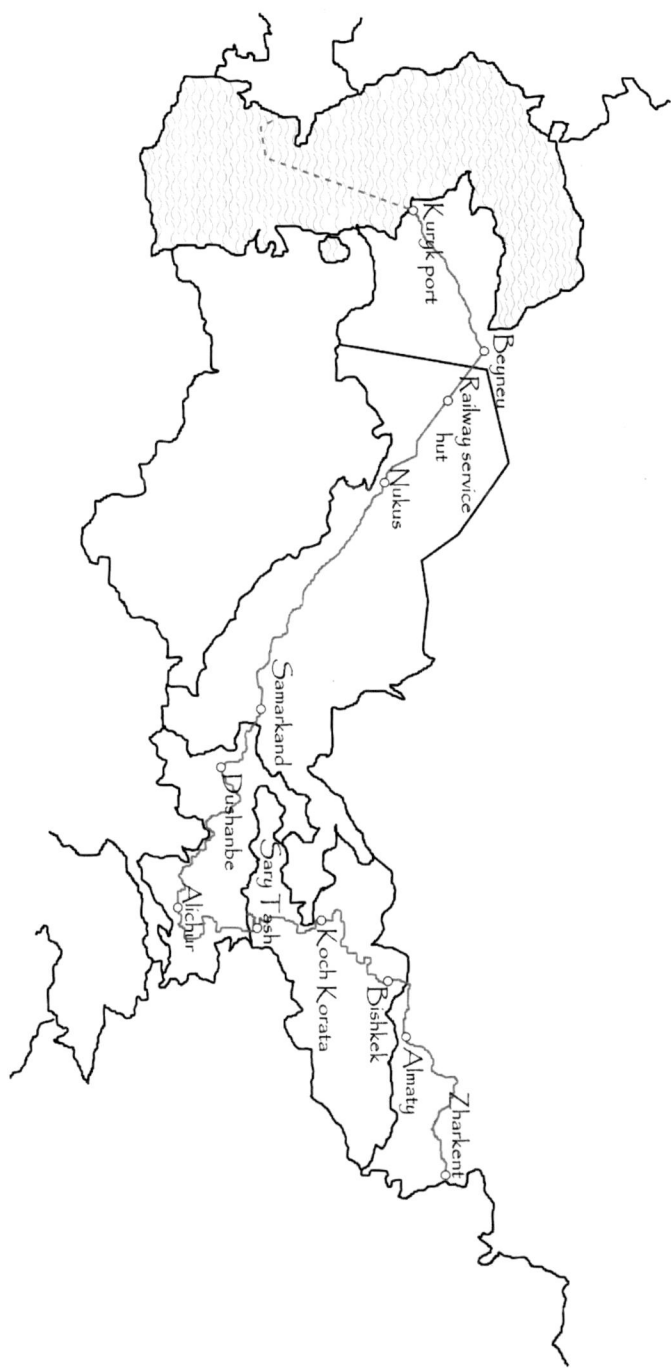

Kuryk port

Beyneu

Railway service hut

Nukus

Samarkand

Dushanbe

Sary Tash

Alichur

Koch Korata

Bishkek

Almaty

Zharkent

Freedom

On The four days to Almaty – Kazakhstan's major city, I felt unrestrained and free, like a dog let off its lead. With the last 1500 kilometres through Xinjiang being bordered almost the entire way with barbed wire fencing, the open prairies and hills and mountains of South East Kazakhstan that stretched boundless to the horizon took my breath along with them. Then, there was the cycling, the camping, the scenery and the people. All were joyous. The restored sense of freedom was tangible. It was the walk onto the grass to find shade for a siesta, or to the clear water of a stream for a drink. When I organised the trip, I had no intention of visiting Kazakhstan, but two days in, I sure was glad that very little has gone according to plan.

The route that Charlie and I had planned was by no means the most direct. It avoided the major highway linking the border town of Zharkent to Kazakhstan's main city of Almaty and instead crept through the steady expanses of Altyn Emyl national park. We sped through a spattering of civilisation tailing away from Zharkent before reaching Altyn's open plains. The empty road beckoned, the meandering strip inviting excitement. Steadily upwards we rose, towards the distant fineline forms of the mountains drawn faintly at the base of the blue sky matted with ambling clouds. Not a car in sight. Just the bicycles steadily rising through wavy rocks rayed in shades of greys, creams and oranges that dampened off towards the horizon. We crossed a stream gurgling and burbling discreetly through the dryness. Wiry shrubs now decorated the roadside instead of Xinjiang's wiry fence. Freedom expounded. We were in central Asia. Kazakhstan! A climb transported us from musty shrub-land, up through lush grassy moguls dappled with purple flowers against a crepuscular skyglow. Here, for the tourists, was a roadside establishment proffering tea and *shashlik*. We were both enamoured by the unexpected conditions that were grinning upon us. I stopped to chat to an ageing man in an even more ageing maroon saloon. "karabala tushniya lakanya pit gorushney," or something that sounded similar was said.

"Ah I see," I replied. "It's very beautiful around here isn't it?" I asked, not expecting a response. Cocked head. Something else unintelligible. The man then took the key from his ignition, and curled off the charm from the ring and put it into my hands with a hearty smile.

"Wow, are you sure?"

"Mozhesti koblents schistleeva puti mala" He said. I understood nothing but his encouraging smile, and took the gift and attached it the only key I owned, lodged in my bike lock. I finally had the perfect souvenir that I had dreamed of on the hills of Northern Thailand.

The scenery seemed to beautify with each kilometre and I was almost disappointed when the sun shod the last of its light for the day. We camped a short walk from the empty road, nowhere special, nowhere secluded. Nowhere else would I rather have been. We performed our evening ritual with great satisfaction. *Find a flat spot. No bumps, ok: plant tent. Strip the bike of the panniers, change clothes. Sleeping bag strewn out carelessly, will arrange later. Carry kitchen bag over to other flat spot with roll mat. Take out pasta, dill, jar of tomato sauce, salami. Run back to tent because I forgot the water. Return and fire up the stove. Crack open beer with Charlie. Stir the pasta. Eat and recline.*

The following day, the scenery grew even sweeter, long green grass sprouted. The wildflowers proliferated, inviting the eye to ogle their vibrant yellows and purples spangled amongst the encroaching slopes. The road itself passed through rising tetrahedral forms, whose rocky shoulders burst from their grassy cladding. For the first 40 kilometres of the day, a perfect tailwind cupped and whistled us along. Already Xinjiang and China and everything that was before it dissolved into an imposturous dream.

On the final stretch of the day an orange form appeared in the distance, like Charlie and I, ambling. As it approached I discerned with excitement the steady motion of another touring bicycle! Francisco greeted us with warmth. He looked battered, with mud-caked t-shirt and baggy shorts falling around his knees, but he exuded a grim joy. Three months previously he had been in his home in Italy. He had ridden only 100 kilometres a day to meet us here, at the Eastern extreme of Kazakhstan. Italy! Three months! The time scale shocked me. I hadn't thought about distance to home in quite some time but after our brief meeting (an evening storm was brewing and we were all keen to move on to sheltered camping spots). I began considering these implications. Europe was no longer a million miles away. Home was no longer an abstract memory. I realised in excitement and melancholy that I had probably already done over half of what I had set out to do.

The brewing storm intensified. Charlie worked himself into an angry state when we didn't stop soon enough to find a good campsite. I didn't mind too much and the rift of our sentiments towards light rage and indifference respectively pissed me off, although I tried not to let it show. We settled for a reasonable spot amongst bushy grass growing between poplars that separated colza fields. Charlie put up his tent in a huff while I remained silent and tried as best as I could to let the storm pass… Rumblings intensified. The sky darkened and lowered itself oppressively. *Pitter.* We retired to our canvas shells without conversation. *Patter.* We rested for twenty minutes and by the time the storm had passed, reconciliation was found over the psht of a beer. Charlie and I were probably going to go separate ways in Almaty so it was stupid to let a little spat come between our relationship that had thus far been so smooth.

At Sary-Ozek we left the infinitude of the small national park (relative to the enormous size of the World's ninth largest country, that is) behind us. The highway brusquely took over and ploughed directly towards Almaty. I was optimistic that perhaps we could make it in a day. *What was 170 kilometres compared to our traverse of China?!* Still high on the massive distances that were regularly smashed out under police-company in Xinjiang, I found myself tapping my forearm gagging for more. Undaunted, I wanted to feel the Earth's curve beneath my wheels. *The fleeting nomad!*

As the road reared on a climb's summit, a change suddenly became apparent. Astraddle the top-tube, I turned to Charlie to see his familiar grim gurn that always accompanied these conditions. Nasty headwind. Cars whooshed past, their following draft billowing through my loose, sweaty shirt. I squinted my eyes beneath my sunglasses.

"Bit rough eh," I posited, receiving a look from Charlie that told me to mention no more.

"Let's take five then crack on," he said.

The wind intensified throughout the day, buffeting us and eventually culling the day when a turn off to a beach by the Kapchagay reservoir presented itself.

It seemed that we had landed in the unlikely Cleethorpes of Kazakhstan. Pot-bellied men stood shirtless outside beach-huts barbecuing shashlik while severe-looking women sat or squatted in semi-circles, gossiping and pointing to their men and what they were doing wrong. Kids ran around and tumbled in the sand. The older boys showed off to girls by spinning donuts in the sand on their dirt-bikes. The girls giggled amongst themselves, mocking, rightfully. Right on the busy beach was an abandoned storage hut and I asked a nearby stall owner if we could sleep there. I'm pretty sure she said something along the lines of: *nobody here gives a shit, the world is your bedroom, take a pick, boys!* We chatted a short while over Google translate and she invited us to come for breakfast the next morning. She tutted that charming Kazakh tut when we told her a few of our stories. The Kazakh tut is always masked behind a half smile and a subtle shake of the head as if to say: *ah, you're nuts.* In contrary to the British tut of snobbery and contempt, this was a tut of respect. It was adorable. Settled into our cosy abode for the night, there was only one outstanding task left…The water of the lake was fresh and we swam away the crass that had gathered on our bodies, before holing up for the night as the classic evening thunderstorm finally materialised. The masses extradited themselves from the beach leaving it barren, and the winds whipped up the shallows as waves licked the shore. One more sleep to Almaty.

Although ninety kilometres of tarmac separated our abandoned beach store by the lapping waters of Kapchagay reservoir from Almaty, I had already mentally transported myself to the city: a real danger for cycle tourists. Mental teleportations do nothing to quell the real distance that remains, and I suffered more over these kilometres than any of the larger days in China. I had told myself in my head *ninety kilometres is nothing.* But it isn't. It's not for waking early that dawn comes quicker. Each of the hours of this day was spent in a mindset akin to waiting. I kept surprising myself that I wasn't there yet. It is the same fallacy as looking inside an oven to make food cook faster. It doesn't work. So, after a full day looking into Almaty's oven, my body finally caught up with where my mind was already set. *Almaty! Apple city! Europe?* From dusty peripheral towns, suddenly, great sentinel trees began to line the smart arteries into the city. The knobbly tarmac was sheened over, and brick buildings were replaced by polished concrete; clinking Ladas and Kamaz trucks by sleek Japanese or European designs, dust and brass by green and glass. Charlie and I checked into a hostel where nobody could speak English. Although there were few words that I could exchange with the *babushka* that ran the place, it was made very clear to me that I should immediately shower and wash all of my clothes or I was to get back onto the street and find another bloody bed! She wasn't over-reacting. Between Charlie and I, we caused quite a stink. My panniers were caked in the filth of thousands of kilometres, my shoes not much better, and whereas the road and I were indifferent to the consequences of socks being worn five days in a row, plump Kazakh hostel owners certainly were not.

Our roomies were also not the travelling sort. They were all of central Asian or Russian descent, and appeared to be lodging here while working jobs in the city, some were seemingly permanently more settled than others and it led me to wonder if some degree of tramping culture existed here, like the famous paragons from Orwell's 'Down and Out in Paris and London'. This line of thought was soon halted when I realised that while settlements in the UK are seldom separated by more than a dozen kilometres, here, Steppe that stretches hundreds of kilometres can separate civilization! They were probably just for the cheap accommodation.

The following day I contacted a Japanese traveller I had met back in Mai-Sot, just after returning to Thailand from Burma. Chizru was full of jovial energy and had since hitchhiked across China to finish up in Almaty working at a hostel. I agreed to meet her that very evening to celebrate my catching up with her with a *cognacsha,* that as the reader may imagine, somewhat entails the copious drinking of cognac. I had initially been discouraged from heading to Chizru's hostel due to the considerable three-kilometre-long incline that leads up to it: which was rather daft since I had just cycled about 12,000 to make it to Almaty in the first place! Nonetheless, once there, it became apparent that this was the hub for rich-country travellers in Almaty. Europeans, Americans and Japanese folk lounged about on comfortable sofas, while a young Kazakh woman – Aigerim, who spoke perfect English with great wit and a charming smile, lazed behind the reception desk, intermittently replying to e-mails and joining the *cognacsha.* I spent the evening there, ran tipsily back to the workers' hostel and in the morning implored Charlie to move with me up the road to where we both wouldn't stick out like sore and smelly thumbs.

The rest of my memories of Almaty are of self-sure blue skies, bursting green trees, and pseudo-summer days spent with Charlie, Chizru, two other British cyclists: Dante and Luke (who were about to embark in the direction of the Karakorum highway: the highest international highway linking the Far West of Xinjiang to Gilgit Baltistan in Northern Pakistan) and Aigerim, for whom my fondness didn't cease to grow. Out of all the inevitably ephemeral connections that the road is paved of, fleeting moments of bonds none less the strong, gasps of still normalcy amidst life in motion: it was the one with Aigerim to which I most wanted to cling. I thought back to Almaty, city of apples, for weeks, after leaving it behind with Dante and Luke in the direction of Bishkek.

On the last morning of the five days spent in the city, it also meant it was finally time to bid Charlie farewell. Riding in his company had been joyous and enlightening. It is so typical that with age grows cynicism, yet Charlie remained refreshingly optimistic about the future of humanity. "People are fatter, more comfortable and better off than they ever have been," he would say. For a man who has visited and revisited some of the most obscure and indeed troubled regions of the planet, I found great solace in his affirmation that the quality of life for many people was mostly improving. Through the mundane, banal and odd punctuation of excitement that is the general epitome of cycle touring, I felt truly grateful for his company, for it stopped me getting too sick of my own. Over the high mountain passes of the Kunlun, to the long stretches of dull desert in Xinjiang where we entertained each with trivia or through being cheeky to SWAT officers, to the evenings at camp where I would be consistently beaten at cribbage: we had been through a lot together. We were ultimately an unlikely pair: a wise balding old man with encyclopaedic knowledge of much of the world, and me, on my first voyage, the apprentice. It worked. I doubt I would have made it through Xinjiang on an unbroken red line without him. We gave each other a hug outside the hostel, and

186

the red line bifurcated, his in the direction of Charyn canyon, and mine towards Kyrgyzstan.

The Fleeting nomad

Luke and Dante had a deadline in Bishkek and so we arrived at the Kyrgyz capital after only one and a half days. We whizzed by the border to a cheery "Welcome to Kyrgyzstan!" The boys were to fly to Osh, a 45-minute jaunt on a dodgy ex-Soviet plane, whereas this section was to take me an entire week. In Bishkek I took a couple more days off, organised my Tajik e-Visa and bought a cheap and bulky but thick sleeping bag from an army surplus shop. I was still slightly traumatised from my experience camping in minus five on the Tibetan plateau with a Decathlon premier prix sleeping bag. I was heading up into high mountain Asia and I didn't want to be caught short. I found extra spares for the bike for the event of everything going tits up in the remote regions where I was headed.

In China, foreign travellers had all but disappeared. Only once, in Chengdu, did I meet another European other than Charlie. Now, on the other side, the European *ferenghi* were of a completely different ilk to those found in South East Asia. Gone were the purposeless and faceless youth, searching for their souls in buckets of spirit at full-moon parties. They were replaced by the gentler, steadier and more wholesome traveller: one that I instantly identified more strongly with. The travellers of central Asia were my people. The all-in-it-togetherness that I saw and had envied so much amongst the Australian backpackers is what I felt here. Everyone was an open book and had fascinating stories and shared them with mirth. I made the acquaintance of Abi, who was beginning fieldwork to study snow leopards in the Tian Shan. I dined with Ian: an eccentric old chap with a permanent glint in his eye taking leave from his husband who was roaming in Vietnam. I met a Siberian girl who mysteriously spent time between Moscow, Dubai, Bishkek and her harsh homeland. Finally, I spoke with Mahabat: another Asian with dreams to travel to Europe, blocked by the steep but slowly decaying slope of global inequality. I left Bishkek having formed and broken off yet more short-lived but intense friendships with folk at the hostel. As soon as I took to the road out of the city, I became aware of gaping hole in the shape of frustrated loneliness.

I was now, for the first time in a long time, forlorn and shod of company. I felt naked and vulnerable, like a snake, moulted and writhing. My only consolation was that I had a goal on which to focus: slither to Osh in seven days. It wasn't long before my spirits lightened, on discovering that ice cream here costs about 15 pence. This would make life far easier, as already, the temperature was creeping back up to mid to high thirties. It was midsummer in the Northern hemisphere.

Kyrgyzstan has been dubbed 'the Switzerland of Central Asia' for its green pastures, grand snow-clad peaks and blustering rivers. It felt so much vaster than Switzerland. It is compact with mountains and so almost all of the roads, most of which are unpaved soviet era tracks, wind their way between the peaks or along ravines or contour the lakes and reservoirs. As a result, the 300 kilometres direct distance to Osh was in fact 670 kilometres on the road that twisted on all scales and all directions, including vertically.

In the midst of lonesomeness, I needed a new companion, an imaginary friend of any ridiculous degree of abstraction. It took the form of pig-headed focus and led me to streamline my way through much of Kyrgyzstan, blurring the edges of some of the most breath-taking landscapes I had ever seen, inhabited by some of the kindest, proud and warm-hearted folk. Indeed, on most days spent amongst the lush abundance of nature, I was given gifts of food and hospitality by jovial families, merchants, nomads, farmers and even a French speaking army officer, who had served in the Legion Étranger Française.

The road began its ascent into the mountains gently. It split through fields of wheat and colza benefiting from the devises of irrigation redirecting the waters of the Tian Shan: the mountain range that I had followed since Xinjiang and now had to cross. It was an immediate ascent up to 3500m, followed by a valley switcheroo and another pass at 3150m. These altitudes may seem high, but by Tian Shan standards they are but mounds. Only 500 kilometres away, at the Kazakh-Kyrgyz-Chinese tri-border-point are the formidable Khan Tengri and Jengish Chokusu at over 7000 m. It took 24 hours from leaving Bishkek to reach the first culminating point: a tunnel that cut through the mountain at 3500 m. I had spent the previous night snuggled away alongside a trickling beck in which a small pool served as a bathtub. The cleanse was made completely redundant the following morning as the heat didn't tarry to build and I was soon, once again, oh-so familiarly sweating and gurning and churning my way up the humbling gradients. At one point I saw a truck, clinging precariously to the hillside some 600m above my head and snorted in bemusement at how on earth it had got up there. I soon realised that I too was bound that way upwards.

The 'summit' tunnel was ill-ventilated, dark, murky, dusty and narrow: essentially a death trap for cyclists. Barely stopping to catch breath, I chanced my way through. I was suddenly suffocated. *Shit this is not cool,* I thought. Dappled headlights emerged from the black stillness like tigers from the jungle. Tiger, Tiger burning bright... *Head down. Make it through. Light at the end! Whew.* I emerged in a tear of light and steered to the gravelled layby to let my eyes re-adjust. I marvelled at my new world. The tight valley road that the hairpins had just guided me through was replaced by an epic expanse of grasslands, with another offset branch of the Tian Shan lining the entire horizon. Green to brown to perfect white, blanketing the rank of perky peaks. The descent took me once more into a gentle valley, speckled with yurts and stands selling Kumus and

Kurut and occasionally Bish Barmak (meaning five fingers, an allusion to the tools used for eating it) and Kuurdak (essentially a vegetarian's nightmare). Horses, whose fore legs were bound together by rope, hopped hopelessly around the encampments from which young kids waved and shouted. It was evident towards the end of the day that I couldn't make it over the second pass that I was steadily and tiredly climbing. As all the grassland around was already taken by happy campers in their yurts, I was obliged to ask a family to share a pitch.

I spotted a chubby old man milling around, watching the hopping horses. "Do you think I'd be alright putting my tent up here mate?" I inquired.
"Of course pal mek yoursen at home," he replied to me in a thick Yorkshire accent. Of course, my imagination was just getting the better off me. Although he did say something that sounded affirmative in that guttural yet somehow fluid Kyrgyz tongue. As I put up my tent alongside their comparatively palatial ensemble of three yurts, the elder proceeded to eye up my bike and take it for a spin. I first thought he might be drunk but as it turns out he was just very excited. After an evening spent playing football (oh universal bond-maker!) with the kids, I slept soundly in my new community before being invited into the main yurt the following morning for breakfast. My first look inside a *proper* one!

The yurt is *the* icon of Kyrgyzstan. Indeed, one need only look at the national flag and realise that in the centre of the yellow sun set to a red background, is the depiction of the top cover of a yurt. The whole flag is meant to show that the sun is often the first thing that a person sleeping in a yurt will see on a given day. Inside, mats and covers of rich reds, blues and gold adorned the whole space, giving it a truly majestic feel. It could have been a room in a Taj Mahal rather than a tent in the grasslands between two branches of the Tian Shan. Bish Barmak was on the menu, as well as bread and assortment of jams and what I guessed was creamy horse butter. Once I smacked my lips and proclaimed, "Full! Full!", the eldest man took me outside to slap a leather bracelet onto my wrist. *I need to return some favours*, I thought, and noticing how my Kyrgyz bracelet now clashed horribly with my Laotian one, I removed the latter and set out to find the daughter. I handed her the bracelet with nonchalance, but the Father, now almost in tears, clasped his hands and shook them to the air, with a "Rakhmat, rakhmat, rakhmat!" The daughter attached the bracelet with a smile and the mother looked on as if I were her new son. I had a moment where I realised that this may actually be what I was setting myself up for and with a quick doff of my helmet I swiftly but politely scarpered back onto the road, before the engagement could be confirmed.

The second pass was easily reached by the end of the morning (it is surprising how warm it still was even above 3000 m) that led to a stunning non-stop descent of over 70 kilometres. *Ah to be on the right side of gravity!* The road levelled off at Toktogul reservoir, whose water was the purest crystalline cyan that one could imagine. It sat snug between a splendid set of spindly hills whose ridges looked more like wrinkles and it was easier to imagine them carved out of wood than rock. A huge pipe ran along the perimeter, by the roadside. On one of the further edges of the reservoir I spied a chap with an enormous Kyrgyz *kalpak* squatting on this girthy pipe and making the most of a crack in the structure from which a fountain of water was wildly spurting. He appeared to be filling bottles. Taking a look down at my own, I decided I might join him. Having set my bike aside I hobbled along the slippery pipe and squatted clumsily alongside him, balancing on the toes whereas he had his feet comfortably planted. "Mozhna pit da?" I tried my Russian.
"Mozhna!" He affirmed and followed up with a bicycling gesture.
"Da," I nodded, "iz Singapore, v Anglia!"
He jumped from his perch and rushed to my bike excitedly before taking it for a customary spin up and down the road. I winced and recoiled as he almost fell while turning, but I just

couldn't resist the ridiculous image of his goofy smile in the shade of a 50 cm-high felt cap rumbling towards me. I filled up my bottles from the crack in the pipe, and, perhaps naively unphased by the brown flecks floating in it, proceeded to down the lot before plodding onwards. First, to Karakol, where I camped by the Naryn River, then onwards towards Koch-Korata where I broke into the fertile flatlands under a blazing sky, by the Uzbek border. Shaded stands were set up by the roadside where folk, like ants, scurried and scampered, carrying and packing melons, squashes, apricots and tomatoes. I asked a farmer to camp in his apricot orchard to which he agreed. I slept under the branches bearing an abundance of ripe fruit. Breakfast was already made.

In the morning, I awoke to a queasy feeling in my stomach. *Uh-oh.* I tried to stomach some of the apricots, which I managed, but hardly with an appetite. I wheeled my bike back to the road and soon make it to Koch-Korata where I sat at a table and ordered whatever the chap next to me was eating: some sort of vegetable potage with a generous helping of bread. It didn't take long for my stomach to cause me to rise in a panic and urgently cry out, "Tualet, tualet, suu suu, please!" I was pointed across the road to the bustling bazaar, in full swing.

As I hurriedly and worriedly waddled over there, a young guy stopped me.
"Hey where you are from?"
"It doesn't matter where I am from, what matters is that I am imminently going to shit myself!" He nodded and led me to the toilet. *Closed. Shit.* "Come with me," he said gravely. With a leap, he sprinted into the crowd ogling the stacked apricots and spices and danced and swished his way through the great unwashed. I gave chase. We arrived at toilet number two, again closed. "No!" He peeped in anguish. "Ok come my brother," and with a skip and a jump he immersed himself once more amongst the people, now examining showerheads and light switches. He threw a headscarf-clad old woman into a crate of

hose clips and swept the legs of a five-year-old kid merrily canoodling a tattered old toy set, before head-butting a protesting vendor who wasn't even in the way to make way for my emergency. We made it to toilet three, which was mercifully open. When I came back out, he was smiling victoriously and slapped me on the shoulder before explaining who he was. "I am the messiah..." he began. But he didn't really. He introduced himself as Tony and told me he wanted to show me around his town and go swimming with me.

"Alrigh then young man", I replied, "why not!"

It turned out this 18-year-old was a bright beacon of humanity. His light-heartedness, love of his town and desire to share this with foreigners (in line with him moving to China to study tourism) lit up my day. I left him and his mother, who had one of the kindest faces I have ever seen, before hitting the road again on a still upset stomach. The surface deteriorated and I spent sixty kilometres cycling and walking on the dirt at the side of the tarmac because it was better than the tarmac itself that looked like it had been hand-crafted by an army of drunken chimps.

On the last climb of the day I finally vomited before trying to stomach some wafers and camping outside the mosque of a minute village, seventy kilometres from Osh. I was laid in my sleeping bag as the call to prayer of the evening began and a couple of mosque-goers came to gander at the oddity of a curled-up human sleeping in the forecourt. They laughed at my expense and even passed me some almost rotten fruit that I was forced to eat out of politeness.

The next day, still feeling a little light headed, I set out for my victory run into Osh. The temperature had cooled considerably from cloud cover and just after midday I finally passed into Kyrgyzstan's second city. Osh! My mission here was to find a 'hostel with a palindrome name' a riddle that some friends back home had set for me over a month ago. Konok hostel fitted the bill, and I entered proclaiming, "I am Jake Johnson, and I think something here is waiting for me…" The confused hostel-worker got up from playing with her baby and turned on Google Translate. She had no idea who I was but I was welcome to a room. I tried to explain that my friends had sent something here, for me.

"Jake Johnson, you know!"

She didn't know. I thought that perhaps this was a sick prank pulled by my witty 'friends' back home. I took a room here anyway and each day asked whether my parcel had arrived. The woman remained just as confused until the end of my stay, clearly thinking I was crazy. A month later I received a picture of a letter, a jar of marmite, an ankle-reflector and a ten-dollar bill.

"I can only send by Whatsapp", the message read. I asked whether the letter, at the very least, could be sent on. She said that it couldn't. I resigned myself to never seeing any of it, left only with the hope that she knew that marmite was for eating, and not for filling holes in plasterboards.

While in Osh, I began taking the final measures to prepare myself for the Pamir highway of Tajikistan. I scooted backwards and forwards to the bazaar, scowling in shadowy tool-boxes for spare bike parts. I visited money vendors to retrieve Tajik Somoni, as I was told that banks in Eastern Tajikistan didn't exist. It seemed all details were taken care of. I had even received my Tajik e-Visa, an official looking document, complete with an emoji and in place of my face (the photo of which I had omitted to send on my application) an anonymous silhouette like some weirdo on Facebook. It was time to check in to Tajikistan.

Ladder to the roof of the world

In Osh I also spent time shaking off the illness that was niggling away at me, draining energy and motivation. At the same time, an ever-growing keenness to get home was growing. It pressed me softly to fast-track my way through the rest of Central Asia, and to hop leap and jump over Europe back to the rolling green hills of my patria! I was missing structure, peer pressure, friends, lasting complicities that I could touch rather than occasionally reach on the other end of a phone call. I missed not having to constantly meet and leave great people. How bittersweet! Meanwhile, the attractive force of the Pamir Mountains was at work, counterbalancing my thoughts of homeward bound. The reputation of *the roof of the world* acted as a magnet for cycle tourists worldwide. Of those I had met on the road, heading East and South, almost all held this arid land of snow and rock in godlike esteem. I had the visa. I had bought all the gear, and I would have almost certainly kicked myself if I forewent the chance to see for myself, being so close.

With this in mind, feeling in relatively good form after four days in Osh, I took the road up Thankful Pass, 3600m high. I was bloody thankful too when I got to the top in the freezing rain. When the road departed from the river and began to twist up to the mountains, the gradient had become too much. I dismounted, dismayed that I didn't have the strength to cycle on. I was sure I had cycled up far steeper. I resolved to push for one kilometre, then cycle for two, push for one, cycle for two, until the summit ten kilometres later. Every time I tried to cycle on, my legs were squeezed of all their motion, and I never managed more than a few hundred metres at once. I trudged seven kilometres to the top and with two kilometres to go, the heavens opened. I rounded the final corner on foot and mounted to cycle the last few hundred metres. I bowed my head under the clips of the rain, gnashing my teeth. The thing I least expected to see at the col, under such grizzly and bone-chilling conditions, were people. But I met some there nonetheless. What I found atop the climb in such dismal conditions was simply heart-breaking.

Two small girls approached me, cheeks scorched red by the sun at this altitude, clothes tattered and faces certainly not happy. They each gave me a yellow flower, then I think they asked for money or chocolate. I asked them where they were going and they couldn't answer. It was evident that the parents had left them up here to beg for money from the truckers, drivers and odd cyclist who stop at the top to admire the immense vista. It was freezing. Icy rain blew in sheets across the pass, striking the girls on their cheeks. I felt terribly sorry for them but had an even greater reservation that giving them money would make the parents continue to condemn them to begging on the pass. On the other hand, perhaps it is the best, and maybe only way for a poor family up here to gain money or supplies. I half-reluctantly handed them all my walnuts as a compromise, wishing them somehow a way out.

Child labour was common in South Kyrgyzstan and these two girls weren't in a standout exceptionally poor situation. I thought back to Osh, when myself, two Poles and two Kyrgyz visited a garage. It was ran by an eleven year old, who sat outside on a chair leafing through bills of cash. The Lada car we were riding in was fixed by a seven-year-old, probably the boss's younger brother. *But when the labour is begging up on a mountain pass... ah sigh.* I was too exhausted to mull this over more and I took an obligatory top-of-pass photo. I couldn't even hack a smile.

That very evening, I arrived in Sary Tash, an ominously quiet crossroad village. To the North is the road back to Osh. West is the Alay road to Dushanbe, cutting north of the Pamirs and into

Tajikistan, but where the border is closed to foreigners. East is Irkeshtam pass, towards Kashgar, Xinjiang, and South is where I was bound: the Kyzyl art pass at just under 4300 m towards Karakul, Tajikistan. In this direction, the bases of the Northern flank of the towering Pamirs rise up from the creeping purple-green tallis. The mountain bodies were cloaked in thick cloud as I descended into the village, but even so, I felt taken back by the immensity of what lay behind.

For the next couple of days, the mountains of the trans-Alay were shrouded in cloud and intermittent storms, not exactly conducive to climbing the pass. With that in mind I opted to visit the base camp of Peak Lenin and sleep there for one night to acclimatise. Sary Tash was at 3300m, and the base camp at 3600 m. After this, I would camp on the South road just before the pass at about 3800 m, in two nights time. The clouds were set to clear by this point. I had visions of waking there in the morning to a crisp blue sky. It was this window I would take to climb the pass.

I awoke from a comfortable night in a Sary Tash guest house to a sparse cloud covering, and although Peak Lenin, towering over 7000 m tall was still not visible, the mountains directly to the South were fully on show. The snowline drew a jagged trace that mimicked the shapes of the real peaks towering a thousand metres or more above. The wall of rock and ice seemed impenetrable and I tried to work out where on Earth a road would even begin to try to pick its way through, with little success. I stood on the grass, appraising, incredulous, transfixed on vast unmovable might. A tall order it was indeed. I sipped the last of a tart and sour kumus before taking to the road to Sary Mogul from where a network of tracks sprouted towards the basecamp, some 80 kilometres away.

The settlement of Sary Mogul seemed even less well off than Sary Tash, although marginally larger. Mud-brick walls supported flimsy tin roofs, children shouted

"Hey you! Money, money!" and a couple of small grocery shops were operating from the interior of shipping containers. I sat outside one of these licking a 20 p ice cream when a couple of kids approached.

"Chocolate, chocolate, money, mister!" They rubbed thumb against forefinger. I offered them a bite of an ice cream that one of them grabbed before scuttling out of sight. "I see."

Equipped with a nasty-looking sausage, a naan, a few tomatoes and 4 litres of water, I turned South onto the tallis from which the distant peaks rose. From this road, the immensity of the Alay valley became clear. Nothing, and I mean *nothing* was around for dozens of kilometres, other than the modest Sary Mogul and the parallel spans of the Alay mountains and the Pamirs on either side of the valley that I felt would never end. I spent the night by the yurt encampment here at the confluence of tallis and mountain foot. The evening light from behind the thinning clouds mellowed the deep purple of the foothills that seeped from beneath the snowline. More and more of Lenin was becoming visible, but it wasn't until the morning after, when I woke at 3600m and descended back down towards Sary Mogul that I finally got a view of the peak, nestled above a line of clouds that covered the lower mountains. Immensity!

By midday, I had arrived back in Sary Tash, content with my sleep at 3600 m. I needed only to replenish myself with a final meal in Kyrgyzstan, pack food for the next 100 kilometres, take a deep breath, and cycle into the Pamir Mountains.

In the Kafesi, where I was sullenly sat, taking in my final Kyrgyz calories, I was startled by the voice of what was clearly an American. I hadn't expected to see one of those here! Anthony sat down opposite me and began to explain that he too was cycling in the region. Alas, humble Anthony was doing far more than cycling in the region. "Have you heard of Kyle Dempster?" He asked me. As it turned out, I had heard of Kyle Dempster. He was an American adventurer who had created a fantastic short travel documentary detailing his solo trip cycling off the beaten track in Kyrgyzstan with a bag of climbing gear, to tackle some first ascents in the Tian Shan. This video counted amongst those that inspired me to take my own bicycle across the Eurasian landmass. As it turned out, Kyle was also a massive inspiration for Anthony. Beyond that, Anthony was a recipient of the Kyle Dempster solo adventure award and was carrying the flame of Kyle's passion for the spirit of unwashed and untainted adventure. The inspiration drawn from Kyle Dempster and others in the adventure community had led Anthony to chuck a pair of skis on his bike, that he was cycling towards two 7000 m+ peaks in Xinjiang and Pakistan. His goal was to climb up and ski down. As if that wasn't enough, his final destination was Manaslu, the eighth highest peak in the world that he was planning to summit solo, without supplemental oxygen, before once more skiing down. He downplayed this in emphatic modesty, but without realising it, he suddenly inspired me to rouse myself from my rut, and to face the Pamirs with a renewed sense of motivation for meeting blindly the unexpected. After a couple of hours with Anthony in his guesthouse, weathering out a rainstorm, I leapt to my saddle and charged onwards down the South road. Murghab 220 kilometres. Khorog 540 kilometres. My next two towns. *Bring it on.*

Vertigo

The very next morning I poked my head out of the tent, perched at 3700 m in the no-man's land between Kyrgyzstan and Tajikistan, five kilometres after the Kyrgyz border. My plan to tackle the pass had seemingly worked. I had acclimatised well and the conditions now were much preferred to the thick shrouds of menacing cloud that plugged the valleys the previous days. All traces of low pressure had dissipated, and the blue pre-dawn sky was being filled in from the east. It was 04:30am. I snoozed for half an hour or so before shuffling out of my sleeping bag. Crawling outside, there was quite suddenly a pang of pain in my stomach. *Oh dear.* I unzipped the outer lining of the tent before immediately chucking up the contents of my guts onto the balding grass outside. My head tingled and I felt weak. *This wasn't part of the plan*, I thought to myself, as I began to throw up again. *Uh oh.* I waddled clear of the tent, as I felt my stomach squeeze, to the unwelcome surprise of diarrhoea. *Shit.* I sniffed the sausage that had been festering in my bag and it reminded me of last night's supper, and that of the night before. The tomatoes too. And the cucumber. They were all off! I threw them towards the river in disgust. I still had a pack of wafer biscuits to see me over the pass. I vomited again, tried to stomach a biscuit, then vomited it straight back up. *Shit.* I lay down on my roll mat outside and breathed the crisp dawn air in perfect matinal silence. I was bathed in ideal external conditions, the sky searing a most intense blue, blanketing the valley in a paradoxically appeasing calmness. I turned to my side to let more of whatever was in me, out. This process continued for the next hour and a half as I slowly took down my tent and laboriously loaded everything onto my bike. It was 500 m of height gain and 15 kilometres of distance to the Tajik border, that I felt was walkable. The Kyrgyz border, on the other hand, was only five kilometres behind, though in the wrong direction. I had to decide which way to go.

I set off up the hill with my bike and barely managed 50 m before having to lay on the stony verge on the side of the track up the mountain. I couldn't do it. I didn't want to go back. I sat for half an hour contemplating my options in between the vomit and diarrhoea. I made Instagram videos to talk out loud to myself, and eventually to share the ludicrousness of my situation with the outside world. I scorned myself! *What are you doing here, in the no-man's land between these two bloody countries, alone, with hardly any food and sick as a dog?! What force possessed you to start this folly? To leave a relationship? To leave friends, family and comforts? For this?* I felt foolish and worn and beaten, but I could afford only bleak and bleary pragmatism. I had to get to somewhere to rest. Uphill was out of the question given that 50 m nearly reduced me to my knees. I had to make it back to the Kyrgyz border and try to get my hands on some tea and bread. It wasn't out of the question to almost expect that from Kyrgyz hospitality, even from border guards. I mounted my saddle and began freewheeling downhill. Even that proved too much, and I was soon reduced to a lowly walk, downhill. It was 07:00am and the summer sun was rising quick, illuminating the peaks on the opposite side of the river. As I was on the approach to the Kyrgyz border, I heard a chugging behind me and turned to see a battered light blue jeep drive past. I barely had the energy to signal it to stop. It drove out of sight.

Upon rounding the corner, the same blue jeep was parked by the roadside where I could make out a family of four Kyrgyz or Tajiks clucking around: a mother, father, daughter and son. The daughter caught sight of me and ran in my direction. "Hello, hello hello!"
"No hello, very sick, very sick," I moaned. "Vomitsaya, illness!" I charaded vomiting by springing my fist into a star in front of my open mouth. Fairly so, she didn't get the gist. I approached the family accompanied by the girl and saluted

them. "Assalam Allaikum, vy ad kuda?" They inquired where I'm from.

"Angliski, I yedu na Tajikistan na velosiped but I'm sick, very sick," I wailed back. They sat me down and placed a cup of hot chai in my hands. I vomited. They were beginning to understand. The father spoke to me in Russian and I gleamed that he lived in Tajikistan, by the border, and if I waited five hours he would give me a lift.

"Rakhmat, rakhmat!" I thanked him and slumped on the verge of the river, with the rest of the family, barely stopping to wonder what on Earth they were doing here too. The father, it turned out, maintained the road of the no-man's land, together with a few other men who throughout the day sprang out of nowhere. The woman, daughter and son stayed by the roadside cooking pasta shells and proffering tea unto me. I barely had the energy to move and each time I needed to be sick, I hadn't the dignity to hide myself and I simply coughed up whatever I needed to, laid on my side. On the other hand, I had enough dignity left such that when diarrhoea came on I could disappear behind a verge rising from the river, away from the family's view. It was gruelling. The woman mournfully draped a blanket over me. It almost covered my head, as if I were a dead body.

Five long hours passed, I was still with the rest of the family, trying my best to be a good guest, despite chucking my guts up. I let them wear my sunglasses and took photos that I showed them. Eight hours passed and still no sign of the man. The family had gone for a walk down the road. Two cars passed. One had room for the bike on the roof, but not for me. Another Tajik man with a mouth of gold teeth just repeated "100 dollars, 150 dollars, 100 dollars, 150 dollars." I launched my sunglasses towards him and told him where to stick his 150 dollars. Ten hours later and the mirage of the father was shimmering and walking back up the road. *It is really him!* He got in the car without greeting me and drove off towards the Kyrgyz border with the family. *Had I misunderstood?* I sat hopelessly and waited.

After 15 minutes the car came back into view, packed full with the family of four, two other workers, a Pamiri woman and a young kid, who was apparently a Japanese-Pakistani hitchhiker. Things could not get stranger. We tied my bike to the rear of the jeep using my bungee cords that I would normally have strapped over my tent and roll mat. Squeezed inside and blissfully against the window that I opened should I need to throw up out of it, we began our ascent to the mystery house. At about 4000 m, we arrived. The house was actually set up as a homestay! Nur-Mohammed was its name. We entered into the kitchen past two scraggly dogs and into the living room that doubled up as a bedroom. There were a few embroidered mats laid on the floor, and as was customary in most Tajik houses that I would later visit, a pile of thick blankets. I took a blanket and curled into a ball in the corner of the room, while the rest of the family, workers, Pamiri woman and 16-year-old hitchhiker began to eat. I intermittently ran outside to clear my body out, before returning to my patch of floor as the amicably curious Japanese-Pakistani traveller questioned the workers in Russian amidst jovial laughter. I felt bitter and jealous and sorry for myself, but the worst of everything didn't come until later in the night.

At about 01:00am in the morning, my body still somehow had stuff to get rid of. I hurriedly hobbled outside, tried to distance myself as much as I could from the house, before dropping my trousers. Unfortunately, one of the scraggly dogs had cottoned on that I might be the source of a delicious meal. So, it was outside in the no-man's land and past midnight, at 4000 m of altitude, on the 8th of July that I closed my eyes, wishing as hard as I could that I could teleport home, as a scruffy Tajik dog proceeded to lap up my diarrhoea.

The following day, the horrors of the night before tucked deep in my Freudian memory box that will one day return to haunt me or friends that hear it as a pub story, I left the house on foot with the hitch-hiker. I felt eternally grateful to the family who had saved me, though I was still rather unwell. With his unlikely adolescent support and frankly endearing yet annoying curiosity, we traipsed up to the top of the pass at almost 4300 m. A statue of the Tajik national animal: the Marco Polo sheep marked the culminating point of the road, before the rudimentary border post became visible. "Welcome to Tajikistan!" It was here that I left behind my new friend, and sailed in the tailwind over the Martian rock of Tajikistan towards Karakul, a village tucked behind the vast lake of its namesake.

Tajikistan is probably the least well-off country I have visited on the trip. 93% of the country is mountainous and so a vast proportion of the land is non-arable, and yet, Tajikistan's economy depends heavily on agriculture. Besides this, most of the country's GDP is generated from remittances from workers – mostly abroad in Russia. Many of the communities and settlements in the high mountain part of the country are oasis villages that are constructed around brooks, streams or rivers. Water here, is the substance not only of life, but of community. Before reaching these parts, however, there was the even rougher Pamir plateau covering the Eastern half of the Gorno-Badakhshan autonomous oblast. Hostile doesn't quite cover it. With dry summers and winters where temperatures reach minus sixty Celsius, life on the plateau is hard. This is coupled with a difficult economic situation, brought partially about by the textbook dictator, Emomali Rakhmon. Upon talking to a man with a decent grasp of English in the village of Alichur, the tragedy of the inescapable poverty became clear. I had just been to the shop to buy supplies for the day totalling the equivalent of $4. My interlocutor was a student at Dushanbe University and was back in his natal village to help his brother to construct a house. He had recently been offered a job as a teacher here but turned it down. When asked why he turned it down: the remuneration. 800 Somoni per month: the equivalent of about $2.70 *per day*. It is impossible to live not in a state of semistarvation on this measly amount. It angers me to think of the opulent luxury that most of us can not only afford, but take for granted, whereas a virtuous man such as this - but typical of so many more – was struggling to survive.

Before Alichur, however, was 220 kilometres of road, including the notorious Ak Baital pass that would be the roof of my entire trip, topping out at 4650m. From Karakul I set off to merciful tailwind. I passed the turn-off down the Bartang valley, an alternative route through the Pamirs that cuts through the heart of the mountains. Most cyclists who go this way pack five days of food and many more supplies and spares, which gives a sense of how remote this is. Still bogged down by illness and pangs of mental suffering, I opted to forgo this route in favour of the conventional passage: the M41 Pamir highway. Shortly after this turn off, the road deteriorated and became 'washboard'. It is exactly what it sounds like. Winding through the cruel landscape, Martian reds and lunar greys, it was surreal to meet Earthlings – especially Europeans and especially Europeans on bicycles. I met at least one group of my contemporaries each day, which in such a faraway place was frankly bizarre. If Tajikistan is the mecca for cycle touring then mid-July was *Hajj*. There were almost as many Europeans on bicycles as there were Tajiks in cars! Most had set off from Europe and were heading to Bishkek or somewhere in Mongolia, while a few were doing longer journeys, some the whole way around! Some had also come uniquely for the highway: Dushanbe to Osh or even on to Bishkek. Although it was great to meet so many like-minded folk, the guaranteed meetings almost detracted from the sense of remoteness and magic of the place. In coming to the Pamirs, I oddly felt much more like a tourist, one of the masses. The Tajiks were fully aware of this fact too, and alongside the road, what must once have been outposts for herders, had become homestays.

This paradox of meeting many folk in the most on-paper remote place of the trip was cemented as I battled my way to the top of

Ak-Baital pass. A surge of cool wind led a fingering flurry of scary-looking clouds through the mountains behind me as I was tackling the last two or three kilometres of the climb. I could barely believe I was over 4000 m as there was a marked absence of snow on the nearby peaks. On the final approach to the top of the pass, a 4x4 mounted ahead of me and slowed as it neared. The rear window dropped to reveal two very drunk Germans in the back seat. "Champagne, champagne!" They harked.

Before I could fathom what was going on, they procured a bottle of sparkling wine that they poured into a plastic cup and handed to me. A slightly concerned Tajik driver was laughing dryly from the driver's seat as I, in disbelief, necked the cup dry. The Germans whooped and wheed and wished me *Gute reise* before being chauffeured off to wherever their inebriated whims would take them.

At the very summit, I was met by another eccentric traveller. This man, a Japanese mountaineer by vocation, was taking a different approach to cycle touring. He had a ten-year old folding bike, with a pedal half-missing. He only rode downhill, and hitchhiked up. He had an inner-city-professional-looking rucksack, the likes that software developers might be wearing on the London tube. He was wearing a bucket hat, jeans, and bloody sandals! Sandals, at 4650 m! We shared a moment on the summit before I headed off in vanguard. This is what I meant by paradox.

By the end of the day, I had made it to Murghab, the highest town of the former Soviet republic at 3650 m. I found it to be terribly poor. The theme of commerce being run out of old shipping containers intensified. Here, the entire market looked like it belonged in a dock, not a landlocked country in central Asia. The water source for the village comprised a few pumps, ironically sponsored by Coca-Cola (given its history of depleting groundwater levels in places like Kaldera, India). I stayed at a guesthouse with a group of Argentinian actors, where I inadvertently became an extra in their film (my second acting engagement of the trip after my role in a Chinese bank advert in Hekou), in between trying to recover from the fatigue and diarrhoea that were still plaguing my body.

The day I set off from Murghab, the sky was bereft of clouds: a perfect blue. A tickling tailwind lazily accompanied me on tarmacked yet bumpy roads up the next col at around 4000 m. All other cyclists I met were in good spirits and I was full of optimism that I had finally battered back my sickness and that I was truly back in business! Hours passed, midday came and went, 01:00pm, 02:00pm and by 03:00pm, I began to grow concerned that I still had no desire to eat or even the motivation to stop and cook. The day's perfect conditions were warming me to the core yet I knew that it could not continue indefinitely. Eat or crash. The crash came at about 85 kilometres when the wind turned and my eyes felt like they had been pushed a little deeper into their sockets. As luck had it, only a kilometre down the road on the approach to Alichur was a café by the boggy mosquito-infested grasslands where I intended to camp. I flaked limply amidst the mozzies and march flies in a bizarre room for almost two hours, demolishing tea and dried fish. I still believed I could make it to Khorog within two days (225 kilometres to go) but at 02:00am in the morning, when I woke in my tent, sweating and shivering and feeling like my entire head was submerged in Vaseline, this was set to change.

The 15 kilometres left to Alichur were pedalled in a groggy haze. With a helter-skelter head, I creaked my way towards the shabby collection of white painted mud-brick buildings. The first homestay I saw, I entered, and with little ado grabbed a blanket from the stack in the corner of the room, reclined on an embroidered mat and let sleep take me until the early afternoon, with the rest of the day spent allowing the patterned ceiling to be imprinted on my retina. I had no energy to muster. No leaving the room bar for when my body pressed me to stumble outside to the cess-hole. This was day one in Alichur. No signal on the phone, no network through which I could diffuse my woes. I oscillated in and out of sleep. Wacky dreams blurrily

208

faded into reality and back again. After a long and sleepless night, I had enough energy to search for a shop and to visit the water pump. Coca-cola, snickers and biscuits were all I dared buy, for four US dollars. It was on my way back from this brief escapade that I talked to the would-be teacher, and the stark and harrowing extent of financial poverty that touched these communities became clear.

I couldn't help but feel like these communities, rich in history and tradition, were being left behind in a world driven by progress towards more progress. Perhaps I see this naively. What would a true 'caught up' Alichur look like? Would the riches of culture and tradition be traded for material wealth: the rests of that small community spirit that once defined all human society dispersed by a greater reliance on other powers? All the same, I felt ill at ease in Alichur. Out of place. I didn't belong in this community that was clearly evolving in any case to cater for the adventure tourists passing through on organized 4x4, motorcycle, or bicycle tours of the Pamirs. As I returned to my room, staring once again at the oh-so-familiar ceiling, I resolved to leave Alichur. I could not stay here. 200 kilometres to Khorog. It was impossible by bicycle in my current state, but by car?

My bike was laid amongst the dust and stones. I was sat in a burnt-out car by the roadside, eyeing up the macadam that stretched far between the distant ferrous hills from where I had emerged over a day ago. I had taken the decision to hitch hike, but not only this: I had taken a deeper decision. I had to get back home quicker and find a new source of motivation. I simply wasn't having fun – and I couldn't imagine that these times would turn into the type two sort either. How could I keep up such a fruitless endeavour by choice? I would hitch a ride to Khorog, rest up in the larger town, cycle to Dushanbe, and from there I had many options. There was a train network through Uzbekistan, a ferry to cross the Black sea. I could bring Europe at least 40 days closer. It was reassuring.

A couple of trucks passed. No luck. A 4x4 approached, brimming with people and with a bleating goat strapped onto the roof. I laughed it by, lowering my thumb when I could see how full it was. It stopped. I walked to the window. "Asalam allaikum!"

"Salam, where you are going my friend?"

"Khorog, are you driving that far?"

"For you, ten Dollars."

10 dollars for 200 kilometres? It was a done deal. With Gulbek's help I strapped by bike and panniers onto the roof next to the remarkably tranquil and pacified goat, before joining the nine others in the seven-seater car. It was a bit of a squeeze. Just before leaving Alichur, there was time for one final stop to pick up Dushanbe, an old boy who squeezed into the middle row. We were set for the 200 kilometres to Khorog. Three in the front, five in the middle and three in the back.

The journey was punctuated by stops every thirty minutes for Gulbek to check on the goat, which if it could speak would politely bleat "Stop bloody stopping and get me to Khorog already so I can get off of this roof!" during these stops, Dushanbe took cheeky swigs of vodka, that on a couple of occasions he shared with me. This culminated in a half hour of him ranting and raving in Russian and Tajik, offering me to stay with him in Khorog, before very suddenly falling into a deep slumber. At that point I took the offer to no longer be valid. The scenery was phenomenal, following the road down the river valley. As we descended, the mountains became closer and more rugged, which, coupled with the gorgeous Tajik guitar music and seemingly hilarious conversations of my co-passengers made the trip a joy. Khorog! We passed the sign that marked the entrance to the town and to better times.

In sickness and in health

Khorog was base camp for adventure tourists visiting the Pamirs. It is substantially lower than much of the rest of GBAO, at just over 2000m. This also means that in the midsummer, locals and tourists alike flock to the swimming pool in the central park for refreshing dips and relaxed swims. From the boughs of surrounding trees, Tajiks somersaulted and dived while Europeans belly-flopped. Unfortunately, it was only the men who swam, while women lined the poolside, too abashed to put their skin on show. After three days recuperating at base camp, with phone signal to contact my family and friends back home, I finally felt truly ready to strike back onto the road and to overcome what remained of the Pamir highway. It wasn't far to Dushanbe now.

From Khorog all the way to Qualai Kumb, the rudimentary gravel road was steeped into the towering giants on the Tajik side of the river Panj: the natural border between Tajikistan and Afghanistan (following the Pamir agreements between the British and Russians at the end of the 19th century). In fact, about half of ethnic Tajiks were found on the Afghan side of this arbitrary separation of what was once the same land. Even now, a large fraction of the folk living on the fringes of the Afghan side of the Panj, are ethnic Tajiks. On both sides of the border, the arid mountainscape supported nothing but the road connecting oasis villages, like knots along a string. On the Afghan side, the road was walked by families or young kids bouncing up and down on the back of donkeys or occasionally a few people squeezed onto a motorcycle. They felt so far, like fleeting comets, as their wheels splayed a tail of ethereal dust. Only a river separated their world from mine. On the Tajik side, 4x4s of tourists continued in a steady stream towards Khorog and the highlands beyond. More and more Tajiks were on the roads too, visiting the evermore dense neighbouring villages or heading to and from Khorog for supplies.

On the first evening from leaving Khorog, I found a perfect campsite right on the edge of the river. A persistent and charming young lad with a complexion that was almost Caucasian had followed me and eventually helped to put up my tent. I was shocked at how many Pamiri people looked much more European than Asian, with fair skin, light hair and the occasional piercing blue eye. I swam in a small pool by the river with him and his uncle, who later delivered over a kilo of mulberries and sweets, before calling it a night in the tent. I drifted off at 09:30pm and a short hour and a half of sleep later, was rudely awoken in the night.

"Hey mister!" I heard a voice just outside my tent.

"What do you want?" I groggily inquired.

"Mister!" I heard men's hushed voices talking amongst themselves, and bootsteps close by the tent.

I unzipped the tent and poked my head out to see who was coming to disturb my sleep. I was met with three Ak47s, hanging loosely from the shoulders of three men dressed in full military uniform. "Pa Russki znaiyesh?" One of them asked, to see if I could speak Russian.

"Chut chut znaiyu, I can speak a little," I told him with bated breath, not having any idea what would happen next. The lead soldier began dictating in Russian, that for all I understood could have been a recital of Pushkin.

"Ne panimayu, I don't understand!"

I was already bored of what they might be trying to ask or say. They were just here for want of anything better to do it seemed. The sense of danger I immediately felt at the sight of their guns eased. I then passed the lead soldier my phone, Google translate open. He spoke into it and handed it back to me. "It is dangerous here near the water, Taliban are across the river. You must move now."

"Taliban!" I recoiled in disbelief. Not out of panic but out of genuinely not believing their prerogative. If the Taliban have interest in subduing the donkey riding Tajiks that I had been waving at all day, then they have been seriously over-estimated. Nonetheless, the soldiers nagged on that I was in danger, and I protested and even pointed over to the black and silent silhouette of the mountain beneath the clear and calm night sky across the river.

"There is no Taliban here!" I protested with indignation. They told me to move, and I didn't want to argue more than 3 times with armed men. I began to reluctantly pack up my stuff from the lush green pasture where I had pitched up for the night.

"Where are you going to take me then?" I stipulated.

"Gostinitsa."

I knew full well there were no hotels nearby, and as I finished racking up the last of my panniers, I saw a threesome of camouflaged jackets walk off into the night. *Unbelievable!* I took to the road and pedalled onwards until I came across a benzene station where the attendant allowed me to camp for the remainder of the night, next to the toilet. The smell was gross and light shone into the tent. *What relegation! What a palaver!*

After the curious incident of the nobs in the night-time, it took two and a half more days to reach Qualai Khumb over broken asphalt and gravel, where there was a choice of two roads to reach Dushanbe. The formidable North which entailed 2000m of steep climbing over 35 kilometres in order to pass into the next valley along, or the more leisurely South road. As I approached the town, I had it in my mind to take the least arduous route possible, even at the expense of the spectacular. This all changed, however, when I met Brigitte Fournier.

Brigitte was a 60-odd year-old French woman, whose radiant smile simply diffused *bien-être* and *bonheur!* She was with a troupe of three other older French cyclists who had just arrived, having taken-on the South road. But not Brigitte, she had split from here group and taken the notorious Northern passage: far more remote, with a bike-crippling surface over densely packed contour lines. In the homestay, with an ineffaceable smile, she told her story of being invited to join a group of people de-mining the surrounding hills and how she cherished this humanistic joy that solo adventure still brought her. While so many steer clear of arduous activity at her age and even younger, this woman, whose face was dimpled to accommodate her constant beam, had taken-on a road on a bicycle that strikes even the young and fit as being too difficult. She had taken it in her stride and with a smile, for the pleasure, without even thinking of the defiant message that her act wrote. She was an example. Of course, after talking to her, I became reinvigorated myself. Inspiration is the fuel for motivation. I would take on the Northern road.

I left Qualai Khumb reflecting on one of the greatest and unexpected assets that this journey had brought me: encounters with amazing people, who in the end, turn out to be more or less 'normal'. When I set out on the trip, I was expecting to be wowed by the nature of our fair planet and to meet and learn from local people. I had hardly even considered that I would become part of the community of travellers: a vast number of open-minded folk who are often brimming with riveting and inspiring stories. I was also shocked by the normality of amazing folk. I had read countless blogs and books of modern round-the-world travellers, holding them in high esteem and considering them to be a rare breed of people, whose openness and drive for adventure unlocked the vast spectrum of the possible. This rendered them somehow different. In fact, as it turned out, adventurers were normal people who had found a reason and a renewable source of motivation to discover. Many almost seemed plagued by imposterism and were themselves shocked at the leaps they had made; how easy it seemed to travel vast distances by human power.

For 35 kilometres I heaved my bike upwards on the loose stony track of the North road. I paused for a light lunch after passing a traffic-jam of a few hundred sheep, herded by a shabby but happy-looking Tajik. He didn't look up as I passed him and continued to march, wrapped in meandering thoughts and preoccupations. Nearing the summit, panels lined the roadside depicting poorly drawn cartoons of little girls and boys with their arms and legs blown off by the mines that were strewn on these lands during the 1992-1997 civil war, following the dissolution of the Soviet union.

At the summit I caught myself getting a little emotional. It was all downhill from here to Dushanbe (more or less). I had conquered the final climb of the Pamirs and for the first time in a long time felt truly fantastic! This sentiment, intensified by a breezing descent on a carless gravel road flanked by the lush meadow-flowers spangled across the green Alps, accompanied me for the remaining 270 kilometres to Tajikistan's regal capital. Mars was behind and I was back on planet Earth.

It was a 06:30am start and a 07:00pm arrival, but I had made it. Dushanbe! The official finish of the Pamir highway and the place I could flake out, have a beer, indulge in a bit of good food, fix my bike and hang out with some lovely people and talk about things that aren't where I am from and where I am going. The city was a world away from the villages. From abject poverty to frivolous decoration of tree lined avenues. Suit-clad men smoked hookah and drank beers. I think I even saw a couple holding hands. Grand palaces and buildings for the use of the esteemed dictator Emomali Rakhmon stood proudly at the head of symmetrical parks. Libraries. Museums. Theatres. Hubs of culture. It seems unfair that everything was here whereas most of the rest of the country were working for a pittance to get by, some not even managing that, subsiding along on bulgur wheat and imported pasta shells. But that's the way it was. No infrastructure was, or perhaps *could* be sustainably put in place to support people through harsh winters and dry summers in high mountain Tajikistan. Perhaps it was just meant, geographically, to be different to here in the oasis of Dushanbe. This havre of rich, relatively comfortable civilisation amidst a country built on dry hostile mountains.

While staying here I made the acquaintance of a British literature professor, who read out Ozymandias, by Percy Shelley. I couldn't help but transpose its allusion to the greed for power and dominion made starkly impermeant by the natural order of the world, to what I saw in Tajikistan. The frivolous grandeur of Dushanbe would surely one day lay to ruin, I felt. The dictator Rakhmon's shattered visage would perhaps protrude from the sand, leaving nothing but idle memories of his forlorn bastion of riches. Meanwhile, goats in the mountains would still peck tufts of grass from the gritty soil. Smoke would still rise from the makeshift chimneys of the clay buildings in the lofty Pamirs. It feels like this way of being is so much more permanent, though so much more tough to live through. Surely, there must be a balance where elements of the comfort of Dushanbe without its terrible frivolity join in symbiosis with those of living on the land, arid and hostile as it may be in some places. For the time being, I found it tricky to reconcile that Dushanbe was only a relative stone's throw away from the Pamir, while the concentration of wealth between these two places was all off-kilter. I was beginning to realise that this imbalance, sometimes abrupt, between the proximity of places and division of wealth between them, is a seemingly ubiquitous hallmark of civilization on our planet as we know it.

Amidst these reflections, I was keen to continue making progress towards home. A measly 280 kilometres was all that remained to the Uzbek border. The devil in the detail was the 3400 m pass in the Fann mountains north of Dushanbe that I still had to cross. I am convinced that nobody who believes the Earth is flat has ever been to Tajikistan. After two days, I was within 80 kilometres of the Uzbek border and about 120 kilometres off the famous Silk Road City of Samarkand. It is also when illness struck again. I couldn't believe my ill fortune! What was I doing wrong to deserve such bad turns? I spent the night in between my tent and the least conspicuous corner of the garden of a disinterested family, who I hope didn't see my sporadic night-time escapades to clear out my body. The following day, in spite of, and in fact *because of* the return of illness, I ploughed onwards and by dusk had somehow made it beyond the border of the country that had almost all the way through seen me in such a wretched state.

I emerged into the land of the Uzbeks and their glorious city of Samarkand. That morning, I had felt the clutches of sickness taking hold and I worried I might not be able to make it anywhere. Yet, I had cycled well over 100 kilometres. It seemed the bike possessed some mystical quality that facilitates equanimity. I had made it. I arrived in Samarkand just as night fell, after an easy border crossing: "Welcome to Uzbekistan!"

I checked into a guesthouse and fell almost immediately into four days of crippling sickness. For two of these days, I couldn't muster the strength to leave bed. It was like in Alichur, or Port Dickson. On one of the days where my energy allowed me out of bed, I wandered slowly around what must be some of the finest and most ornate structures of the world of Islam. I also managed to talk my way into writing and recording a rap in English and Russian with a SIM card salesman-cum-music producer. During this period, well and truly fed-up with my body, I finally got round to taking the stomach infection antibiotics that I had carried with me since Australia, a welcome gift from my Auntie Trisha! I was sick of being sick. This sickness made me seriously take stock of my situation for the first time in a long time, and consider my options forwards. It would be possible to take a train from Bukhara all the way to Aktau on the Caspian Sea, before a small 1000 kilometres or so traverse of Azerbaijan and Georgia would bring me to Batumi or Poti port on the black sea, which could take me all the way to Romania! Within this time scale I could be in Europe within little over two weeks! It was a startling shortcut. My thoughts in that sad, sad Alichur room were beginning to materialise into a plan. At the same time, it seemed a shame to stop the break the red line at this point. Flashbacks of obstinacy against the well-meaning Xinjiang security forces came back to mind. *The red line, unbroken.* It felt in Samarkand as if it would be the red line or myself that would break. While it would be regrettable to break the red line, the most regrettable thing of all would be to sulk my way home miserably. The turbulence of indecision rattled my mind. Illness didn't help. Neither did beer. In any case, a decision wasn't necessary straight away. I would cycle to Bukhara and then the rest of the story would be written.

Within four days, the antibiotics had worked miracles, I was back on my feet, abound with energy. I even had it in my head that I would ride à la Mark Beaumont (on his first world tour that is) and smash out 100 miles a day, by compartmentalising each day into sessions. Contrary to Mark's four sets of 25 miles, mine would be divided primarily into a morning and late afternoon-evening session. With the bulk of the midday period dedicated to the siesta: necessary in the 40+ Celsius heat of the blazing flatlands of Uzbekistan. As I left Samarkand, with its marvellous Registan cluster and other madrashas and mosques, I felt like a new chapter was beginning.

Reflections

Before moving on with my journey through Uzbekistan, I feel it is worth a brief analysis of my time in Tajikistan, as large amounts of it seemed to be spent in a state of almost unnecessary hardship and certainly illness. Was it a country where one is destined to suffer, or is there something I could have done to alleviate some of the suffering? If I did things differently, could I have embraced and truly enjoyed exploring this fascinating, remote recess of civilization?

Firstly, with a now great degree of hindsight, it is easy to identify a positive feedback loop of negativity. Since leaving Bishkek, all the way to Samarkand, I wanted to 'hurry' home because I felt bad, for one reason or another. *I must hurry, or else I'll be in a rush,* I thought. Hurry, in this sense, simply means taking the most direct route possible and doing it in the shortest amount of time possible on the bicycle. This may have sounded like a sterling idea at the time, but it meant that during periods of illness, I almost certainly didn't give myself the time to fully recover. For example, I could have stayed in Murghab until I was sure to have no more ailments. Or from my night in the no-man's land, I could have returned to Sary Tash (if the border guards were well-meaning, that is!) or even in Osh I could have spent another couple of days recuperating. But, because I didn't take the time to recover (because I was hurrying), I still felt bad, sometimes even worse. Because I felt bad or worse, I wanted nothing but to hurry home even faster: herein lies the feedback loop. It meant that from Bishkek to Samarkand, I was never truly in good form for more than a day at a time. There are a few more off-shot consequences of the feedback loop that I believe contributed even further to my perceived woes. Tajikistan, and Kyrgyzstan boast an abundance of remote beauty, little of which I visited. In Tajikistan in particular, there was the opportunity to cycle the spectacularly remote Bartang and Wakhan valleys. There was Iskanderkul and a series of Alpine lakes in the North. There was the Zorkul nature reserve, where lucky ones might hope to catch a glimpse of a Marco Polo sheep. In Kyrgyzstan, countless lakes, rivers, and passes were passed by, ignored. Moreover, a person in a hurry is hardly going to stop to chat to many locals. That was me and I lament that I passed up many an opportunity to discover more of Tajikistani and Kyrgyz life simply from being in a hurry, as if I was on a commute rather than a voyage of discovery. I rode my bike through these countries, but not much more.

It may seem that I am being rather harsh on myself, but I truly feel like the rush curdled my experience of these countries. It is only now, revisiting my blog, the photos and reading amazing stories of other travellers, that I regret not taking more time. Of course, at the time, in my ready-tuned and channelled mind, I would have heard none of this. But next time I am in such a ridiculous hurry, I would love to be able to remind myself that the best thing to do is to pause and breathe and utterly crazily and paradoxically, take more time.

There are also, of course measures I could have taken to not become ill in the first place, or at least, avoid its horrible recurrence. I had a water filter with me for the whole trip, so why I did not think to filter the brown flecked water from an unknown pipe I do not know. Why I drank from large streams in Kyrgyzstan without filtering, when there could well have been cattle or sheep on higher ground, I do not know. The same goes for other slightly suspect sources. Why I did not take antibiotics for my stomach before Samarkand when I was suffering with the shits in Murghab, I do not know.

As I was fresh-legged and bodied, leaving Samarkand under the already searing sun on the 2nd of August, all of that was shoved to the side to make way for what would hopefully be a new period of boundless positivity in a new country amongst new landscapes. Either that, or the train.

One small steppe

In the two days upon leaving Samarkand, great progress was made. The 300 kilometres or so to Bukhara was completed by lunchtime on day two. I rocketed along flat roads, waving to melon vendors and napping in teahouses. Truly, it was a joy, and the Uzbek people had been extremely generous to me over this stretch. I was having such a great time that when I reached the old Samanid capital, the thought of getting a train seemed simply out of the question. Over a delicious Uzbek naan with egg, I contemplated my next steps.

After Bukhara was a large stretch of desert with an oasis island in the middle of it. About 450 kilometres of desert and 100 kilometres of irrigated oasis land to be precise. This would take me to the city of Nukus, the last bastion of life before the very remote desert stretch to the Kazakh border town of Beyneu. My plan to ride à la Mark Beaumont would continue all the way to the Caspian Sea. Ride 90 kilometres before midday. Eat and sleep the early afternoon away in a Chai Xona (teahouse) or some sort of shack selling *samsa* to beat the squeeze of the heart. Ride 70 kilometres into the evening. Even if it got dark I would not stop. I would not stop until I reached 160 kilometres. At that point I would erect my tent in the desert or sleep in a teahouse, if one was within a few kilometres.

For the first two days, I matched my expectations, and managed to sleep in a teahouse each night. The set up was ideal: a big plate of meat and potato for a couple of dollars. The name of the dish made me laugh: Jizz. I would then ask the proprietor whether I might also sleep on the raised platform where I had eaten. I can think of few other places in the world where this was totally acceptable. Of course, the night's sleep was never totally comfortable, with truckers coming through all hours of the night for refreshment and a chat and the odd insect that came to take a hearty meal from my bloodstream. All the same, it was novel and great fun. It also helped massively to maintain my newfound impetus. Everything except my valuable bag was left on my bike next to my table-cum-bed for the night and for a few hours I simply became an accessory in the corner of the teahouse. At just before sunrise, I could leap from the mat and within two steps and five minutes I would be on the bike, beating the day to it in the competition of who could be the first to wake.

The desert was not only searingly hot, but it was truly beautiful. There was a real tangible, and I suppose rare sense of what a day is from the propos of the planet. The sun, whose gaze was unimpeded by mound, rise or hillock, arced across the sky and didn't shy between its bounds of dusk and dawn. Meanwhile, on the roadside, shadows of low-lying shrubs danced adiabatically. They reeled themselves in from their morning maximalism to a shy of midday introversion before venturing out once more into the late afternoon, much like myself. The still dancing shadows were cast on the canvas of the sands in which serpentine shapes rested, ribs and ridges folded by the winds into the rolling dunes. And the quiet! When the road was absent of *marshrutkas*, loaded Ladas (one of which had a full-grown cow in the back) or nexus cars, naught could be heard save the breath of light wind and the satisfying hum of my galloping tyres.

I began to make short videos of my cycle through this vast steppe of infinite horizons. I had once again decided to promote my journey for Newlife and to try to boost donations to my fundraising page, having done almost nothing since my time in Thabarwa for this. I had been enraged by the disgusting level of care that was afforded to disabled people in Myanmar, and I was filled with self-contempt at seeing this with my own teary eyes, All the while, a couple of thousand pounds that I had raised was being sent to Newlife to buy battery assisted wheelchairs for a few English kids. I had since processed to some extent the brutal inequality and decided that not all causes that blight our world could be fought at once. The suffering of some of those in the Thabarwa didn't detract from the fact that life could be difficult, albeit in a very different way and in a very different context, for families with disabled children in the UK. I would never forget my experiences in Myanmar, but for now, as I was sweeping across the Uzbek desert, I put it to one side.

On the second evening since departing Bukhara, just before nightfall, I met Jeroen and Menno who were suffering the low energy blues on the roadside. I was in relatively good spirits, charmed by the serene expanse of the desert and having almost reached 145 kilometres for the day. I chatted with them and it so happened we were heading the same way. The first cyclists doing so since an odd chap called Dimi in Tajikistan and before that, Luke and Dante. After they had briefly refuelled, we reached a Chai Xona ten kilometres up the road and ate fish supper before being led to a mercifully air conditioned room to sleep alongside a couple of other truckers, making the classic trip from Moscow to Tashkent and back. Dunya, one of the tea house inhabitants or staff members or artefacts was sleeping in an adjoining room. For some reason her phone began to play a song. On repeat. From 02:00am to 05:00am. My tentative knocks on her door and quips for her attention had no effect. The vodka of the evening had her well and truly out for the count. Little sleep was had that night, especially given the alarm that sounded at 04:30 am. *Wakey wakey.*

The day with Jeroen and Menno made me drop my Mark Beaumont aspirations. Nonetheless, progress was strong and it was a delight to converse freely with these two fantastic chaps. They had ridden their bicycles from Beijing to Almaty, before being obliged to return to the Netherlands. They left their bikes in Kazakhstan, however, and had come back to finish the job of cycling from far Eastern China to Utrecht. They each had wonderful stories and personalities, that made getting on with them seem as natural and easy as ticking over the pedals in the steady tailwind of that day. Jeroen was still feeling low on energy, after his wobble of the previous night, and stomach issues seemed to be plaguing both of them. I, naturally, could heavily sympathise. When there was a slight rise, Jeroen began to struggle a little, and when he did, Menno would ride alongside him to either chat or joke or place his hand on his partner's back, pushing and urging him onwards. We made it to Tortogul that evening for a celebratory *plov* and beer, with another 130 kilometres or so ticked off on the campaign to meet the Caspian.

I parted ways from Jeroen and Menno that morning, not knowing whether I would see them again. They were heading to another of the preserved Samanid cities: Khiva. I would forgo the touristic jaunt and pedal onwards to Nukus, little under 200 kilometres up the road. The day brought headwind. The wuthering desert gusts blasted me like a furnace pump during a horrendous puncture experience, prolonging my exposure to the brutal 40+ °C heat for almost an hour longer than I would have liked. I got over this by glugging down a litre and a half of Pepsi cola. Despite these nightmarish scenes, my takeaway from the day was a heartfelt meeting with a man waiting for a *marshrutka.* I told him about my journey in pig Russian, that I was slowly learning with the help of a Pushkin book I picked up in Dushanbe. He almost went into shock and gave me a gift of 10,000 Somoni (£1) for 'energy'. He was a good guy. I found a great camping spot to consolidate on these events in an abandoned building, 40 kilometres from Nukus. I tried to cowboy camp. Mosquitoes soon put a stop to that idea and it wasn't long before the tent was back up. The following morning, I arrived in the westernmost Uzbek city after taking only seven days to traverse the vast majority of Uzbekistan.

Nukus. I had honestly expected to get the train before here, but I was in great form. My sails were still full of my second wind and I set my sights to cross the desert solo. Jeroen and Menno were still sightseeing in Khiva and I wasn't going to wait. The beans had finally arrived after what felt like a long hiatus of real motivation. I hadn't felt so positive since Bishkek but now it was time to drive it home in what little remained of the Asia before the Caspian sea, that was now just under 1000 kilometres away.

I prospected the situation from Nukus to Beyneu from the shade of a gorgeous courtyard in my guesthouse, in which ornate and decorative flags swayed melancholically in the mid-August breeze. It reminded me of Tulufan and those dulcet days. Looking at the map, upon leaving Nukus there would be roughly 100 kilometres of minor civilization. Probably consisting of roadside shops and hamlets and perhaps melon patches. After this, there was about 50 kilometres of nothing followed then by a roadhouse, similar to those in Australia whose sole purpose is to provide a point of repose and replenishment for motorists. There was then a singular straight line striking out North-westwards for 130 kilometres before reaching another of these roadhouses. After surely and hopefully stocking up on *samsa* and *plov*, a 140 kilometres landing-strip of asphalt remained until the Uzbek- Kazakh border post. The distance then looked to linger at around 50 kilometres between roadhouses up until Beyneu. The total distance summed to some 520 kilometres. I mused thoughtfully over this harsh stretch that ran alongside the old Aral Sea and through the heart of Karakalpakstan province, that even the Soviets had barely bothered to take over. I had been in contact with Charlie who had only one week ago taken this route. He warned me to pack at least ten litres of water for each of the long stretches between roadhouses. It sounded grim. I flicked to the weather app on my phone. The temperature seemed mercifully cooler, rarely even reaching into the high 30s. It was the wind, however, that would pen the story of the next few days. The following day a strong plumb South-easterly was set to whisk through the Karakalpakstan steppe. According to predictions, it would stay in that rough direction for 48 hours, before weakening and doing a complete U-turn. At least three days of ensuing strong North-westerlies followed, that would almost entirely halt all progress. I mulled all of this information over as I gorged on honey melon and sipped ayran.

As far as I was concerned, I had essentially two choices. The first of these was that I should set off in the morn, aiming to cycle for as long as I possibly could until the winds turned. I predicted I could quite possibly manage 400 kilometres, which would take me clear of the remote stretch in Uzbekistan. From there, even with slow progress, I would have plenty of amenities to survive the two days or so to Beyneu. My other option was to wait for a few days in Nukus while keeping an eye on the winds.

In practice, I did not decide on either of my options in favour of socialising with the other cyclists, all of whom had taken the train here from Beyneu. I left on an impulse at 11am the next day when I realised that the winds were just too sweet not to ride. That very same day I covered just shy of 200 kilometres, before pitching my tent in the isotropic steppe with about 75 kilometres left to go down the first 130 kilometres stretch of nothing. I would have loved to have cowboy camped here beneath the clear night sky were it not for almost all the locals warning of the dangers of scorpions and venomous snakes.

My route of the day had taken me past a salt encrusted basin. This had once upon a time accommodated the fourth largest lake in the world: the Aral Sea. From the viewpoint of my saddle, I managed to gleam in the distance an abandoned congregation of rusting fishing boats that at one point contributed to an enormous local economy producing 20% of fish consumed in the Soviet Union. The sea was fed by two of Central Asia's longest rivers, whose sources were in the Pamirs and Tian Shan respectively: the Syr Darya and the Amu Darya. In fact, I was shocked to discover that much of the flowing water I had seen over the last two months would have once made it all the way to the Aral. To the Syr Dara, the Naryn is a major tributary: the very river that I followed from the breathtaking Toktogul reservoir most of the way to Osh. As for the Amu Darya, it receives contributions from the Bartang, the Panj and the Vakhsh. The Bartang has its source in the Pamir, not far for Murghab, just like the Panj that I followed for days along the Tajik-Afghan border. The Vakhsh (also known as Kyzyl suu, the red river) flowed by Sary Tash and Sary Mogul in Southern Kyrgyzstan. I also followed it for a couple of days on my approach to Dushanbe from the North road out of Qualai Khumb. I felt a connection to all of these rivers, but I never quite realised that they once all met here in Karakalpakstan.

Alas, these days their waters are mostly dispersed between Cotton fields in the Ferghana valley or along the Turkmen-Uzbek border in a crazy irrigation project that began in the '60s, under Soviet rule. It still carries on even now, as the Islam Karimov administration continues to divert the waters for Uzbekistan's biggest export, helped along by drafting in doctors, nurses, students and soldiers to reap the annual harvest for the good of the nation! As for the soviets, they were bent on producing this white gold. The project of irrigated cotton fields went ahead despite acknowledgements from some of the former mega-state's engineers that the project would inevitably lead to the depletion of the Aral Sea as well as the societies and ecosystems strongly coupled to it. So as the seeds of prosperity were sowed around Tashkent, zephyrs rippled in the fluffy white flags of surrender of the Aral Sea. The water receded from the former stable shores. The salinity increased, along with the concentration of grossly over-used pesticides and fertilisers that slurried from the cotton fields and into the river system. Now, all that is left is 10% of the water that was there 70 years ago along with the remains of the once thriving Karakalpak, Uzbek and Kazakh communities. These people are now plagued by health problems like certain cancers and outrageous child mortality and birth defect rates. Not all is lost though! For the flow of water has been replaced by a steady flow of selfie-stick armed tourists visiting the boat graveyards, gagging for Instagram likes on their newest photo captioned "abandon ship"…

The next day, substantially beyond the old Aral Sea basin, I wanted to hit out another 200 kilometres or so in the pleasant winds to camp close to the roadhouse at the end of the brutal 140 kilometres stretch of straight road, flanked by a void of infinite and flat sand and rock. This plan never quite materialised. The first 75 kilometres passed in ease, with the winds loyally remaining on my back after my tardy 05:30am start. They gently willed me onwards towards the roadhouse that I reached by mid-morning for a filling of *samsa* and *plov*. Groups of truckers were already huddled, sat cross-legged around the low tables, putting the world to rights amongst themselves, or snoozing after a couple of litres of coke and tea that lay spattered across the tablecloths. I filled up on tea myself and bought a few more litres of water. Although the atmosphere in the roadhouse was one of constancy, of safety and of refuge, the outside world was changing. Across the battered rocky shrubland of the Uzbek steppe, the wind of promise was slowly being extinguished, the exhale from Nukus to Beyneu was about to be sucked back in.

As I walked out of the door, I immediately felt the change. The wind was blowing across rather than behind. I got on the bike and geared down a notch. As the wind direction switched into my face, I geared down once more. And after a short siesta under the scant shade of the largest shrub I could find, at around 01:00pm, I was cycling into a less than appetizing headwind. The blue sky that seemed to almost sparkle above the road lost its sheen and a quilt of beige haze loomed. I squinted into the distance as squalls whipped up almighty dust devils that dizzied themselves across the ground. The sky hazed further. The wind pumped harder. The haze was approaching rapidly. I began to feel flecks spatter on my cheeks, but not from any rain. I soon worked out it wasn't in fact haze at all. It was dust. An immense cloud of it hundreds of metres high pummelling its way towards me. As it came closer and closer, the wind blew harder and stronger. The flecks pattered more frequently on my cheeks. I looked around for shelter, but the steppe was devoid of form. Just earth and rock and shrubs either side of the empty open road, down which the cloud rushed like a stampede of fluid cows. I hurried with my bike to the first mound of dirt I could find and I squatted behind it to shelter from the dust and wind that was now rushing past with considerable ferocity. It continued for ten minutes. Twenty. One hour… I drifted in and out of sleep as I waited there, curled in ball behind this pitiful shelter, for the dust to stop. After two hours the dust had subsided and the gusts had calmed. The wind however, was still being sucked back down the road. There would be no 200-kilometre day for me and indeed in the next three hours only five kilometres of cycling were done. The wind rattled my very skeleton. I found another mound and considered my options.

1) Sleep on this mound until the night falls then cycle through the night in lighter winds.
2) Sleep on this mound until early morning.
3) Find better shelter and actually pitch the tent somewhere.

In any case I needed to make it towards some sort of rest stop by the following day for water. I opted for option three. I laboriously groaned through the wind on my ever-sore arse, praying for something to appear. As I creaked forward, I noticed a railway line had appeared from the western horizon, running parallel to the road. As the sun lowered, In the shivering distance was a building, hugging close to the line, around three kilometres from the road. I made a beeline. It looked like I had found my shelter.

I approached slowly, trundling over a makeshift track through the resilient shrubbery of the steppe while shifting my bum about the saddle to find an elusive sweet spot that didn't put too much pressure on my by-now rather painful saddle sores. I could hardly believe my luck at this find! I could merrily pitch my tent out of the wind and wait until morning by which time it should have died down a little. The building looked to be some sort of service centre for the railway line that I had barely paid attention to before, with antennae poking up from beyond the white-painted wooden structure. As I neared, I began to hear laughter! Voices? Who on earth would be occupying this far-flung outpost in the middle of the desert?

I was greeted by a group of men, lazily reclined about the decking on the side of the shelter, gesticulating wildly, roaring with laughter while rapidly depleting a vodka bottle of its contents. I tentatively presented myself. After enduring a good hour of banter, mostly at my expense I imagined, I was invited into a room for chai, pasta soup and bread by one of the senior 'engineers' who looked like they were more kitted out for a stag-do than they were to maintain a railway.

I couldn't relate my tales of struggles through the dust storm more than gesturing wind by blowing and proclaiming, "Vetter, niet karasho!" Any other feeble attempt at more advanced Russian merited a *ne panimayu* and the banter and laughing amongst them continued. What an unforeseeable change in dynamic of the day. In all credit to the 'engineers', I was allowed to stay inside for the night, in a separated room with a bed in the railway service shelter. When I woke in the morning at 05:00am, the same engineer from the night before was there. He brought a wholesome breakfast of naan and chai. I wandered outside to prospect the wind. It had certainly died down, but not by as much as I had hoped. It was rideable, just. In any case, I had little choice.

I set out half an hour before sunrise to do at least some cycling in lighter winds. In the next five hours I managed only a pitiful 35 kilometres. Inevitably, as the heat of the day reared, so did the winds. I had very few supplies left and there was no prospect of reaching that next roadhouse by the end of the day. It would have been a mission worthy of a real trooper, something that I had almost resigned myself not to be. Exhausted, I squatted in an area of slightly depressed ground where I tentatively cooked the last of my instant noodles, as my stove struggled to remain alight. In between forkfuls of noodles, I mentally noted the call to hitch hike, knowing that the wind would not stop for probably another 48 hours or so. I had no desire whatsoever to spend them having the energy sapped from my legs as I struggled against the movement of the atmosphere.

Thumb outstretched, it took a surprisingly short time before a car stopped by my side, with plenty of room for a bike to be strapped onto the roof. The driver was a generously fleshed man who, for the four hours or so that I spent with him, was almost constantly chewing *khat*. In the car with him was his younger 'brother'. I ascertained that brother was used in the Asian sense of the word, which just means some lad that he vaguely knows. They were on their way to Moscow from Bukhara to pick up a working family and bring them back to their homeland. I managed to grasp that this was quite a common journey for many drivers on this road. It was a service to transport workers and seemingly their entire lives from ex-Soviet countries to the Russian capital and back. I say their entire lives, as the cars coming the other way were full of families, while the roofs were precariously plied with an abundant amalgam of household objects. The poor Ladas and nexuses were groaning under the weight of washing machines, bikes, barrels of cooking oil, chairs and other items that looked out of place. There was, however, no need for worry or alarm, as the tumbling tetris of tat was securely bound in heavy-duty cling film to stop it from falling. On a 3000 kilometres trip over pothole-wrought macadam passages, what could possibly go wrong?

100 kilometres later, we reached the border, where after a rather lengthy ordeal, including a disgusting display of non-voluntary white privilege, we were allowed to continue. I was fast-tracked through the bustling crowd and given special treatment by the

Kazakh guards. "Welcome to Kazakhstan, again!" They ushered me through the border gate, making me skip ahead of the waiting Uzbeks before forcefully closing it in their faces. Despite my protests that I was in no rush and had to wait for my 'brother' anyway who had cast me a dejected glance as the door was shut on him and the rest of the great unwashed, I was pressed onwards. Clearly, the guards had been told to make a good impression on the wealthy Europeans, probably to increase tourism prospects. I found it rather abhorrent and frankly unwarranted.

That very evening, my two companions and I arrived in Beyneu. The driver, who was almost certainly called 'something-Bek', let me down in a chai kona before continuing onwards to Moscow 30 hours up the road. While waiting for four hours at the border earlier in the day, I had already concluded that I had made the right decision to hitch hike as the wind rattled through the lifeless surroundings of the outpost. *It would have been a fool's errand to continue,* I thought to myself, as I fell to sleep in another teahouse alongside impressively symphonic snoring and farting truckers who trickled in through the night, talking loudly and stealing the room fan to put in their own corner, surely just to waft their sulphuric trumps around for everyone else's indulgence. I was back in Kazakhstan and the Caspian lay a mere 500 kilometres away.

Masters of the Universe

Jeroen and Menno, my favourite Dutch couple, arrived the following evening on the train from Nukus to join me for the 430 kilometres remaining to Kuryk port: the gateway to Azerbaijan. We took in the thrilling sights of Beyneu town including the train station and the high street featuring shops such as 'bread', 'hat' and 'shoe'. Beyneu wasn't at all a bad place, but after two full days allowing my saddle sores to partially recover, it was time to leave.

For some reason or other, it felt like the Caspian was a massive milestone in my trip. It felt like the end of Asia proper before passing into the Caucuses and Turkey and baby Europe. The closer I got to it, the closer I felt to being at peace. I was hungry for the sprint into its shallow waters and thirsty for the sense of closure that it would give to Central Asia. Whereas the end of South East Asia was marked with a land bridge between Lao Cai and Hekou town and the end of China had been marked by a geographically arbitrary border crossing on a line drawn somewhere between the mountains and the Steppe, the end of central Asia was marked by the world's largest inland body of water. It felt more real.

The first day out of Beyneu was a joyful breeze with Jeroen and Menno: 155 kilometres were taken down in relative ease as the road rose at a miniscule gradient of about 0.5 degrees up onto the Ustyurt plateau. The alentours were devoid of all traces of civilisation save for the telephone lines, an odd Muslim cemetery and droves of wandering horses or camels. The homogeneity of the steppe made choosing a camping spot exceedingly simple. We walked a few hundred metres off the road and found ourselves one of the many flat patches, away from shrubs and prickly three-finger jacks that would not be pleasant to sit on… The steppe or desert became my favourite place to camp. As the day came to a close and the sun blushed above the shimmering horizon, the sky's colours silently seeped from blue and purple to pinky reds, while a darkening blanket was slowly draped over from the East. Sitting on the dusty ground. Dicing onions with a blunt, rusty pocket knife. Arcing my gaze over the panoramic spectacle. The steady whistle of the gas stove. Checking around for scorpions. Jeroen and Menno struggling to put up their tent. Bliss. It was hard not to feel like masters of the universe.

Day two out of Beyneu and according to the map there were no villages on the road, but a pockmarked trail of chai konas should see us through the day in terms of nourishment. The first was closed. The second was closed. As we approached the third, some 80 kilometres into the day, it wasn't without a hopeful rumbling of the stomach. Closed. Luckily, by the third one was a run-down old shack around which a scruffy man was lumoxing. "Chai xona yest?" I inquired. He eyed the three of us up with his wise eyes set into a haggard face. We probably looked and smelled like we needed something. Our clothes were incrusted with salt-stains from the sweat, beads of which were still dripping down our brows. Taking pity, he incited us to sit in the shade of his shack, while he called his wife to bring tea. Tea came, along with hundreds of flies swarming to the bowl of sugar like sperm to an egg. Drinking politely was a challenge of endurance.
"Mmm delicious tea," I hollered above the buzz as I wafted away a couple of clouds of flies.
"Ne Panimayu."

The shack here was perched right on the far edge of the plateau. The land simply ended here! At the edge was a single road whooshing down through the rock like a rollercoaster. The drop took us on a breath-taking and exhilarating descent into what used to be another inland sea. The rock surrounding the basin was weathered into curvaceous forms and the lower few tens of metres were encrusted in salt. We shot along the old seabed and the sense of geological time was condensed into seconds. A long time ago we would have been underwater at this point. It was an incredible thought. Interspersed along the road, we each savoured the wind on our backs coaxing us onwards until we came across what looked like a small town: Atlantis (ok, it was actually called Sayotesh). We investigated. A building that looked an awful lot like a chai kona was at the forefront of the village. We rapped on the locked door and peered through the dusty windows. Not a soul was to be seen or heard neither here nor amongst the buildings beyond. Suddenly, from nowhere, a khaki-clad man hobbled towards us and jingled some keys in his right hand. His left arm abouted in a stump. "Chai?"

"Oh with pleasure you saint!" We unanimously squeaked.

As it happened, there was no food stocked in this chai kona, but what was instead served, was a DJ set of global 80s classics. He brought out disco lights and set the disco ball on the ceiling spinning. A four-man disco in a house under the sea with myself, Jeroen, Menno and a Kazakh ex-soldier, who claimed his hand had been shot off by the Taliban in Afghanistan. We danced in Atlantis, fuelled by strong chai, losing ourselves to the woozy otherworld of flashing lights and Gunther's ding-dong song.

After that brief interlude, we exited Sayotesh and arrived back to the real world, not less absurd. We began to climb out of the seabed. The climb, despite the otherworldly surroundings, was of a similar calibre to the ones in the peak district: a good couple of kilometres at about six or seven percent. If I closed my eyes I could have been taking on Winnat's pass or part of the Snake pass or Holme moss. I was in my element and my legs felt like they could spin forever. The road was a travelator. Amazing. After pulling out my emergency snack of dry naan and peanut butter and distributing it among my puffing and panting comrades, we tackled another descent back to sea level and entered what we dubbed 'Camel valley'. It felt like somewhere from walking with dinosaurs. Menno and I began imagining gentle herbivorous stegosaurus sipping from the oasis pools, honking at each other. T-rexes stomped along the road, one just missing us with its wayward left foot! Brachiosaurus and diplodocus plodded noisily amongst the sporadically strewn rocks and boulders on the meagre grass, eyeing us up curiously… The light from the soon to set sun slowly began to dapple across the rock ahead. A smooth empty road bisecting a pit of history. We had it all to ourselves. Emotions were high.

Finally, as twilight encroached, a teahouse came into view, where, hungry and thirsty, both Menno and I decided to down a litre of ayran yoghurt each to kill two birds with one stone. It wasn't long before we were both sprinting to the loo while the affable yet smug Jeroen was slurping his borsht. Distracted by the sublime scenery and dealing with ayran poisoning, I had barely registered that we were less than 150 kilometres from Kuryk port on the Caspian! Two days to go!

Early on the third day from Beyneu we arrived in Shetpe, where we would wait for a friend that the three of us had met in Beyneu. Reenat was a proud man of Mangystau province and had promised to meet us in Shetpe on this day to show us some of the region's formidable sights. He had impeccable English through working on the huge construction project of Aktau's oil pipeline and through completing an MBA in consultancy. We waited for hours until finally, late in the afternoon just before sunset he arrived in a shiny 4x4 with his wife and daughter. He apologized for being late but he had an excuse. In the last 24 hours he had driven over 1000 kilometres including a 200 kilometres detour to take us to Sherkala mountain near to his ancestral village. We arrived just as the sun was setting. This majestic rock, in what was called the 'valley of balls', was surely amongst the most magnificent standalone natural features I had seen, even at a tiny 332m. As the sun receded beyond the valley of balls, I was reminded that size isn't everything.

On the fourth day, hardship returned, with gruelling headwind that meant that we didn't quite make it to the Caspian. Beyond the land of nodding donkeys sucking up oil from the rich crust, we camped one last time on the steppe, with thirty kilometres to go to the Caspian Sea.

Then, after a steady morning of contemplation and excitement, on our last stretch to Kuryk port, the sea finally revealed herself. We descended into Kuryk like a pack of dogs with two dicks, tongues flapping in the wind and tails wagging uncontrollably. We blasted through the town on a beeline for the Caspian. I took the lead. I dismounted the bike in a trance and stepped from land to water. Dipping my toe into the water for the first time, I felt like a selfish Neil Armstrong.

It's hard to condense all this. But in a way it makes the world feel small. Like it fits in the palm of my hand. Yeah I've been through a lot to get here but I'm here. And before I was in Singapore. And (With the exception of a couple of 100ks of hitching) I've arrived on a pushbike. The world is small. All these millions of people between Singapore and here, on this great continent, can be seen from the saddle of a pushbike.

Everyone from everywhere that had before seemed so foreign: the Tibetans, the Thai, the Chinese, the Tajiks, the Uyghurs, the Kazakhs, the Burmese, the Malays, the Yi, the Wa, the Shan, the Karen, the Hui, the Vietnamese, the Lao, the Kyrgyz the Uzbeks and all that is in between seemed to dissolve into a single memory as I reached what I regarded as the end of Asia proper. It seemed like all these people were so close to me and to one another. As if the bike was a stitch in the cloth of the people of this continent. A stitch that weaves another strand into the fabric that remains mostly unchanged but I felt like somehow I was a part of this land now. I had definitely been marked by the people of this place and as I ran into the waters of the Caspian I smiled and rejoiced in what these people had unknowingly given me: a sense of connectedness. From

238

Singapore to the Caspian, these many worlds were one and the same.

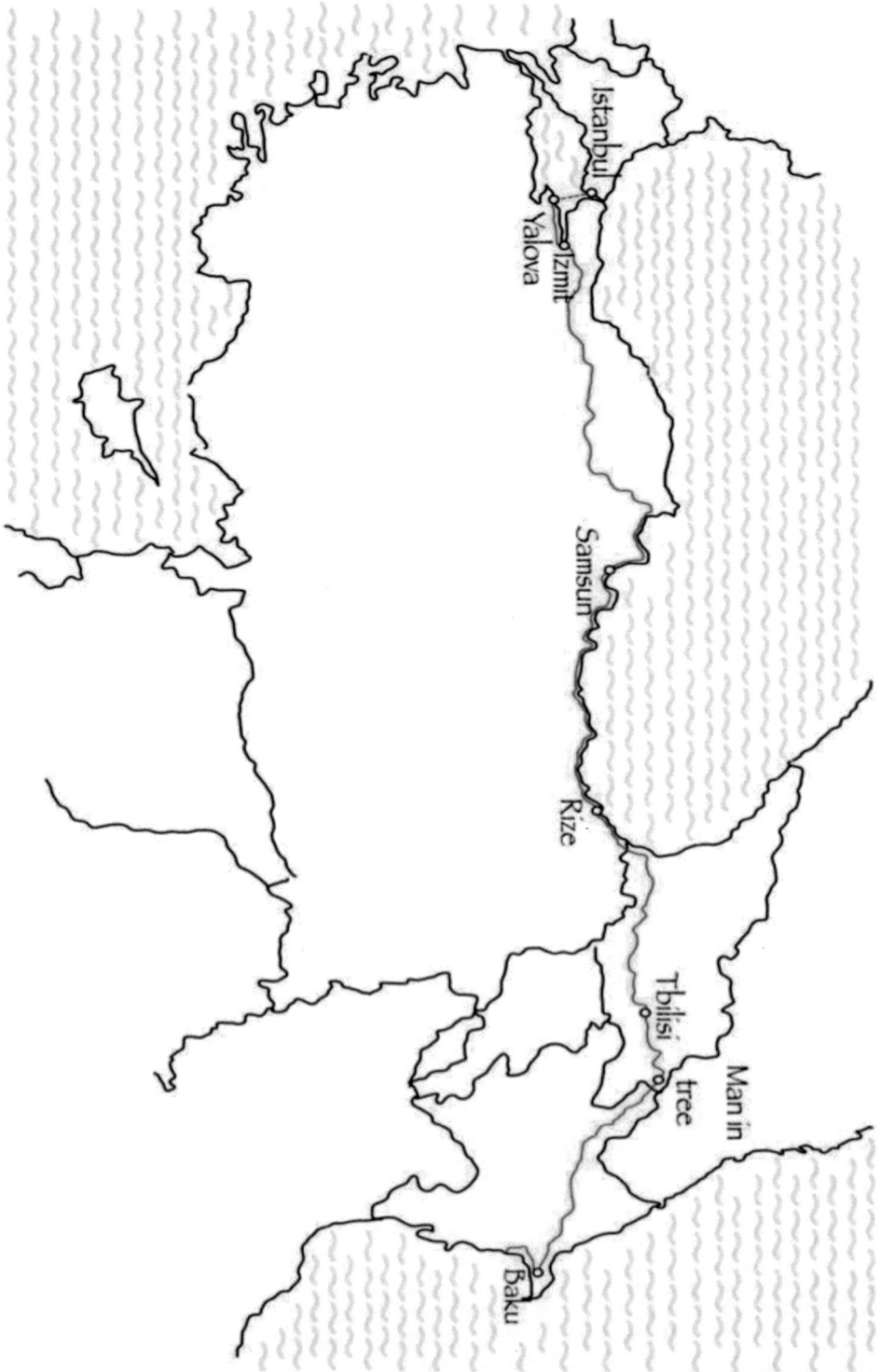

Istanbul

Izmit
Yalova

Samsun

Rize

Tbilisi
tree

Man in

Baku

Inbetween days

The Caspian ferry is a freight boat transporting logistics minions and their cargoes in between Central Asia and Turkey. The odd tourist is also to be found on this ship whose timetable is pretty much a function of weather, how many people turn up at the port and apparently a whole host of other factors that are shrouded in mystery and enigma. A fleet of three Soviet vessels operates between the ports of Kuryk, Kazakhstan and Alat in Azerbaijan. Rumour told us that they appeared and disappeared like ghosts in the night. After the characteristic ramshackle town of Kuryk, It was easy to imagine that the port would be a rotting wooden pier, and the ferry would be a bobbing dingy, lashed to a post and captained by a stoney-faced oar-wielding Kazakh, beckoning us on board for a few hundred Tengge. So it was a massive surprise when a super-modern and airy port complex came into view, resplendent with hotel, canteens and waiting areas. A day and an evening were spent milling about the terminal. Sloth had slowly begun to set in. Word had been circulating amongst the few other waiting travellers of a vessel docking at 1:00 am and departing soon after. At 4:00 am I woke up from a light rest on my roll-mat installed across a few chairs. Nothing had changed. I grew impatient and decided to take matters into my own hands.

I headed to the local decathlon to purchase swimming goggles and armbands to go with my ice cream patterned budgy smugglers with which I had already offended so many people. I looked at all the truckers idling for the ship that might not even be here for another couple of hours. People were sleeping slumped on chairs in the waiting area and Jeroen was even sprawled uncomfortably on the canteen floor. Fools. I asked Jeroen and Menno to keep my bike safe. "Where are you going?" They chimed. Saying nothing, I turned my back to them and strutted seawards before stripping down to my budgies. With my back to all these losers, feeling the fire of their eyes against my white skin, I confidently inflated my bright orange zoggs armbands. I snapped my goggles onto my face and I crowned myself with my swimming cap. I intrepidly dipped my big toe into the water. Shrieks and jumps! *Damn, that water is chilly! Ok. 3 2 1. Go.* I waded in from the rocks then dove below the crystalline surface rippling like satin in the night, before my arm bands brought me back up above the surface. I heard whistle blasts from Kazakh immigration and spotlights danced and illuminated a circle of water around me. I was an aquatic virtuoso. No time for bowing, I began breast stroking my way to Azerbaijan. The commotion behind me was exhilarating. Shouts, sirens and whistles. I turned on to my back and blew a raspberry while sticking my finger up at the bone idle dossers standing on the jetty shouting hopelessly at me to come back. I laughed and turned back onto my front before swimming through the next day to get to Baku port 500 kilometres later where I drip dried and waltzed through Azerbaijan immigration who, agog, with limp mouths, stamped my passport that I pulled from my dripping trunks. "W-w-welcome to A-a-zerbaij-j-jan"

Although this was just a fever dream, I still managed a quick dip in the Caspian with Jeroen and Menno before the battered ferry came at about 07:00 am and took us over glassy water all the way to Alat. It wasn't long before Jeroen and I (Menno had to take a ride because of a problem with his tyre) were navigating towards the centre of Baku, a city whose majesty rivals that of any European capital.

Baku has always been a convergence point of cultures. In the past, the Persians, Russians and Turks have all bridled the Azeri capital, which has led some Azeris to feel disenfranchised from their national identity. What did it mean to be Azeri anyway? From my few days in the country, the impression I got from

Azeris, at least from a foreigner's perspective, was the perfect balance of politeness and forward curiosity with a certain pride that shone through, be that about their food or lush nature. It has to be noted, though, that most of the country differed dramatically from Baku, more so than other capital cities I have visited, with the exception of perhaps Dushanbe in Tajikistan. While Azerbaijan is known as the land of fire, it is Baku where the fiery oil and gas money is invested. It has created a mega city of incredible contrasts, with startling modern skyscrapers that light up the night, set behind the buildings of the restored 11th century old town. A common theme that ran through the capital was an almost sterile cleanliness. There wasn't a trace of grime on even the oldest buildings. It rivalled Singapore.

Waking bleary-eyed and mildly hungover, following a night with Jeroen and Menno scouring the city for elusive, and in fact non-existent gay bars, I resolved to leave the city alone and pick my pace back up to something of the level that I had set myself leaving Samarkand. Humming through the streets of barley-shaded buildings with Jeroen and Menno filled me with joy, but also a false sense of security that I had made it. As far as I was concerned, I had just conquered the crux in crossing the Caspian Sea. I had cycled 18,000 kilometres even though I had set out on this journey expecting to do only 16,000. Alas, 7000 kilometres of road still separated the oil fields of Baku from the green hills of Sheffield.

With renewed focus on the task that I had set myself, I left Baku crawling over the bold brown hills northwest, surrounded by half of the world's mud volcanoes. For such a tiny country, Azerbaijan lay claim to startling scenic diversity. There are none less than 13 different climate zones present in this thumbnail state. From steppe and desert, to polar tundra in barely 100 kilometres. Within a day, I had passed from harsh arid badlands to quaint forests of rustling oak, set beneath the peering snow-capped Caucuses. The beautifully paved road ran over the mountains' feet, rising and falling in meditative rhythm, diaphragmatically. Gentle climb to a bridge across a gushing torrent. Steady descent through golden oaks sponging up afternoon light. Gentle climb. Steady descent. Climb. Descent. Gentle. Steady. I was almost sad when after two and a half days, the extent of this country came to its end at the Georgian border. During the last few kilometres, I mused on a nugget of Charlie's observation. The joy felt while bicycling through glorious nature is down to the traverse. It is not beautiful scenery that makes the skin shiver, but beautiful scenery in motion. A palatable stew of what is before the next corner and what is after it. 'That feeling of just passing through'. It was as if it were the wheels of the bicycle that span the film reel of reality. The bittersweetness in this is that the more the pedals are span, the sooner the end will come. This summed up well my traverse of Azerbaijan. The cycling was so delightful, I could barely stop myself from doing it, but the more I did it, the faster it came to an end.

Crossing the border to Lagodheki, I realised I was pretty much an intercontinental cycle tourist myself. I suspected that this put me in good stead to spout my own romantic nonsense about what cycle touring meant. Whereas the car or the train might be the opera box of the spectacle, the saddle is the front row seat. As the curtains are drawn open each day there is the palpable excitement of being involved in the show at any moment. At once, spectacle and spectator, cycle touring, was above all, balance. The bicycle is slow enough to salute and be saluted by the innocuous passer-by, yet fast enough to be a fleeting enigma. It allows for observation in depth of the goings on of the tiniest of settlements, while allowing the breadth of entire countries to be experienced through the wandering eye. It is a mediator between physical exertion and mental nourishment. At once a statement of self-sufficiency and a desire to be part of something bigger.

The wanderings of my over-active mind were cut off when I heard a shout and a cry, 10 kilometres down the first Georgian road. "Pilemini starzhiniya, balalashi kebab karadaglic (or words to that effect)!"

I slowed my pace, looking around for the source of the noise. "Oi! Shashlik bilasht, oi! Khachapuri!" I stopped. The sound was close and yet there was nobody to be seen. "Oi!" I looked up. In the tree by the road was a very old chap amongst the branches. He seemed very, very stuck and very, very drunk.

"You alreyt pal?!" I shouted up to him. He gestured towards a big stick on the floor.

"Do you want this? khochush da?" He appeared to nod and so I passed him the stick.

"Moi brat Russki ne borsht i Moskva!" He was completely unintelligible.

"Do you need a hand down mate?"

He rasped away in his language and didn't seem to want to descend and so I cycled towards my first campsite in this new Caucasian country, to the soundtrack of yelled ramblings of a drunken old man stuck up a tree. *Welcome to Georgia.*

Following on from Azerbaijan, Georgia had big boots to fill. It did not disappoint, with its beautiful mountains, food and for the first time: Caucasian people! The country felt extremely European, only accentuated with the EU flag draped everywhere there was a flagpole spare. The people no longer well-wished at every possible occasion and instead kept their distance, preferring to observe and form their opinions from perception rather than conversation.

By the time I arrived in the bustling and comfortable capital of Tbilisi, I had covered a stonking 650 kilometres in only four days. I was on a roll, and barely tarried in the city save for trying to fix a problem with my rear derailleur and to purchase cycling shorts that would hopefully relieve the torture of turning my undersack into a carapace. Armed with a new pair of ten-dollar ¾ lengths that left little to the imagination, I set out on the road to Turkey. By this point, I had completely abandoned my idea of watching the black sea coast pass by from the deck of a ferry from Batumi to Bulgaria. I was having far too much fun again on the bike. After almost 19,000 kilometres of cycling, one would imagine that my legs would be like tree trunks and that my core pebbledashed with muscle. Alas, I had only succeeded in losing five kilograms. Nonetheless, my legs felt stronger than ever and I engulfed mountain pass after mountain pass, swallowing up the kilometres like plankton in the mouth of a whale.

After passing by the gorgeous Paravani lake region, where the hills rising into a thin mist reminded me of the beloved Lake District, I was heading for Akhaltsikhe (meaning New Castle). I had camped in the rain twenty kilometres out of this small city and awoke to find something largely amiss with my bike. My rear rack had snapped! It must have been on the heavily potholed road late yesterday, but I don't know how I didn't notice it the previous evening. In any case, out in the woods here nobody was going to come to my aid, so I attempted a rudimentary bodge with satellite ties and bungee cords. I judged that my fix would last a day at the most. I had to find something more long term. In Akhaltsikhe, my mission was to find a hardware store, which was difficult with all the shop signs written in the Georgian Script that looked like a cross between Burmese and Thai! But if words didn't give away a hardware store, then the sight of four balding men stood chain-smoking in power stances did. I approached them. "Hello! Velosiped, problem!" I gestured towards the snapped rack as they began to crowd round the bike. "Problem yest, zdyes." I hoped that speaking Russian would not offend them. "Ah yes problem problem," they agreed and took the bike inside the workshop. *Bingo.*

Within minutes, there were all sorts of attempts at a magnificent bodge. My favourite was a plait of metal wires lodged into the tube either side of the fracture. One of the lads tried to drill screws through the rack and into the plaited wires to brace the whole structure. It could have been beautiful, but the end result was simply a very holy rack. I began to feel a little concerned, seeing the boys scratching their scalps and running their hands through their thick beards in deep thought. Hrant, who I perceived to be the leader, soon began to talk of a 'svarka'. Svarka, sparker, welder. He took me in his car to the scrapheap of Akhaltsikhe, where my suspicions were confirmed.

"Aluminium mozhesht?" Having heard that it was nigh on impossible to find aluminium welders in many countries, it seemed too good to be true that the first chap I came across could do it. "Mozhna, mozhna!" Affirmed Hrant with a manly slap on my shoulder. I left my rack in the hands of the man who appeared to live in his workshop and within ten minutes, I had a sturdy spanking rack in my hands! Hrant refused to let me pay and on the journey home I glimpsed that he was part of a motorcycle club based in Akhaltsikhe. Arriving back in town, a crew of five other riders were soon assembled and we made our way to the motorcycle club's garage hangout. Posters and calendars of Valentino Rossi hung from the wall, as well as a flag of the gang's emblem. Empty bottles of Staropramen were strewn in a corner next to a couple of open toolboxes. Centre stage was a Honda superbike next to a scary-looking concept machine. The cave simply oozed manliness.

Hrant emerged with a beastly 1200cc BMW tourer, joining the superbike, concept machine and two other slower-looking bikes. The plan was to ride to Vardzia. We flew along the road like streamers. I kept an eye on the speedometer. 150, 160, 170 kilometres per hour! The river, the trees and the rock faces that I had been admiringly at length on this very road the day before passed by in a singular blur.

Vardzia was an impressive ancient city built into a mountain. It was commissioned by a 12th century queen to be a stronghold against the Mongols advancing on Europe at the time. Workers dug into the mountain and hollowed it into separate rooms, like a rabbit warren but with enough room for thousands of Georgians. Now, hundreds of years of weathering along with one devastating Earthquake have taken away much of the initial mountain and only a cross section of the former system remains. It was impressive to wander amongst the ancient 'apartments' and to visit the monastic halls. But perhaps most interesting of all was how well preserved the stone toilets were. I was almost tempted…

We rounded off the trip with an obligatory round of honorary beers in the man-garage. The boys wanted to persuade me to swap out my bumbling bicycle for 'a real bike' but even after the high-octane adventure, I couldn't disagree more. Ok, so it was great fun swerving round Georgia's beautiful mountain roads on these massive machines, but it didn't feel any more exhilarating than taking the road on by bicycle, although it was twice (ok, five times) as slow. It was also startling how much less I could take in from the motorbike. We had driven down the exact same road as I had cycled down the previous day. On the bicycle, I had noticed the birds flitting between the trees: Barnes Wallis swallows bouncing along. I could hear the rush and gush of the river. All of this resolution was lost to the blur of speed on the motorbike.

I tipsily thanked the boys, especially Hrant, for everything. They had authored yet another tale of the abundance of generosity and goodwill that is proffered with almost predictable regularity unto the humble cycle tourist. This one made his way onto his penultimate Georgian camping spot before leaving the beautiful Caucasus behind.

On the 2nd of September 2019 I arrived at the Turkish border and crossed into the final country of Asia. "Welcome to Turkey!" Although it felt like I had left Asia behind on the other side of the Caspian, Istanbul, the official watershed civilisation in between this mighty continent and baby Europe, was still about 1200 kilometres away. I planned to cover this distance in ten days to be able to cross into Europe on my Birthday and to meet my Dad who had booked a flight to be there that weekend.

Bridges

There was one common thread that seemed to pull the Turkish nation tight. In a word: *Çay*. This country's tea flows in abundance from the *Çaydanliks* and *Semavers* installed in every building, like water from Mountain springs. It seemed to be the lifeblood of the nation and nowhere could be visited without the suggestion of a coaxing "Çay çay."

"Oh, go on then."

From the smallest villages to the thronging Black sea coastal communities, the humble *çay evi* was never absent. They were immediately recognisable from the congregations of plump men whose smart shirts were open one button too much, revealing a tangle of proud chest hair. These men passed their hours looking at, but not reading newspapers (I knew this as the pages of the paper were never turned), or surveying ruminatively the façade of the other *çay evi* across the road. Occasionally, these havens of gravity and pensiveness were punctuated with animated discussion, which I assumed were mostly arguments of wanting to front the next round.

"Çay çay çay, çay, çay, besh çay !"

Within seconds, a bearded fellow would come with a trayful of five tulip glasses, strong *tavşan kani* or rabbit's blood for the initiated, or the diluted *açik* for novices like me. Like dummies for babies, the teahouse dwellers would soon settle down into their pacified pensive states within the first few sips, before getting back to their games of *okey* or watching the world pass by.

I entered Turkey on the Black coast road that ran almost completely flat along the northern flank of the dominating Anatolian plateau all the way to Sinop, after which it undulated on the mountainous coastline. The newly constructed road with only the gentlest of rises and declines meant that progress was swift. I autopiloted along at between twenty and 25 kilometres per hour on the way to Rize on the first day, freeing up my senses to what Turkey had to offer. The bitter freshness of the Rize tealeaf cultivated on the surface of all the hills receding southwards wafted in the air. The tangy saline air! There were crashes of thunder that boomed from the black storm on the black sea and not before long, the torrential rain arrived. It soaked me to the bone. With blinding water streaming into my face, I pedalled like a madman possessed. The hairs on my arm threatened to stand on end each time the sky quaked above. On one instance, the hairs on my arm very much *did* stand on end as a bolt of lightning struck the hillside about half a mile to my left side! Being a little *too* close for comfort, I took refuge, completely bedraggled, in a coffee house. I sipped away with a smile, perched on a chair prepared with an ingratiating bin bag as strobes of lightning barely warned of the shaking thunder.

The five days to Sinop fell quickly into a settled rhythm. I raced past developed cities: Trabzon, Giresun, Ordu. High volumes of traffic buzzed around these populous settlements, which made the cycling rather stressful and so when there was the occasional choice of a smaller road that scrambled along headlands (while the main road tunnelled through the rock), I took it. Very suddenly, the bustle would cease and I was regaled with sea vistas and silence of all else but the wind and the waves. I stopped in smaller towns at kebab or *pide* houses for lunch, took my breaks in the settled atmosphere unique to *çay evis* and camped on a beach each evening. There was always a secluded spit of sand off the road and the Turks didn't mind my camping there at all. In Samsun, a city of about 600,000 people, I even pitched up on the main beach, completely hassle free. I had assumed that camping wouldn't be such a big deal in Turkey, given the massive number of campers along the coast, tending to their *findik* or hazelnuts, drying out in the late summer sun. Turkey is responsible for 73% of the world's hazelnut production, which after five days on the Black Sea coast was completely believable. For kilometres on end, shells of hazelnut were drying out in the roadside. Entire families were camping out in the ubiquitous lay-bys where they drank tea from *çaydanliks* and occasionally traipsed their bare feet through their crop, turning them over in the sun. My sole takeaway from what must have been over 100 square kilometres of drying nuts, was a jar of *findik* spread that I bought from a roadside vendor. It was the source of inexhaustible fantasy for the black coast stretch. Twenty kilometres until the next *findik ekmek* pause, 10, 5, 2, 1…

About thirty kilometres before Sinop, I decided to leave behind the black sea in favour of the coastal mountain range to Kastamonu. The climb was an unexpected epic. I had been lulled into a false sense of security by the ubiquity of Turkey's food stores and cafés, namely, civilisation. So when the road turned up the hillside I was shocked to find the landscape suddenly and absolutely devoid of human construction. In one way it was refreshing to find myself in an environment of untempered nature again after the hubbub of coastal life. Great pine forests like bristly blankets covered the Pontic range on the north flank of the Anatolian plateau. Life suddenly lost its frantic pace and instead only the odd farmer would amble by on a chugging tractor. I had not even paused for a minute to foresee these rather natural consequences of leaving the coast behind. On the other hand, after the mammoth climb taking me a kilometre closer to the rainclouds above, I began to feel pangs of hunger and had no supplies left in my panniers. Even after so long on the road, it was clear I was by no means a cycle-touring grandmaster. The road flattened. A sign for a town. Hanonu, 30 kilometres. My stomach rumbled and I readied myself for a big slog until a *pide* feast. Just as I began seeing mirages of the *findik* spread floating over shimmering hillcrests, I clocked a trailer full of sweet, juicy melons. My pupils dilated. I had barely stood my bike alongside the trailer when a haggard old woman, face weathered by a lifetime in the elements, appeared from round the side. She offered me a hearty smile and a small honey melon. My heart melted. I sat in the shade of the trailer,

251

carving up the fruit ravenously when she came around again with bread, tomato and salt. I could have kissed her.

I carried on along the rising road to Hanonu reflecting on why, time after time, in hours of need, people came, people helped. How was it that all these strangers conspired to tend their hands? Was it through pity: the sight of a bicycle, laden with sagging bags and ridden by a weary traveller being the epitome of vulnerability? Was it empathy? What would I do if that were *me* on that bike in this heat on this empty road? What if it were my son or my grandson? Was it pure curiosity: A shake-up from the mundane and a foray into the life of a foreigner? Was it through seeing a part of themselves in me: an impossible wish or dream to travel that finds its means only vicariously? Some other form of altruism, unfamiliar to me? Simply a manifestation of white privilege? Religion, *zakat*, doing unto others as one would have done unto themselves, giving alms? It seemed to me that any combination could be possible. I was sure though, that in all of these cases, the power of travelling humbly cracked open the nutshell of the stranger and allowed these astonishingly good attributes of humanity to come forth. It is *the humble* that opens up the world and writes the stories of a hundred thousand incredible adventures, every day, that succeed only with unlikely helping hands.

The mountainous landscape of Turkey seemed it would never flatten after taking the inland road. Col after col after col led on to Kastamonu, Karabuk, Düzce and eventually all the way to Izmit, on the Eastern extreme of the Sea of Marmara. The constant undulations made me feel like I was on the 'big one' at Blackpool pleasure beach, except that the ride was about 50 times slower and 500 times longer. The clock had been ticking. For all of Turkey I had raced along, never taking a day off and consistently topping 120 kilometres, but as I approached Izmit, the race was all but won. It was the 11th of September. A tiny stretch of only seventy kilometres would take me on the quieter road to Yalova the next day, from where I could get a quick ferry into Western Istanbul. I would enter Europe on my Birthday.

On the speedy Yalova to Yenkapi ferry, I made sure that I stood at the bow to allow the wind to whip my face and drown everything else out from beside and behind me. I wanted to contemplate the odyssey that I was on the cusp of completing. Cycled Asia. Going to cycle Europe. As is often the case when one wishes to contemplate, all thoughts that entered my mind consisted of either nonsense, or what I was going to fill my belly with upon arriving in Istanbul. Ignorant to my existence, the wind whipped on, as the boat moved assuredly forward. It skirted around an island on which gnarled stone pines and contemplative olive trees clung tentatively to the hillside, poring over the lapping waves. As we swept by the island, the fuzzy outline of Western Istanbul was revealed: a sprawling mess of colours (roses, reds, whites, pale-creams, baby-blues and mustard-yellows) and buildings that looked as if they were all on top of each other. Mosque towers could be seen reaching skyward. Wriggling Turkish flags revealed that, as advertised, we hadn't changed country just yet. From getting off the ferry until the moment I would see my old man for the first time in almost a year, I had about 28 hours to indulge in the finest and simplest of pastimes. The one that is the common thread between the long-distance traveller and the Turkmen: watching people behind a teacup.

I would always opt for the least conspicuous haunts. By preference and paradox, those in which no other Western folk sat or would choose to sit. Main squares and long avenues were immediately out of the question. It was a matter of finding the right balance of grit and charm. A place remarkable only through being the shortest of deviations from the ordinary and unexceptional. A place where a few plastic stools and mini-tables, adorned with sugar cubes and ashtrays were disposed out front. The interior: lugubrious but not uninviting. A tacky laminated menu stuck to the wall was a bonus. The waiter should look disinterested – slightly aloof but not unkind. The clientele's faces should be obscured by tea steam, only revealing a distant rumination between the wisps and the sips. A place where people passed but seldom stopped. A place settled on the cusp of feeling lost. In between nowhere, and the bustle.

I didn't spend *all* of my 28 hours in such places. Most of the time was spent meandering around the thronging Istanbollu backstreets trying to find the bloody joints! When I was there I watched and pondered and observed and thought. *Wow, look at those binmen – how respected they are and how diligently they work, maybe I should look into that when I get home. Huh, that woman is carrying a lot of different spices! I'm enjoying myself, I wonder if I have enough money left to cycle through Africa or the Americas. Shit, I should perhaps try and organise a job for when I get home. Dad's getting here tomorrow! Why are the binmen back again? Why is my mind constantly embarking on thought trains and then losing, oh wow, it's getting late!*

Finally, on the second evening in Istanbul, my dad arrived. He had been a massive source of support throughout the trip. He made sure he 'liked' my blog posts within the first hour they were put up and was always on the other end of a phone to let me dissipate my travel woes. It felt fitting that he was now, really and in person, part of the physical journey, even if this part did consist of filling up on *çay, pide, börek* and the other usual suspects. It clearly meant a lot to him to be here, to travel once more to such a landmark city. Especially one that he had been to before, forty years previously, at the start of the magic bus hippy trail. My dad's nostalgia took us to a small establishment called 'The pudding shop', that he had once visited with his best friend, Martin. Back in the '70s, it was a focal point of congregation for travellers, a last iconic hangout before the overland route into Asia. It was famous not so much for its food, but for its notice board. Here, letters of romance, memos of plans and hopes of future meetings were left by travellers for those following in their wake. 'Tim, hope you're well mate! Let's meet in Delhi in 2 months time, Fabien.' 'Linda, I can't wait for our Rishikesh nights in 50 days, Fred x.' 'Looking for 2 more free spirits to share a ride to Kathmandu, Katie. x' After our meal, my dad wrote a note of his own, pinning his memories of 40 years ago to the board with the permission of an apathetic and otherwise unmoved waiter. I guess he had a lot of nostalgic fogies doing the same thing every day. After three relaxed days, it was time for my old man to head back to the UK, while I still had the small business of cycling across a continent to consider.

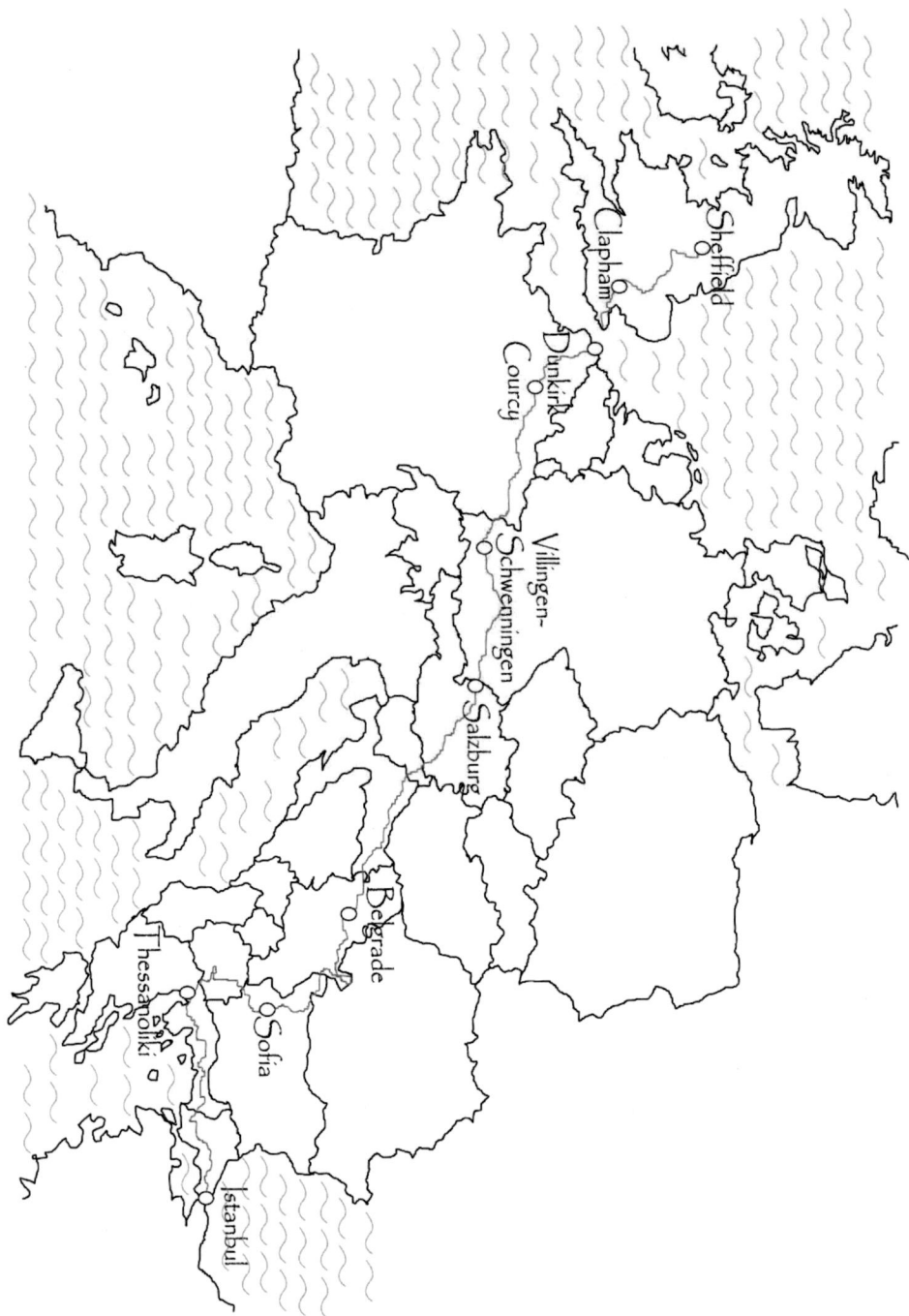

Clapham

Sheffield

Dunkirk

Courcy

Villingen-

Schwenningen

Salzburg

Belgrade

Thessaloniki

Sofia

Istanbul

256

Catch-up

I had heard horrific accounts of cycling out of Istanbul. Twelve-lane highways on which speeding cars snake indiscriminately. Three-lane slip roads leading to inadvertent games of chicken. A haze so thick, that one can barely see their impending death. Frankly, I found it rather tame. Compared to say, the outskirts of Trabzon, or the road towards Johor Bahru on the way into the Asian continent, it seemed relatively calm and orderly. After fifty kilometres, the traffic had completely thinned on the route to the border with Greece. I had promised to meet my mother and my nanan in Thessaloniki in five days and I had 700 kilometres to cover. "Easy, I'll be waiting for you!" I had told them in the phone conversation when they asked if I could make it. I barely had time to stop and take an extra breath. It would require every minute of daylight at my disposal to make the distance to Greece's second city in this time.

Within only two days, whizzing by the stilling undulations of fields of wheat, I had reached the Hellenic border. Men with moon faces and bristly moustaches milled around the quaint border post, ushering me through with utmost nonchalance. One eventually decided to skim my passport in between sips of coffee. "Where you go?"

"Thessaloniki, then back to England!" My dazzling plans merited what was either an approving or contemptuous grunt. "Welcome to Greece."

It was the first time I had gotten through a country since Singapore with my passport unstamped. I was almost woeful of this abrupt discontinuity in my passport journey. *How would anyone know I had cycled across Europe if I had no stamps in my passport?* If no stamp was the first indicator that I was back in a union country, then the next was the suddenly extortionate prices. *A euro for a bottle of coke?! A euro for even a bottle of water?! Coffee? That'll be three euros!* I was gobsmacked at the hole that was being slowly drilled into my wallet by the wonton greed of western capitalism. It eventually became clear to me that I had to change my model of food sourcing. Throughout all of Asia, food can be bought from markets. Be they stalls on the street side, shipping containers in the high mountains or simply Chinese or Turkish shops. In all of these market places, groceries are to be purchased fresh and at a fair price. If the food is not fresh, it is generally not bought and if the price is not fair, it can become fair with respectful barter. In European markets, or 'convenience stores', the price is not fair, the food often not fresh, and no amount of boycott or barter can hope to change that. For the business lays its foundation not on being a store, but on being convenient. I soon stopped relying on these European 'markets' as I did the Asian ones. I had to place my allegiance with something that had been absent from my life for nigh upon nine months. Something bigger, transcendent even. A Klein bottle of loathing dependence. *You can try to get out, but you will always come back.* An ouroborus of consumerism. Yes, in Europe I was faced once more with the horrors of shopping at the supermarket.

Aside from this minor culture shock and a gruelling headwind that impeded progress to a frustrating grind, the Greek regions of Thrace and Macedonia were lovely (as it seems, is most of the planet). I spent my hours now cycling past Mediterranean villas with their characteristic orange tiled roofs, dry hillsides sprinkled with shrubs and vast groves of olive trees, cicadas humming excitedly in the shade of pines. Eventually, I even came to join the tranquil slosh of the Mediterranean itself. It seemed almost intractable, 260 days ago in Singapore, that I would arrive at the seas of the med, by bicycle! Every day on the bike was just business as usual, but now the sum of these infinitesimal atoms of the journey were beginning to add up to something to be proud of. It seemed that the trace I had drawn on the map was very suddenly of global scale. I thought back to the moment I looked at the map two days into Malaysia, near Batu Pahat. How I had winced and despaired at the pitiful and

258

meagre line I had drawn! My mouth was full of too much to chew. Now it felt like I was letting dainty mints melt on my tongue, while my stomach bloated in contentment.

Coastal towns came and went. Alexandroupolis, Kavala, Asprovalta. I passed through in haste against non-stop blustery headwind, stopping only for a daily coffee, *spanakopita* or *bougatsa*. On the penultimate night, with only 90 kilometres left to Thessaloniki (after a 160 kilometres day to ensure that this was the case) I fell asleep soundly in my tent on an empty beach near Asprovalta, almost sure that I could make it. What I did not expect, was a thunderstorm to develop above me in the night, delivering with it a harsh residual headwind that greeted me the morning after. Not a single one of them 90 remaining kilometres could be called enjoyable. I cursed in oaths beneath my breath as I gritted my teeth and sullenly sunk my head to meet the handlebars. It was the fact I had an absolute destination that made it such a task. I had fixed unalterable expectations of myself, which given any other circumstances, would have changed in wake of such adverse conditions. On this day they simply couldn't. I arrived in Thessaloniki completely bedraggled. I was barely even satisfied to see my own mother!

Spending three days with my mother and nanan equated essentially to being pampered. We slowly wandered the quirky streets to the grand seafront, where people whirred along on communal electric scooters. This gave my nanan an idea and with ten minutes, we too were whizzing along, screaming in fright and at civilians to shift. A 74 and 24-year-old charging full throttle along the main walkway caused quite a commotion. That very evening, my dear friend Martha, along with her boyfriend Alex arrived in Thessaloniki. They had been travelling overland through Europe and as coincidence conspired, they arrived in Thessaloniki for their flight home on the same day as that of my nanan and mother. We lounged and chatted away in a cacophonous courtyard shared by many heaving *tavernas*, aided by karaffs of wine and a beer that made my nanan laugh: the infamous '*vergina*'.

On Monday 23rd of September, my mother and nanan left in a taxi for their flight back home. The unlikely tidal crash of worlds bringing Martha, my mother my nanan and myself together in Thessaloniki receded. Once more, only me.

The next stages were almost all written in plan. There was room neither in my headspace nor on the map for meanderings. I was to meet my friend Seb in Sofia in just under a week's time. Seb is another of those people in my entourage whose zest for life is one of my personal inspirations. He is one of those chaps who always have a way of getting things done. This was especially great since most of the 'things' that he deemed worthy of getting done were often wonderfully absurd and brimming with quirk. Be that organising his own half marathon where it was mandatory to wear hi-visibility jackets and a bicycle helmet, or leaving graduation early to drive from London to Kyrgyzstan. He had now somehow managed to procure a bicycle and find the time to fly out to meet me in the Bulgarian capital. Our aim was to cycle together to Belgrade. It promised to be full of outrageous misadventure and I was ticking with excitement and anticipation. Sofia was really only a stone's throw from Thessaloniki – I had one week to cover some 250 kilometres (as the crow flies) and so I decided to take a long detour onto the little travelled roads of North Macedonia. I'm glad I did. The roads going up into the mountains here would often suddenly cease to be tarmacked, replaced by earthen tracks and trails where no vehicle but the odd tractor or oxen-drawn cart would be present, each of whom greeted me with warm salutations and sometimes a laugh.

On the first instance that I was acquainted with these tracks, it was towards the end of a day of constant drizzle: the kind of dreach curtain of low-lying cloud that one might expect of a nice day in the Scottish Highlands. The road snaked up through a couple of tucked away villages: the sort where red tiles form unintentionally curvaceous roofs on the buildings and headscarf-clad old dears peer nosily through cracks in the shutters, if they're not out beating a rug. At the end of the road was a single earthen track that soon bifurcated chaotically into a network of trails that spanned the space between the encroaching hillsides. This is the way I took, just as a heavy thunderstorm set in. The sky darkened in an instant and thunderclaps brought a great deluge, flooding the way and softening the clay that constantly stuck between my mudguard and wheel. I couldn't cycle 100 metres without having to find a stick to dislodge the pesky congealed earth. Lost and filthy and wet I decided not to go any further. Although there was no real risk (other than the improbable event of being struck by lightning) in continuing, I simply couldn't claim to have had the desire to camp in a muddy puddle by choice: the very first night of camping in Australia with Pierre having put me off for life. I headed back the way I came until I reached the water trough I had remarked earlier. Washing the best of the mud and crass off my body and bike, I found a place to camp. It was certainly a favourable position here, on a hillock above the village shared by a few roaming cows. The sunrise the morning after was glorious: soft light fed through the last of the low-lying cloud that sailed wistfully along the lake below. I sat in the open doorway of my tent, taking it all in, undisturbed and at peace. Within an hour or so, the socks that I had left hung on a tree to dry would be ready and I would set out to find an alternative route to the sure-to-be flooded tracks that I had wished to take.

Through the rest of Macedonia and Bulgaria, I was surprised at the topography. Especially Bulgaria, whose peaks in the Rila range towered towards 3000 m. In both countries I was delighted by the quietness of the sinuous country roads that lazily stretched from sleepy village to sleepy village. In fact, I would go as far as saying that the seven days between Thessaloniki and Sofia, were amongst the most pleasant and serendipitous of the whole trip. I rolled into Bulgaria's capital feeling pretty pleased with myself. Relaxed, at ease, satisfied. Almost enveloped in a wispy nonchalance of invincibility. I was pervaded with an urge to constantly hum and smile, knowing everything was going well and that I was finally to be reunited with Seb.

Until Seb's arrival, I was happily churning out days of 120 kilometres. We had planned to cover some 500 over the coming week. On the first day, we accomplished thirteen. It wasn't that Seb was particularly unfit, on the contrary, he was quite capable and although at the time I tried to hide it, I worried as we headed out of Sofia up a hill and I struggled to keep up with his fiery pace. Alas, Seb's speed was at the detriment of his endurance, and after ten kilometres of said struggle, we pitched up for the first time together, sharing stories of what had happened in our wildly different lives.

Heading north, we laughed and chatted our way to the Serbian border while munching down the kilometres. Eighty in a day became pleasant and easy, giving us plenty of time to enjoy each other's company and converse with the locals in a mixture of pig Russian and perfect Polish, hoping it somehow equated to Bulgarian and later, Serbian. We mostly got across what we wanted.
Within only two days, we reached the legendary Danube and within three, we had reached the border with Serbia. There was a slight delay as the border guards were investigating a suspect German man trying to import an enormous quantity of legumes for an estranged uncle… We wished him good luck, as the border guards eventually ushered us on through, keen to crack on with the field day they were having.

Crossing the border we noticed plenty of brown signs depicting the promising and overly wholesome symbol of a bunch of grapes. We had entered Serbian wine country. On our merry way towards the border town of Negotin, we agreed that we couldn't pass through this region without paying a visit to one of the vineyards. We contracted the help of a lady with whom I instantly fell in love at the tourist office of Negotin. She dubiously put a word in for us with a local vigneron, fifteen kilometres or so up the road. Over the sound of my furiously palpitating heart I gleamed that we should get there as soon as possible for a look around before they retire for the day. Seb dragged me away as I hopelessly searched for further questions satisfying the balance of charm, wit and genuine interest to win if not her heart, at least another of her reassuring smiles. Seb ribbed me as we pootled towards the vineyard and I shrugged off his jibes, secretly seething with melancholy. *Ah, futility of fleeting love!*

We arrived at the vineyard a couple of hours before dusk. Contrary to what the love of my life cum tourist informant had told us, they didn't seem to be expecting any sweaty lycra-clad cyclists with cheesy expectant smiles. Nonetheless, we were duly shown around their impressive cellars and fermentation vats. A few characters joined us on the tour. There were a couple of family members of the wine-maker, all humble and warm-faced. An English-speaking aficionado of wine and *rakija* came along midway through the tour. He was there that evening to give a business presentation on roof tiles (yawn). Finally, mostly at a distance, we were joined by Noddy. He was thin and his wrinkled skin seemed to flap about his face, and yet he was barely touching forty. His stooped mannerisms were almost servile and he wore tattered work clothes. When he talked, he seemed to struggle to articulate and most of what he said came out in rasps. It was hard not to think of him as a relic of serfdom.

After the tour, indulging in a couple of obligatory glasses of wine and *rakija*, the tile merchant took the parole and our yawning soon ceased. He explained that that very evening, after his business presentation there was to be, in true Serbian style, a great banquet and a party, where the wine was to flow like water to facilitate the making of business arrangements between the punters invited. He wanted to make us two punters of honour. The vigneron agreed to let us stay in a guest room upstairs and asked for a contribution of ten euros each for the food. Deal, done. We had a few hours to beguile and in that time we accompanied Noddy to the animal enclosure. He was enthusiastic to show us around.

The hazy sky dulled the heat of the day that was slowly easing anyway as the sun set behind the ranks of vines in front of the grandly understated chateau. I took a walk to fill myself with the cool evening air and reflect on what an incredulous world it is that we share: and how it is the way it is shared that makes it incredulous. Indeed, in such a situation, it's almost easy to feel guilty to have been lathered with so much undue privilege. Was there a catch to all this kindness that runs as a constant theme? Experience told me that surprisingly, no! Human interaction is something that has constantly opened my eyes on this journey. It has been the source of almost all incidences of serendipity. Although the networks, concepts and ideas that people build in this modern world through interaction can sometimes be terribly alienating, it nonetheless remains the source of a rich and beautiful complexity of experience and emotion, that can be tapped into from something as simple as a smile, a hello and a conversation shared with a friend or a stranger. It seems so odd and irreconcilable. Emergent from human interaction are beastly systems and entities that compete for power, monopoly and control. While on a fundamental level, human interaction is almost always centred on sharing and goodwill. I feel it is important that societal organisation exists on these large scales, at least insofar as there is no sign of going back to simpler times. But a shift away from focusing on the rigmaroles of society, towards taking solace in the elements that make up society, which is to say, us, humans, is certainly something that I have found greatly comforting and reassuring in this otherwise wild world.

I was distracted from my thought train as Noddy came around the corner, blurting out something that was obviously funny in Serbian, as he laughed and smiled at his own joke. I laughed and smiled too and headed in to join Seb in getting ready for the big party…

After the tile-merchant concluded his two hour-long discourse on the advantages of his *krepa* above the competitors' *krepa*, we were invited to take to the dining hall and were seated at the long oak refectory tables. Immaculately dressed waiters brought out platters of grilled vegetables and mountains of barbecued meat that pervaded the hall with a smoky lust for stuffing one's face. At first all the guests picked at it with trepidation, feigning to be absorbed in their own thoughts while savouring the scrumptious meal. But soon, as more and more wine was consumed people began to laugh and joke and grab at the thick sausages and shamelessly shovel down rashers of bacon. Alas, the merriment truly began when the accordion came out and most of the men, who at this point in the evening, were flushed as red as tomatoes, grinned broadly from ear to ear while belting out Serbian folk. Around Seb and I were sat Sinisa and his Franco-Serbe relative, Fred. In the jovial forget-all-else spirit of the evening we made a wager with each other, reminiscent of Philleas Fogg at the reform club albeit with slightly lower steaks. Sinisa barely believed that I had cycled across Asia and prospecting the map he scoffed at my idea of getting back to the UK within a month. The challenge, then, was to make it to the foot of big ben in this time. The date was 2nd October. I reckoned I was going to make it to London before the 26th and so, a bottle of fine Serbian wine against a bottle of fine French wine (England being devoid of such quality) was put on the line and once again, a ticking clock was mounted in the back of my mind.

Suitably hungover, we hazily stumbled down the stairs rubbing our heads and surveying the immaculate hall that was the playground of raucous and jovial activity just a few hours ago.

Clearly, the cleaners were slightly over-zealous or the whole party had been a crazy dream. We were seen out by the son, who ran the business side of the Vinerija Boirescu. We bought a couple of bottles for the road, and boss junior slipped us a couple extra with a cheeky wink. With that final show of staggering kindness, we headed out of the vineyard gates, and towards the iron gates.

The iron gates are huge cliffs that suddenly encroach on the Danube on its course between the lands of Romania and Serbia. Before arriving there we fought hangover and headwind to advance northwards. In a provincial village, we stocked up on snacks and were called over by a group of men congregated outside the small store, some swigging beer, others - whisky and the eldest, something stronger. At least one of our matinal woes was cured by the moonshined shit that they procured unto us, laughing as we reacted to the harsh liquid evaporating or combusting on its burning tirade down our throats. Some sixty kilometres later, we approached the impressive 'gates'. Staunch Silvery cliffs stood proudly on both sides of the mighty river, mottled with fiery autumnal trees. The issue that this brings for the touring cyclist lies herein: if impressive tall cliffs are feasts for the eyes, then legs are the feasts for impressive tall cliffs. Cycling over the iron gates certainly didn't come without challenge, but we both agreed that this was more than compensated for by the sweeping vistas of the Danube and the blustering descents that ensued.

The weather was continuously getting cooler, making camping a rather chilling affair. At the time Seb arrived in Bulgaria, the thermometer was still reaching into the high twenties, and the nights were pleasant. Now, as we woke shivering and dirty from another light sleep, on the flat edge of a wheat field 120 kilometres from Belgrade, the mercury was struggling to stay afloat the freezing mark. As we cycled along that morning, the air packed a punch of frost that hit straight into the lungs and for the first hour we barely warmed up. Five days of constant cycling had taken its toll on Seb, and although his spirits remained mostly intact, his body was screaming out to put a stop to this ridiculous nonsense! In a cruel and wicked throe, surely associated with the cold and the fatigue, Seb's leg gave in halfway up the first climb. It sounded like a muscle injury of some sort. With over 100 kilometres left to Belgrade, this wasn't the most welcome news. We broke fast at the first village we came to, again, finding a sombre group of men gravely sipping from beer bottles. We identified two options for the day, weighing up Seb's prohibitive leg against both of our preponderances against spending another shivery night in the tent. Option 1 was to take it easy, 'the reasonable option', and make it to Belgrade on Sunday for a night's rest before Seb's departure. Option 2 was to grit the teeth, clench the butt-cheeks and smash out 110 further kilometres to Belgrade in the day. 'The stupid and potentially dangerous option': in other words, the one that we could not resist choosing.

With dusk approaching, we summited the last of a succession of three steep hills, exhausted. Our faces, though flushed with sweat and telling of our effort, betrayed a complicit proud smugness. Catching our breath, together, we rode onwards. The light splayed between the young boughs of leafy oaks that lined the now gently descending boulevard. Buildings began to get closer, higher and grander. The road split to accommodate rails that curved in from a busy intersection. To the chime of an evening tram wagon, we passed the sign: Beograd! We had made it! We fully savoured the last decline towards the city centre: past parks, museums, theatres, and already bustling restaurants. We had made it to the capital in emphatic style with a full day in hand. This meant we had plenty of time to 'relax' by cracking open the wine that I had carried in my bottle cage for the past three days… It was odd that we both once more found ourselves heavy-headed after our steady evening in Belgrade. We wandered hazily and steadily, almost floating through the Sunday morning streets that seemed so gentle and tender compared to the evening before. The city was just seeing-in the end of the summer to autumn transition and from a café, disguised behind our books, we observed the first of the falling leaves and hunched church-goers sauntering out of Sunday-service. I missed such simple delights as these and my short time in Belgrade with Seb was not only relaxing and joyous, but a reminder of the idealism of home-life that I cherished. Imbibed with café-lounging thoughts and longings, my focus was more than ever sharpened on home. I left Seb on the Monday with one thing on my mind – the dash to France.

I was content to have swept aside the rest of Serbia in that half day, as I set up camp just beyond the Croatian border 140 kilometres beyond Belgrade. The route was rather fluid but largely, I was aiming for Slovenia, Austria and a route through Bavaria and the black forest to Strasbourg. The 'west' had begun.

Dash

It took me two days to clear Croatia – it being flat and boring and very conducive to big days. I just topped 200 kilometres on my first full day, stopping only once to be accosted by a man walking through the manicured grounds of a castle in the small town of Valpovo. "Ad kuda ty?"

By this point I knew the drill and had even levelled up from being able to say 'England' to being able to say 'Great Britain'. "Iz Velika Britannia," I replied almost proudly.

"Ah, Velika Britannia, velika problem!" He chuckled and plodded on his way. Ah yes, now I was back in Western Europe I was open and defenceless to the justified Brexit jibes. The fact that Croatia was perceived to be so boring is appreciated in noting that this brief encounter was my most in-depth interaction with a local. I was lost in a whirlwind of solitary speed that precluded any conversation or learning of the Croat ways. It regrettably became just a tick on the list. On the other hand, if I were to judge my success and satisfaction by the criteria of how swiftly I was moving, I could certainly be proud of myself.

In only four days I had transported myself from Belgrade to Austria.

Like Croatia, Slovenia became a tick on my list, a feather in the cap, and a flag badge metaphorically stitched to my sash. Only a grey but beautiful morning was spent in this country, amongst the bucolic green hills that hinted gently *'we are the foothills to the alps!'* Indeed the Alps were approaching. The houses were now all painted magnolia blossom pink or custard cream, crowned with orange tiles like scales of terracotta fish. Vibrant colours accentuated windows and cantilevered roofs cast sharp shadows. I hummed my way along, picking up on all these familiar idiosyncrasies while gradually gaining height following the road to Graz. I passed without pomp into Austria, where quite suddenly there seemed to be a five-fold increase in petrol stations, hardware stores, supermarkets and traffic. *This* was Western Europe as I knew it. The landscape was unaltered at the imaginary line between Slovenia and Austria, but now, coaxes of temptation were everywhere. Huge billboards decrying the potential shopper from passing the liebmarkt without coming in to purchase the garden chairs that they simply *must* have. A Billa markt with thirty cars parked, but space for 270 more. Purchase your seventy year loyalty card and get five years free!

I was, in general, rather jarred by the new order of Western Europe. There seemed to be far less scope for the unexpected and everyone, instead of loafing or taking time to indulge their curiosity, was highly focused on some sort of mission. In one instance, I was cycling along a busy road, which soon became a fast dual carriageway and more cars came out of nowhere (explainable by the increase in speed limit). Suddenly, cars began to beep their horns. One driver, with his window down, face like a tomato under uniform compression, belted out a string of what I assume were profane expletives. I shrugged him off and showed him a gruff finger. Not long after this unmemorable incident, at a layby, the same car was waiting and the driver motioned angrily for me to come. I was ready. He began by shrieking something in German.

"I. Do. Not. Understand. Your. Language." I replied trying to sound as patronising and rude as possible.

"You cannot cycle on zee highvay! Vat vere you theenking?" He pointed and flapped to a sign depicting a cyclist encircled in red.

"Ah, that one…" I smiled and changed tack, while he carried on spouting about the dangers of the road.

"Look mate, I've cycled on far busier roads than this and I'm safe in the hard shoulder, but thanks for the concern."

He began to cool down and we shook hands. Although I was miffed, he was right. It did seem that suddenly the road had become a motorway and clearly, I wasn't going to get the same reception on motorways in Austria as I did in Singapore or Xinjiang. Rules were back.

While in Austria, one of the most expensive countries of the trip, I couldn't help but make a few comparisons to countries I had been through in the last year. I sat reflecting on this in a mediocre café during one unfortunate instance where I got stung with a 4.50€ coffee. This is about twenty times the price of a roadside coffee in Thailand. I remarked that that same sum could have almost paid for two nights in a hotel in some of the cheaper guesthouses in Burma. It is also almost the sum that a teacher in Alichur, Tajikistan might expect to earn for two days work. Global inequality is startling isn't it? I couldn't afford accommodation in Austria. I inquired as to the cost of a *zimmer* at a few *gasthofs* that I had passed. Returns of 40-50€ made me laugh and move on to a place I could put up my tent. 50€ was enough to live on for about a week as a traveller in much of Asia. Although the night in the tent was chilly, its pure simplicity and reliability felt in the end almost preferable. I woke to a crisp morning on a quieter road, taking on my first alpine mountain pass that rose to 1544 m before a racy descent to Judenburg.

There is and always will be something special about the Alps for me. Beyond the stalwart legions of spruces that rise up the hillsides from the brilliant green pastures to the proud buttresses of rock that burst forth at higher altitudes in the East. Beyond the jagged aiguilles on knife-edge ridges in the western massifs. More than the majestic bust of the Matterhorn or above the glacial heights of the Grand Combin or la Meije. Transcending the lunar peaks of the Queyras and lost in the forests of the Chartreuse there is some oxymoronic comfort in these inhospitable places. I suppose that recent history has seen the Alps become more and more civilised and populated. Nonetheless, even out of the way of the quaint and quiescent Alpine villages there is a sense of these mountains being at once inviting and unyielding. Like the prettiest girl or cutest boy in school for whom everyone had a palpitating crush. In contrast, the Asian ranges were simply of such sublime brash unattainability, that they could only be compared to a TV model, startlingly beautiful yet so far removed from emotional investment, at least for a Joe as average as myself. As I reared on the summit of the col after a long morning of significant climbing, my heart leapt at the vista, as if the prettiest girl had just dropped me a wink.

I rejoiced in the billowing descent before joining the valley tainted by Austria's obsession for billboards and hardware stores. The ubiquity of civilisation here meant that I couldn't find an out-of-the way place to camp for the night. As dusk began to draw in, along with the twilight chill, I approached a chap who was hanging around outside a house near a flat and well-mown plot of grass with a stunning view onto a nearby peak.

I asked in my best German, "Kann Ich hier schlaffen?"
He seemed a little confused and ran away, returning two minutes later with a set of keys. He spoke pig English and between his tentative linguist skills and my own, we managed to have a half-satisfying conversation. We touched quickly on the philosophy of life on the road and the romance of the kindness of strangers, etc. The keys were for his shed where he let me stay for the night on a plank of wood. It fell a little short of the Schloss Belvedere but he claimed it would be warmer than my tent. It almost certainly wasn't. Even in the warmer sleeping bag that Seb had left for me, I awoke shivering in the night a few times and from 05:00 am I stayed awake, praying for dawn to hurry along. When finally it did, it brought with it an absolutely enchanting morning. Low-lying cloud bumbled along the bases of nearby peaks, giving the incredible illusion that they were floating on their midriffs. Spruces and pines waded through the shrouds of mist that were slowly dissipating in the morning sun, while the clink of cowbells arranged about the veiled pastures played an ethereal and soothing melody. I

revered and revelled in this fantastic Alpine beauty all day: over steady passes and towards the cluster of shimmering sapphire lakes by Bad Ischl and finally into the city of Salzburg, right on the German border.

On the 13th October I crossed into Germany. At least, I noticed I had done so only after five kilometres. There was no indication, no welcome to Germany or inscribed stone or enormous flag proudly flying in the wind. No grumpy border guards hungry for passports. The transition was seamless. With regards to my running wager, I was, boringly enough, well on track for arriving in London before the 2nd November. So much so, to the extent that I began making plans with friends to meet them in Dover on the 26th of October.

The first few hours in Germany were promising. It was a Sunday morning and hardly a car was to be heard on the roads. There was the noise of distant strimming of grass and the odd tractor lazily ploughed the post-harvest fields. Cyclists of all ilk passed and were passed by me: from the vigorously gurning huddle of roadies, looking down at their Garmin power metres in between winces of pain, to the more recreational old dears on sit-up-and-beg bikes, surveying the Austrian alps that were the backdrop of the surrounding green country. Fit families flitted across the criss-crossing lanes, the kids not only putting up with the likely enforced Sunday outing, but actually enjoying themselves! It all seemed far too utopian.

In the first village, I came across the only shop that was open: a waffle and ice cream stand, not exactly a cause for complaint. It seemed that the whole village was congregating here, delighting in a welcome spoonful of frozen joy or four. A few men were wearing traditional Lederhosen and a couple of young girls with pig-tailed hair even donned the dirndl. Again, with no evidence of contempt for their elders who had clearly dressed them so. It seemed no bad could abound in Germany. Until that is, I was once again lambasted on the road: this time, by a shouting police officer. The German language sounds quite threatening when it is yelled and as before, my instinctive reaction was to rudely and unjustly shout back.

"I. Can't. Understand. You!" I thought that my interlocutor was making things unnecessarily dangerous, trying to have such a discussion with me as I was cycling. Especially as it distracted me from my riding no-handed in the middle lane of the motorway, heading the wrong direction.

Ok, so I was just checking my maps while riding on a minor road on the correct side. "No handy!" he cried. I giggled, recognising that 'handy' was German for mobile phone, before putting it away until the cops had driven out of sight.

The German infrastructure is perfect for the recreational cyclist. Unfortunately the same cannot be said for the cyclist in a hurry. There are completely segregated cycle lanes alongside almost every minor road, but they seem to detour indulgently into every little village and point of interest. I wasn't interested in every point of interest so sometimes opted to take the road, at the great displeasure of many a stuck-up driver. In fact, it was here, by German drivers, that I felt the most threatened on my entire trip. Even on the border of Afghanistan I felt safer. I suppose that they weren't used to people not following the maxim *cycle paths are for cyclists, roads are for cars.* I was subjected to the odd angry beep of the horn and further admonishments from the most zealous of the outraged passengers. I wish I could say that I let all this pass me by, but in truth I felt mounting pressure to rejoin the less efficient cycle lanes. I ended up seesawing between the two: taking the cycle lane until the windings and sudden steeper gradients irritated me sufficiently to take the road, and staying on the road until horn blasts and shouts irritated me sufficiently to take to the cycle lane.

In such style, I had soon seen by Munich, Augsburg and a whole host of other towns and villages on the way to Villingen-Schwenningen, where a charming chap by the name of Leroy

McAdoo that I had met in Belgrade invited me stay for a night. After a rather horrible time camping in the rain, I was appeased to flop onto his plush sofa bed, arriving there just before nightfall. More so, his flatmate worked part-time in a greasy burger restaurant, so it would have been rude not to visit this fine establishment. The next day, well-rested and now with a dry tent, I finally set my sights on Strasbourg and the country at the end of the Eurasian landmass: France.

The final *Deutschland day* took me through the mythical black forest that bore in mid-October the full robe of Autumnal glory. The thick stilled darkness of the evergreen vegetation was riddled with other trees fickle to the seasons. Gentle yellows and rough reds wantonly interspersed the black of the black forest. It was a joy to descend the 1000 m or so that I had climbed over the last few days amidst such gorgeous colours, right down to the Rhine river which marks the natural border between France and Germany all the way from the tri-point with Switzerland, to Karlsruhe. I, however, was not planning to stay in Germany that far north. I longed to be in France, to rejoin a country to whose customs I was familiar, and for whose cheese and bread I was positively frothing at the mouth. My get-out point was the bridge across the Rhine to Strasbourg that I approached mid-afternoon. When I reached the border bridge to Strasbourg, my eyes welled with tears. I wore a smug smile on my face as I thought back to the hours spent talking with Pierre over Skype. *Cycling from Singapore to France! Ha!* What had before been both the dream and folly of two naïve, over-optimistic and broke students was just about to become history. It had been achieved in emphatic disregard to our initial plan, in a way that was simply unforeseeable, including detours that had added on some 9000 kilometres to the initially planned route at the time of reaching Strasbourg. Of course, another massive difference was that I was alone in passing into France.

Pierre, in the meantime had not simply stopped in Myanmar (where he eventually got on a flight to Mandalay from

Tachileik). He had been safely back in France for the last month and a half, having many a story to tell of his journey there to boot, quite enough to fill an entirely separate book. From Mandalay he had cycled to the Indian border to meet his Sister, with whom he realised one of *his* dreams by taking a train across India to New Delhi. From there, he flew with his bike to Teheran, before tackling the frigid mountains leading to the Anatolian plateau of Turkey. He cycled and hitch hiked his way back into Europe before, again, realising his dream of cycling across Europe like a man possessed, putting even my swift journey across the continent to shame in terms of the little time it took him. This brief overview completely downplays the hardships, highs and *galères* that took him back to his *patrie*. I was contented though to know, that in the end we had both made it to France in our vastly different fashions.

Monotone

"Un café allongé s'il vous plait."

I sat in a bougie café in a Strasbourg side-street, feeling utterly chuffed. I called as many people as I could to announce that I had made it back to France, finding as many outlets as I could for my elation. After putting the phone down having spoken to the last of the people willing to listen, I couldn't help but feel a pang of emptiness. It was that demonic lack of someone with whom to share this intense moment of happiness. This whole trip was a foolhardy and selfish endeavour and it meant so much to me, which is part of what made it so special. The decisions, risks, experiences and encounters were mine and I was glad for it, but I must admit to feeling hollow, when in this Strasbourg café, there were no bells and whistles and nobody to hug saying *hey, we made it.* It may seem odd to the reader that I felt this in Strasbourg of all places. Why, I wasn't home yet! Indeed that was the case and I slowly pulled myself together, failed to find lodgings in the city, and set out in the dreary rain to unceremoniously pitch up in the first suitable field I could find.

France is a country that can happily and confidently lay claim to boasting one of the vastest varieties of incredible landscapes and cultural heritage in the world. The towering heights of the Alps in the South East. The sun-soaked Côte d'azur. The Calanques between Cassis and Marseille. The salt flats of the Camargue, the suks of the Ardèche where the Loire has its source. The wine regions of the Rhône valley, Beaujolais and Burgundy. The extinct volcanoes of the Massif Central. The charming cityscapes of Paris or Lyon. The gallo-roman remains of Vienne, Nîmes and Arles. The wild expanses of the Garrigue. The rugged Brittany coastline, lashed by Atlantic winds. The verdant slopes of the Pyrenees. The lazy Dordogne valley. The Cévennes, the Verdon gorges, the Jura, the Vercors plateau. The diversity is frankly, startling. So how I found myself cycling in incessant drizzle through endless farmland, I am not quite sure. I could happily tout the joys of France all day long, but two breaths seemed to me to be more than exhaustive for the Grand Est. The drivers here were much more relaxed than their uptight German contemporaries and even then, the roads were wonderfully quiet. I could sail through the stout, curvy hills of grazing-grass, maize and wheat at my complete leisure.

Another point of diversity in France is the cheeses. These blocks of fermented milk curd are the source of immense regional *fierté,* to the extent that many unique types are fabricated and thus the country has been dubbed *'le pays des 400 fromages'.* So again, why I always settled time after time on supermarket Camembert to fill my baguettes is likely a reflection of me grasping for security and familiarity, feeling nigh upon truly shod of the curiosity that I possessed at the start of the Asian continent. Or it could simply be that one can never go wrong with camembert, fresh juicy tomato (the likes that one cannot get in England) and the baguette *tradition,* for which one pays 10 centimes more but derives infinitely more pleasure.

My trajectory was set between the two large cities of Metz and Nancy, not wanting to get ensnared by traffic while finding the most direct route to Reims, where my friend Charlotte had agreed to host me at her family home. I passed through a promising-looking 'green patch' on the map, which I hoped meant a change from the farm fields. I was suddenly regaled with *more* farm fields, now occasionally bordered by thistle and thick *buisson* that I assumed warranted the green map marker. 140 kilometres of not necessarily unpleasant monotony brought me to the outskirts of the small village of Luppy at dusk, where there was a freshly-mown football field presided over by a humble-looking club house. I tried all the doors, thinking that in the depths of rural France, nobody would bother locking them. That was found to be untrue, but nonetheless, there was a fine roof overhang that provided more than ample shelter for my tent that would benefit from being dried out before being slept in. As I was pitching up, a woman wandered by on a twilight stroll and I hailed her with a bonsoir! "J'espère que ça dérange à personne si je plante la tente ici?" I inquired.

"Mais bien sûr que non, mais tu veux pas venir à la maison boire quelque chose?" My ears perked up at this quick offer of a drink. I couldn't refuse but it still wasn't completely clear if it was a drink only, in which case I would leave the tent safely pitched. "Non non, tu peux démonter la tente aussi."

I had won. With a promise of a warm bed and wine, I excitedly began packing away the tent so as to quickly rejoin the woman at her house, just down the road. *Snap. "Merde!"* A little of my excitement now spent, and one tent pole poorer, I freewheeled down the road to Nathalie's place.

The French are often ribbed for many of their mannerisms: constant droning complaint, laziness, snobbery, making much ado about nothing… But there are at least two qualities for which the French can never be teased: their *discussion* and their *hospitalité*. Whereas many peoples discuss to come to the ends of an issue: cattle prices, women, men, alcohol, occasionally philosophy etc, the French people enjoy discussion for discussion's sake. Especially when boosted along with the fruits of their hospitality, there is nothing finer and more fulfilling than an evening in their company, face slowly being flushed with warmth in between sips of delicious red wine all while heavily engaged in *la discussion*. The evening with Nathalie and Claude was certainly no exception, and the world was affably put to rights before a restful night in their plush guest bedroom, with my tent happily drying in the garage.

In the morning I asked Nathalie why she had been so quick to invite me to her home and she rather bashfully opened up about an event that had occurred far in the past. Many years ago, a Belgian cyclist in much the same situation as myself approached Natalie, asking if she could pitch up the tent in the front garden. A bit forward, indeed, but not unheard of. At the time, Nathalie's daughter was young and suddenly thoughts of fear and what-ifs rose to her mind. The mothering instinct took over. She hesitated for a short while then told the Belgian cyclist that she couldn't stay and would have to find somewhere else.

For the Belgian, I am sure that this event will have been almost completely unmemorable. For if you don't ask you don't get, and if you do ask, well, there is still very much the possibility of not getting. But, for Nathalie, this episode remained ingrained in memory. She regretted not having let the cyclist stay and for turning away a person who she later thought would surely not have been a threat. When Nathalie saw me, she thought back to the Belgian, saw an opportunity for moral redemption (of course, she didn't have anything to redeem) and seized it. I found her story hilarious and I stipulated that really, I should be thanking that Belgian cyclist for the Nathalie's hospitality, rather than Nathalie herself!

The following day brought, *quelle surprise*, more drizzle and more farmland, this time through the *Parc Naturel Régional de Lorraine*. I failed to see how this part of France had obtained its *naturel régional* status, especially when compared to those I had visited in the South East: the Haut-Jura, the Chartreuse and the Pilat seemed to be in a different league. In any case, the riding wasn't difficult, the roads remained quiet and I had plenty of time to contemplate the essence of travel, human nature and the deepest mysteries of the universe, none of which I used for that purpose. At Nathalie's place, I had inserted some bracing wire into my tent pole and duct-taped around the snap. I put my tent up in the rain on the edge of an abandoned rail-line near the hamlet of Récicourt and stood back to marvel at my jagged palace-for-one: more humble than ever. With a sigh I entered the tent, for what would surely be one of the last times.

The next day I arrived comfortably in Reims (pronounced Rranss), or more specifically, Courcy, where Charlotte and her family lived. There, I was pampered by the whole family to the tune of wine and *raclette* and spent the evening catching up with Charlotte. On the very next day, she was to embark on her own journey to Greece, to *wwoof* at a stable in the countryside. That left me in the hands of her parents, who were a couple of chalk and cheese. Didier was perhaps the most relaxed man I have ever met. He was a poet and surely enough, almost always seemed to be tapping into a higher level of existence. Fabienne, on the other hand, was down to Earth. She organised events for a local brasserie and exuded a non-stop energy for getting things done. It was amazing how they were so asynchronous yet so congruous. They, like many other great French hosts, were bound by their desire to *faire plaisir* to their guest and I spent my first rest day since Belgrade in luxury. Not being able to thank them enough the morning that I left for the last stint to Dunkirk, I wrote a short poem.

I had booked my ferry across the channel, now certain that I could make it for the weekend, even if I were reduced to a walk or crawl. It would take only the cruellest twist of fate now to stop me making the 260 kilometres to Dunkirk in the four days at my disposition. As such, I took my time heading North, dipping into the gothic city centres of Saint Quentin, Cambrai and Lens, lounging in parks with a book (when weather permitted), taking the liberty to detour down quiet country lanes and lunching on crusty baguettes with white wine.

I spent a final evening in my broken but beloved tent on the grounds of a deserted *complexe sportif* before making my way to Hamel, where a *Warmshowers* host called Manu had agreed to host me. His kindly face instantly appeased me, as did his stock of Grimbergen and Leffe that we shared with his in-laws who ceremoniously came round every evening at 05:00pm for a tipple. Manu was disappointed that I was already well accustomed to the two giants of Belgian abbaye beers and so resolved to find something to which my taste buds were unacquainted. He brought out a beer called la Raoul, in homage to Raoul de Godewarsvelde, a singer of sea-shanties from the

60s who was born in a village some 50 kilometres away, made locally famous by his raspy *Quand la mer monte*. He was pleased that it was sufficiently niche that I hadn't tried it and *I* was pleased that it took something so niche to introduce me to something I didn't know.

Manu had recently cycled the French divide, an unsupported race across the unpaved roads of France. He was shocked at how little cheap accommodation was on offer on his route and thus set out to remedy this for other cyclists passing by his house. He and his wife were also, for some reason, in love with Britain, or at least the British image. As such, they seemed honoured when I left them the union jack that I had been flying on my bike through all of Europe, alongside that of Yorkshire and the European union. Well-fed and topped up on *eau-de-vie*, I set out for my final day on the Eurasian landmass to Dunkirk.

In true cycle touring fashion, the last day was suitably mundane. I headed straight north, willed on by a perky tailwind. The main features of the day were enormous piles of potatoes, swedes and parsnips by the roadside and a deserted, flooded muddy car park, where there was a sign warning against picnicking. *Piquenique interdit!* I looked around to see if nearby there was a charming lake or some benches in the shade of majestic elms. Alas no, there was just the muddy car park. I wondered who, without the sign there to stop them, would stroll into the middle of this place swinging a wicker basket to and fro, deploying their checkered blanket in that sweet spot next to the flooded pothole where the gravel was slightly thinned. Northern France was not like the rest of France and I rather liked its grim charm.

Approaching Dunkirk, I passed by some of the villages I had passed on my first cycle trip from Sheffield to Amsterdam four years earlier. Signs for Quaëdypre (I cannot offer advice on how this is pronounced) Rexpoëde and Bergues lit up sequences of neurons that hadn't fired in a long time. In Bergues, pulled in by nostalgia, I stopped for coffee in the café de la poste, made famous in the hilarious film *Bienvenue chez les ch'tis*. What a different journey had led me here this time.

In the late afternoon, still encouraged by a now hefty tailwind, I emerged at the North-western end of Dunkirk and of Eurasia. That was it. The sea. La manche. The English Channel. I was less emotional than I thought I would be and seeing that the water was about a kilometre out from the beginnings of the sand, decided against a re-enactment of chariots of fire. I simply nodded, smiled, took stock of its significance, asked a family passing by to snap an obligatory picture and turned around to find lodgings for the couple of nights until my ferry.

On the morning of the 26th October I caught the ferry to Dover. There is a British border control office before getting on the boat, where passports are checked. I had long awaited this moment that my wandering mind had simulated many times. I approached the booth and trying to sound as English as possible, bade the officer a jolly good morning. "So where have you come from on that thing?" he inquired, gesturing to my bike. Liking where this was going, I replied, "Singapore mate, all across Asia and Europe, took me the best part of a year it has."
 He looked up at me, eyebrows slightly raised. Folding my passport and handing it back, he pronounced the words that I had dreamed he would say. In a clear and familiar accent…
"Oh, well congratulations… and welcome home!"

Oak trees

Waiting for me at Dover was a collection of familiar faces: Sam, Lewis, Sally, Liz, Piers and Ben. They had been waiting for almost three hours, which was the delay that my ferry incurred after a storm rocked the coast the previous night. After a copium of warm and emotional hugs, and drenched in prosecco, I set off with my cycling friends on a two-day stint to London. Now it was time to savour my country, although it did seem absurd that it should take me a week to get back when I could have easily done it in four days… or have gotten the train. Furthermore, savour isn't particularly a word I would have chosen, with the skies being grey and the roads being wet for much of the way. It was cold, Autumn would soon pass to Winter and I was certainly glad to be on my way back.

We revelled in our collective wholesome spirit, taking in the Kent downs under blustery skies. The road rollercoastered over the rolling green hills of my country. Sparrows and starlings flitted in the hedgerows and country folk washing their cars for the second time of the day saluted us with full and familiar hellos. I deeply breathed in the fresh air in between conversations and catch-ups, on the bike as much as with stories! It is indeed odd that no matter how long friends may be separated, regardless of what they might have done in that time apart, after an hour or two, everything becomes so normal. I had felt that almost every day of my trip would equate to at least a day of story-telling when finally, I would see my friends. On many days I simply burned with a desire to share my experiences, only to almost forget them a few days later. In all truth, full details are never related, and while I might well have accumulated 300 days-worth of words to share had I noted everything, two hours was plenty before I felt exhausted of tales. More pressing topics were to be discussed: food, alcohol, plans and most importantly of all, the absolute shite talk that binds good friends together.

As that first day back in England drew to a close, we were still none the wiser as to where we would all spend the night. I spotted an inn of sorts on the map, in an old village pub. Apparently, there were no vacancies for the night. How that was the case, I'm still unsure, as the place was mostly devoid of life save for a few fat old men who sat nursing their pints and playing pool. One of them claimed to have cycled across Africa to get here. His stomach flowing over his belt said otherwise. Having little success with finding beds, we instead opted for a round of whisky. We whipped ourselves into a frenzy and took to the dark rainy night outside to gallop in exhilarating fashion full speed down an A-road into the town of Maidstone where there was sure to be hotels.

So many of England's cultural institutions were visited on that first weekend, made all the richer in the context of indulging in them for the first time in over a year. A quaint café in a Kent village, where ladies with pushchairs were sat nattering about the turn in the weather. It served up fresh pastries with 'proper' tea (that would make at least half of the world's tea drinkers gag) and scones. A greasy take-away pizza joint owned by Kurds who called everyone boss and offered chilli sauce and garlic mayo. A Wetherspoons showing a rugby world cup match at 10:00am, where somehow there were more South Africans than Welshmen, all of whom were already merrily drunk. And of course, the real, quintessential British pub. Fat chips with gravy and HP sauce and Sarson's vinegar, all washed down with a good old pint of landlord. Could life be sweeter?

Joined in Maidstone by Martha and George, the peloton made its way North-West across the inexhaustible lumpy greenery of South England, until the M25, that is. Suddenly, lush fields, Tudor villages and ancient woodland were replaced by housing estates and high streets of familiar outskirt towns that melted into the thronging boroughs of South London. We pedalled on through the traffic, stretched in a long and probably rather annoying line in the dark. Through Lewisham, Brockley, Peckham, and Brixton, finally reaching the Yuppie paradise of Clapham. We slumped on settees in Sally and Liz's flat, exhausted but content. Liz was on tea duty. It was beginning to feel more and more like home.

After a delightful weekend with my friends, and another couple of days in London to get that all important photo in front of Big Ben, taken on the 28th October - five days in hand, I set off on my victory parade across the England that lay between London and Sheffield. First stop, Cambridge. I followed the Lee valley across landscapes not dissimilar to Northern France, but a *feel* that was completely different. That evening, Lewis, Magnus and I sat on the sofa, tea in hand, to watch the Great British bake off final. The British tirade continued with fish and chips washed down by ale with my dad and his friend Nick at lunchtime the following day, not far from Peterborough. That night, I lodged with Ann and Dennis, Sally's lovely parents, in Leicester. Dennis's family was from a small village a stone's throw from Kingaroy, Queensland, where I had cycled almost exactly one year ago with Pierre. We delighted in sharing our stories of this unlikely land that linked us. We also watched the news with a *cuppa*. In Nottingham I was united with Tom, Sam's older brother who had followed me through my Polarsteps blog all the way from Singapore. I had never met Tom in person, but knocking on his door, I felt the same anticipation I would if I were meeting a good old friend. I felt privileged to be perched on the comfort of the same settee from which he had orchestrated his unfaltering support, where I was now drinking tea to wash down the treat of a takeaway curry.

Life had taken back its slowness and the sublime essence of adventure was slowly reclining into the *mou* of British autumnal comforts. On Saturday the 2nd of November, I rode on eerily quiet roads to Chesterfield, owing to the rugby world cup final that finished at 11:00am. After this time, the traffic angrily retook to the route. I could sense that England had lost.

From Chesterfield it was the slow and final stretch to the peace gardens of Sheffield, my hometown. I descended from the edge of the peak district into the city centre in driving rain. Down Abbeydale road, past the Asian takeaway district of London road and up the Moor where the town hall and finish line came into view. I cycled in front of a crowd of students protesting against the tyranny of the Chinese government, in between a photographer and the ensemble of a wedding that were clearly alarmed by a passing wheeled vagabond ruining their group photo, and finally towards my family and friends who had been in wait for a very long time: I arrived at 15:02pm and they must have been stood there for at least quarter of an hour. I dismounted my bike here and hugged my parents and all those who had come to see me. I dismounted my bike here for the last time, for now.